MAKE MONEY

=== *with* ===

FIXER-UPPERS

AND

RENOVATIONS

MAKE MONEY

with

FIXER-UPPERS
AND
RENOVATIONS

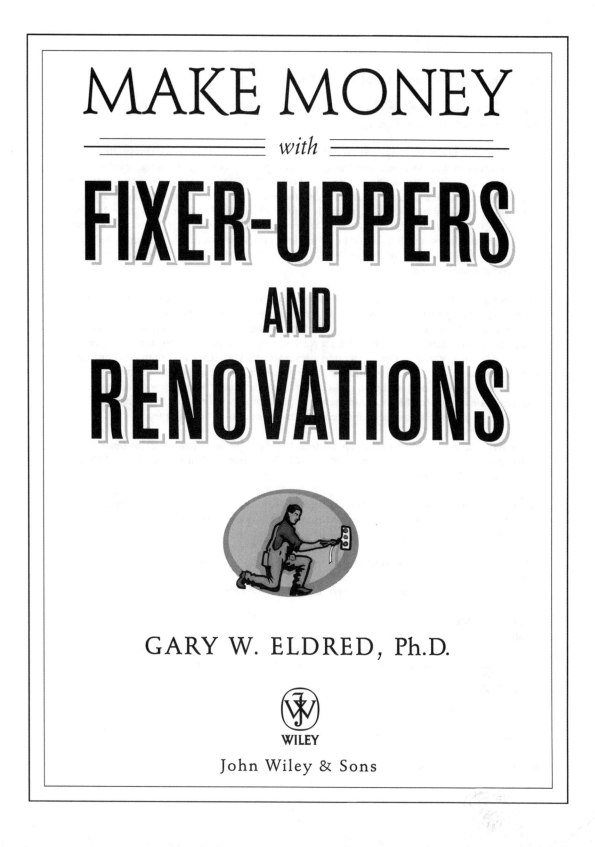

GARY W. ELDRED, Ph.D.

WILEY

John Wiley & Sons

Published by John Wiley & Sons, Inc., Hoboken, New Jersey.
Published simultaneously in Canada.

For general information on our other products and services, please contact our Customer Care Department within the United States at (800) 762-2974, outside the United States at (317) 572-3993 or fax (317) 572-4002.

Wiley also publishes its books in a variety of electronic formats. Some content that appears in print may not be available in electronic books. For more information about Wiley products, visit our web site at www.wiley.com.

Library of Congress Cataloging-in-Publication Data:
Eldred, Gary W.
   Make money with fixer-uppers and renovations / Gary W. Eldred.
      p. cm.
   Includes index.
   ISBN 0-471-43342-X (pbk.)
      1. Real estate investment—United States. 2. Dwellings—Remodeling—United States.
   3. Housing rehabilitation—Economic aspects—United States. I. TItle.

HD255.E37523   2003
332.63'243—dc21   2003045091

CONTENTS

1. **Your Quick Path to Profits: The Entrepreneurial Approach**   1

The Entrepreneurial Difference   2
　The "Bargain Price" Approach   3
　Stretch Your Creativity and Imagination   5
　The Entrepreneurial Approach   6
　The Browns Create Value in a Down Market   6
　My Awakening   8
　Unlimited Potential   9

Multiple Ways to Profit   13
　Fix and Quick Flip   13
　Fix and Flip Slowly (Two Years)   14
　Fix, Hold, Refinance   14
　Fix, Hold, Trade Up   15
　The Home (or Neighborhood) You Can't Afford   16

Vanquish Your Fears: You Can
　　an Entrepreneurial Fixer   16
　Yes, You Do Need Some Skills   17
　My Promise to You   18

2. **Market Value versus Market Strategy**   21

Market Value Defined   22
　The Comparable Sales Approach   23
　The Market Value Conclusion   25

Strengths of the Appraisal Process   25
　Common Denominator   25
　Disinterested Third Party   26

Weaknesses of the Appraisal Process   26
Rearview Mirror   27
Narrow Focus   28
The Appraisal Process Shuns
Entrepreneurial Vision   30
Summing Up the Appraisal Process   30

You Need More Market Data   31

3.   Your Formula for Profits   34

The Pieces of the Puzzle   35
Minimum Improved Value (MIV)   36
Purchase Price   37
Acquisition Costs   38
Improvement Costs   38
Financing Costs   38
Other Holding Costs   39
Selling Costs   39
Opportunity Costs   40
Oops Factor   40
Income Taxes   41
Profit Formula in Action   43

Getting the Work Done   43
Know Your Limits   44
Clearly Distinguish the Personal
from the Profitable   44
Plan Your Project, Work Your Plan   46
Secure Bids   48
Secure Lien Releases   51
Stay Legal: Obtain All Necessary Permits and Comply
with All Zoning and Building Codes   52

4.   Make Regulations Work for You   54

Sources of Rules and Regulations   56
Governments   56

Homeowners Associations   59
Private Contracts Also Restrict Property Owners   61

Zoning and Related Ordinances   64
The District Concept   64
What Kinds of Restrictions?   67
Be Wary of Nonconforming Uses   78
How to Challenge the Zoning Rules   83
Building Codes   86
Environmental Laws   87

5.   Discover Your Possibilities   89
The Copleys Make Half a Million   90

The Baglivis Discover a Bargain   90

Put on Your Rose-Colored Glasses   91
Don't Quickly Reject a "Fixer"—You Could
Mistakenly Pass Up a Bargain   91
Your Second Set of Glasses (Buyer's Eyes)   92
The Critical Balance   92

Inspecting the Site   93
Site Size and Configuration   93
Site Quality   96
Fences, Driveway, and Sidewalks   99
Curb Appeal: Attending to the Details   99

The Outside of the House   100
Appearance   101
Exterior Condition: The Professional Inspection   103
Materials and Maintenance   104
Site Placement   105

6.   Enhance the Interior   107
Scrutinize Square Footages   107
Watch Out for Errors of Measurement   108
All Space Doesn't Count Equally   108

Make Sure All Like Space Does
     Count Equally   109

Floor Plan: Does the Layout of the House Work?   111
     Livability   111
     Target Market   112

Aesthetics: How Does the House Look, Feel,
     and Sound?   116
     Create Emotional Appeal   117
     Check Noise Levels   118
     Clean Thoroughly   119

Condition: How Much Time, Effort, and Money Will the
     Property Require?   121
     Legal Compliance   124
     Estimating Costs of Repairs and Improvements   125

Utility Bills (Energy Efficiency)   127
     What Utilities Are Available?   127
     Identify Ways to Reduce the Utility Bills   128

Save on Property Taxes   129

Save on Property Insurance   129

Enhance the Safety and Security of Residents   130

Special-Purpose Uses   131

7. Add More Living Space   132

Work the Numbers   133

Attic, Garage, and Basement Conversions   133
     Target Market Needs   134
     Aesthetics   134
     Integrate the Conversion into the House   134

Create an Accessory Apartment   135
     The Zoning Obstacle   135
     The Mortgage Helper   139

What Type of House Works Best?   141

8. Revitalize the Neighborhood   144

    Neighborhoods Can Get Better   144
        Entrepreneurs Improve Thorton Park
            (and Make a Killing)   147
        Every Neighborhood Has Potential   147
        Community Action and Community Spirit Make
            a Difference   149
        Become a *Neighborhood* Entrepreneur   150

    Add to Neighborhood Convenience   150

    Improve Appearances and Aesthetics   151

    Zoning and Building Regulations   152

    Eliminate Neighborhood Nuisances   152
        Invoke Your Local Ordinances, Deed Restrictions, or
            HOA Rules   153
        Sue in Small Claims Court   153

    Upgrade the Schools   155

    Safety and Security   156

    Lobby the Politicians   156

    Add Luster to Your Image   157
        Accent Something Special   157
        Talk Up the Neighborhood   158

    Get the Banks Involved (Affordability)   158
        Homes for Dallas   158
        Easier Financing Means Appreciation Potential   159

    Buy on the Bad News   159

9. Market Your Property for Top Dollar   161

    Whom Do You Want to Reach?   162
        Why So Many Questions?   162
        Sell Benefits, Not Just the Property   163

Sell the Sizzle   164
    Crafting a Newspaper Ad   165
    Prepare a Property Brochure or Flyer   168
    Make Your Sign Stand Out   177
    Sell with Honesty   178

Sell the Property, Don't Just Show It   178
    Prepare to Sell the Property   179
    Not an Isolated Case   181
    Sales Success: Your 12-Step Program   181
    More Tips on Financing   185
    Avoid Deception   186
    Back to Financing   186

Should You Employ a Realty Agent?   187
    Co-op Sales   191
    What about Lawyers?   192

10.   Buying Your Property   193

Finding Good Properties   193
    Real Estate Agents   193
    Newspapers   196
    Drive, Bike, or Run Neighborhoods   199
    Networking   200
    Foreclosures and REOs   201
    The World Wide Web   205

Search for Agreement   206
    Deal Points   207
    Reduce Seller Anxiety   208

Win-Win Isn't for Wimps   210
    Develop a Cooperative Attitude   211
    Learn as Much as You Can about the Sellers   212
    A Win-Win Example   214
    How to Bargain for a Low Price   216
    Don't Compromise, Conciliate   216

Learn the Sellers' Reasons and Reference
Points 219
Use an Agent as an Intermediary, but
Negotiate for Yourself 219
The Deal's Not Over 'til It's Over 222

11. Easy Money for Owner-Occupants 225

Owner-Occupied Financing 225
Passable Credit 225
Attention *Current* Homeowners 226
FHA 203(k): The Homebuyer's Best Choice
for Financing 227
Owner-Occupied Purchase Loans 230
Owner-Occupied Assumptions 237

12. Money for Everyone 240

"Subject to" versus Mortgage Assumptions 240
Is This Technique Legal? 241
Should You Worry? 241
Short Term, Not Long Term 242
Risks to Sellers 243

Your Borrowing Strategy 243

Seller-Assisted Financing 244
First Mortgage or Deed of Trust 246
Buy on the Installment Plan 247
Lease Option a Property 250
Lease Purchase Agreements versus
Lease Purchase Options 252

Easy Money—Hard Terms 255
Predatory Lending 255
Why Would You Want to Deal with
This Type of "Easy-Money" Lender? 256

The Optimistic Entrepreneur   256
Where to Find This Easy Money   258

Cash to Close   258
Personal Savings   259
Sell Unnecessary Assets   260
Obtain a Home Equity Loan (or Downsize the House)
    and Free Up Investment Capital   261
Bring in Partners   262
Second Mortgages   264
Cash Advances   264

Summing Up   266

Index   267

MAKE MONEY

with

FIXER-UPPERS

AND

RENOVATIONS

CHAPTER 1

Your Quick Path to Profits:
The Entrepreneurial Approach

Would you like to double or triple your money in 12 months or less? Would you like to build quick profits of $10,000, $20,000, or $50,000—even though you lack cash or strong credit? Do you want to learn a money-making skill that you can put to work anywhere in North America (or for that matter, anywhere in the modern world)? Would you prefer to work full- or part-time without set hours and without a boss looking over your shoulder? Would you like to achieve mid- to long-term financial freedom and personal independence?

If you've answered yes to any or all of the preceding questions, then this book's for you.

In this book, you will learn how to earn big profits as you entrepreneurially create value for the buyers and tenants of your properties.

> **To maximize profits, entrepreneurs strategically improve their fixers.**

As a real estate rehab entrepreneur, you will search out properties that offer opportunity for profitable improvement. But you won't just slap on a fresh coat of white paint, lay down new beige carpet, and wash the windows. You will *strategically* improve the property to favorably distinguish it from its competitors. You will explicitly shape its features toward a select and

1

profitable target group of buyers or tenants. You will work with your mind, not necessarily your hands.

As you follow this strategic approach, you will learn how to ferret out those properties that offer the most profitable potential for change. You will discover how to create synergy: The value of the whole improved property will greatly exceed the sum of the parts (your input costs).

The Entrepreneurial Difference

> **Profit with the entrepreneurial difference.**

Amazingly, no other book on "fixers" adopts an entrepreneurial approach. Other authors tout fixers because you can often buy these properties at a bargain price. In fact, in his best-selling book *Buy It, Fix It, Sell It, PROFIT!* (Dearborn, 1998), Kevin Myers writes,

> Some real estate authors have perpetuated the myth that the desirable return on rehab is anywhere from $2 to $4 for each rehab dollar invested.[1] Under this theory [sic], a $1,000 investment in rehab would increase the value of the house by $2,000 to $4,000. This is both preposterous and irrelevant to the rehab investor. (p. 149)

Myers then reprints figures from an article in the *Wall Street Journal* that ostensibly shows that paybacks from rehab or remodeling typically yield returns of only 30 percent to 80 percent of the amount invested. "Just glancing at these [figures]," Myers says, "You can come to only one conclusion: Remodeling a house is a losing proposition" (p. 149).

---

1. I am one of those authors (see my *Investing in Real Estate,* 4th ed., Wiley, 2003, pp. 165–186), but my analysis is neither "myth" nor "theory." It derives from reason and experience.

In fact, if you will take the time to work through the "fix-it" examples that Myers presents in his book, you will see that he made money only because he supposedly bought properties for 60 cents on the dollar. True to his word, he makes no profit from the property improvements themselves.

The "Bargain Price" Approach

Unfortunately, if you do adopt the bargain price approach favored by Myers and other "fix and flip" authors, you most likely will either fail or you will get yourself involved in fix-it work that does not add even one cent to your profit.

The Path to Failure   To follow the bargain price technique, you are told to locate motivated sellers with problem properties (the right things wrong). Ideally, if the current as-is value of a property totals $90,000, you take advantage of the seller's distress and "steal" the property for, say, $60,000. Next you put in $30,000 to cover the costs of acquisition, fix-up, and an eventual sale at $120,000 (the property's market value as improved). Accordingly, you exit the deal and pocket $30,000.

Sounds pretty good until you realize that your total profit hinged on buying a $90,000 property for $60,000. Now ask yourself, why would a distressed (motivated) seller be willing to leave $30,000 on the table? Yes, $5,000, maybe $10,000, on occasion even $15,000 or $20,000—but you will rarely find discounts and bargain prices that even come close to those amounts suggested by Myers and other like-minded authors.

> **Contrary to the hype, you will rarely find sellers who will give you a 30 percent or 40 percent discount.**

Moreover, many (perhaps most) motivated sellers are drowning in debt. They cannot offer you a steep discount because they owe nearly as much (if not more than) their property is worth. On occasion, in depressed housing markets, lenders will accept short payoffs. But these deals generally require much time and trouble. It's best to pursue them only during those times when foreclosures begin to pile up.

What about REOs (real estate owned)? Will lenders sell the properties they take back from foreclosures for 60 cents or 70 cents on the dollar? Well, anything's possible. But that's certainly not the policy followed by the Federal Housing Administration (FHA), the Department of Veterans Affairs (VA), Fannie Mae, Freddie Mac, or any of the other big players in the mortgage market. Every one of these organizations tries to sell for a price that comes as close to market value as possible.

In sum, if you try to develop a real estate investment program that depends on bargain prices discounted 30 percent to 40 percent off the current as-is property value, you are setting yourself up for failure. That's why the authors who advocate this approach encourage you to persist against all adversities. Then, if you do fail with their system, it's not the system's fault. It's your own fault. You just gave up too soon.

Why Fix It?   To further illustrate this point, let's say that your lottery ticket really does pay off. After fighting the odds, you convince a property owner to sell you a $100,000 house for $65,000. The question then becomes, Why fix it? If, as the examples in Myers's book show, rehabbing fails to yield a positive payback, why bother with rehab? Simply quick flip the property at a price of $80,000 to $90,000. You've still made a fast $20,000 to $30,000 profit and you haven't even lifted a hammer.

> **Only use renovations to create value.**

That's precisely the approach William Bronchik and Robert Dahlstrom urge in their book, *Flipping Properties* (Dearborn, 2001). However, like Myers, Bronchik and Dahlstrom never satisfactorily explain why sellers will leave so much money lying on the table for you to rake into your pile at their expense. Nor do they seriously address the issue of mortgage payoff. Selling for a quick, cash sale doesn't explain such deep discounts. To sell quickly and net substantially more, the distressed sellers could simply hold an auction.

Stretch Your Creativity and Imagination

Kevin Myers, Robert Irwin, and other authors err in their writings about fixers for two reasons: (1) As noted, their fixer profits heavily depend on buying at a bargain price; and (2) correspondingly, they define the term *fixer* too narrowly. To these authors (and most others), a fixer simply denotes a property that's run-down.[2] It needs work. It gives off bad karma. Weeds, odors, out-of-date colors, broken windows, rusty gutters, you name it. The house looks bad. It smells bad. It lacks appeal inside and out.

> **Many fixers show little or no physical deterioration.**

Certainly, such properties may very well hold promise for profitable improvement. But the most frequently recommended fix-up approach fails to adequately tap your imagination, intellect, and creativity. Indeed, the traditional fix-up approach almost encourages you to stifle yourself. "Appeal to the largest possible audience," the authors advise. "Keep everything neutral. Don't offend anyone. Don't venture into the unknown. Sure, you might throw in a few 'gee whiz' features like a skylight or hot tub, but for the most part, just focus on clean and fresh."

Although such an approach can sometimes generate profits, it doesn't require an entrepreneurial vision. It doesn't come close to maximizing profits. This common approach only steers you to run-down houses that you can buy at a steep discount. If no repairs are necessary, no deal. No bargain price, no deal. Consequently, if you adopt this bland, thoughtless approach, you will pass by many properties that could yield great returns.

---

2. For another author (in addition to yours truly) who knows how to create value—not simply buy at a bargain price—see Suzanne Brangham, *Housewise* (Harper & Row, 1987). Although now out of print, this excellent book can be found in most public libraries or through interlibrary loan.

The Entrepreneurial Approach

In contrast to the traditional view of fixers, here's the entrepreneurial approach:

> As you compare neighborhoods and properties, keep your eye out for ideas you can use to improve the houses and apartments you evaluate. Although most books and articles on real estate investing tell you to buy fixer-uppers, keep in mind that a fixer-upper is *any* home that you can redecorate, redesign, remodel, expand, or romance. The name of the home improvement game is profitable creativity. You can make nearly any home or apartment live better, look better, and feel better. To profit from renovation, the houses you buy need not look like they've been mistreated and neglected for the past 20 years.

> Throw away the notion that only run-down houses and apartments fit the definition of a fixer-upper. Sure, poorly maintained properties can offer good potential for value-enhancing improvements. But to keen observers, even meticulously kept properties aren't immune to profitable change. When you stay alert to opportunity, you can always find ways to make a property more desirable to potential buyers or tenants. Consider the experience of Raymond and Annie Brown.

> **Entrepreneurs can even create value with "perfect" properties.**

The Browns Create Value in a Down Market

When Raymond Brown and his wife, Annie B., bought a vacation retreat home they call Woodpecker Haven, Raymond says, "I thought it was a done property. It was only five years old."

Annie B., though, viewed the home from a different perspective. As an interior designer with a forward-looking imagination,

Annie B. simply said the home "had great potential." As Raymond tells the story, "Here are some of the improvements my enterprising wife accomplished to transform a livable property into an exquisite home:

◆ Landscaped the front and rear yards.
◆ Installed a drip irrigation system.
◆ Built a stone fence around the pool.
◆ Added decks around the rear of the house.
◆ Installed in both bedrooms French doors that led out to the decks.
◆ Remodeled the guest bedroom and bath to create a master bedroom for visitors.
◆ Built in a fireplace, bookshelves, cabinets, and track lighting in the living room.
◆ Trimmed overgrown trees and shrubs to enhance a picture-perfect view from the front porch."

Although Raymond and Annie B. invested $75,000 in these and other improvements, they added around $175,000 in value—throughout a falling market. "We bought our Sonoma retreat," says Raymond, "just as home prices were peaking, and sold several years later, two months before prices bottomed out. . . . Yet we made a $100,000 profit. Our secret? Woodpecker Haven was a fixer-upper we renovated inside and out."

> **Build wealth in a falling market.**

As the experience of the Browns demonstrates, a fixer is any home that could look better, live better, and feel better than it does. (Remember, at the time they bought the property, Woodpecker Haven was only five years old. Recall, too, the Browns made their big gains in a *falling* market.) To fix up a home or apartment building may require you to scrape encrusted bubble gum off floors and counters, patch holes

> **If it can look better, live better, or generate more pizzazz, it's a fixer.**

in the roof, fight a gnarled mass of weeds and debris in the back-yard, or pull out and replace rusted and obsolete kitchen and bath-room plumbing fixtures. But fixing up a property also can mean visualizing ways to redecorate, redesign, remodel, expand, or bring romance into the property.

In fact, to profit from fix-up work, you don't necessarily have to get your hands dirty. Yes, your sweat equity can pay big divi-dends, but creativity, imagination, and market research pay much better. So, to create value you can: (1) Look for houses that obvi-ously need work; (2) look for properties whose creative possibili-ties would be overlooked by most buyers; or (3) look for properties where you can improve both the physical condition as well as the overall appeal and livability. The better you can envi-sion opportunities that other potential buyers fail to recognize, the greater your potential for profits.

My Awakening

Like the great majority of property owners, at one time I followed the traditional fix-it approach to buying and improving my rental properties. Then, when I was enrolled in my doctoral program at the University of Illinois, I chanced upon a talk about real estate with one of my professors. He told me that since building a new home he had unsuccessfully been trying to sell his previous house. After a year on the market, the house remained unsold. He asked me if I would be interested in buying it. I agreed to take a look.

Great House, No Appeal   The house was located in a de-sirable neighborhood only a short bike ride from the U of I cam-pus. As to physical condition, the house showed virtually no disrepair. No buyer would have called this house a fixer. Yet, when I thought about making the property my home, I was not enthused. The house lacked warmth and cheer. It was too dark in-side. The color schemes made army olive look bright. Heavy

Earn a 5:1 payback for creative cosmetic improvements.

custom-made drapes (of which the professor was especially proud) in the living room and bedrooms also added to the home's dreariness.

"Thanks, but no thanks," formed my initial reaction. But fortunately, a more creative friend who visited the house with me immediately began to visualize the changes that she would make to the home if she were to live there. With just some relatively minor changes, she thought that she could transform the property's look, feel, and livability. She proved to be right.

I did buy the property, made the changes, and subsequently sold the house at a price significantly higher than my professor had been asking. My payback on out-of-pocket renovation expenses was about five to one.

A Home, Not a House From that moment on I dramatically changed my perspective on fixers. I realized that to most profitably improve a house (or apartment unit),

Create a *My Fair Lady* makeover.

you must first think of it as a home. Then you must abandon the mere fix-up mentality in favor of transformation. Don't merely dress the property up in a new outfit. You must think of your work as a Sally Jesse Raphael makeover, or perhaps as Henry Higgins thought of his Cockney drudge in the movie *My Fair Lady.*

Unlimited Potential

As you apply the entrepreneurial perspective, you will recognize that profitable properties may come in all sizes, shapes, and types. Rather than merely judging a property for its fix-up potential, you will inspect it for a much more extensive range of improvements. Likewise for the neighborhood.

Most importantly, you will evaluate your potential improvements through the lens of market strategy. You will persistently try to create that combination of features and amenities for which targeted buyers (or tenants) will gladly pay a premium. Through market research you will discover the most profitable ways to favorably differentiate your properties from those of your competitors (other sellers or owners of for sale and for rent properties). Throughout this book you will learn to ask and answer many detailed questions that will help you exploit opportunities that the majority of investors and homebuyers frequently miss. For example:

> **You can even improve "perfect condition" properties in a dozen or more ways.**

1. *Livability.* How can you improve the floor plan, traffic patterns, resident privacy, egress, and ingress?
2. *Living space.* Can you add living space through a room addition or conversion (garage, porch, basement, attic)?
3. *Storage.* Where are the dead spaces that could be enhanced for storage? What ideas can you borrow from the California Closet Company to add storage capacity without necessarily adding new storage space?
4. *Income potential.* How might you create auxiliary independent living space such as an in-law suite or accessory apartment? Can you create private living space for a teenager or live-in help?
5. *Roommate living.* If you plan to hold (or sell) the property as a rental, how might you modify the space or living areas to more pleasantly accommodate roommates or other types of shared living arrangements?
6. *Rightsizing.* Are some rooms or areas too large or too small? Does the room count and functions (bedrooms, bathrooms, great room) best match the needs and wants of your most profitable target market? What changes are possible?

7. *Operating and maintenance costs.* Can you switch from high-maintenance materials to low- or no-maintenance items? What can you do to reduce the utility bills?

8. *Capital costs.* What steps can you take to minimize the costs of property taxes, property insurance, assessments, or mortgage interest for your buyers (or yourself)?

9. *Aesthetics.* How can you romance the property, add pizzazz, or enhance a bright, cheery, or warm feeling?

10. *Views.* Can you enhance or create a drop-dead view? (No, you don't need mountains or lakes. A flower garden or ivy-covered trellis might also provide a pleasing respite.) Can you eliminate any ugly or distasteful view? Can you add or subtract windows?

11. *Landscaping, trees, shrubs.* What can you add? What should be cut away? Can you improve the yard's appearance with fertilizer, mulch, walkways, fountains, fish ponds, or fencing? Would a different type of grass grow better or look better?

12. *Security.* In our crime-conscious world, what can you do to diminish the home's susceptibility to break-ins?

13. *Safety.* Can you enhance the safety of the home for children, seniors, or just plain everyday living?

14. *Special-purpose use.* Can the property (or any part thereof) be profitably adapted for use as an office, artist's studio, or rentable storage area? Can you profitably adapt the property to better serve the needs of the disabled?

15. *Site.* Can you rightsize the site by acquiring part or all of a contiguous property or by subdividing or splitting off part of the existing lot? Does the size of the site allow for additional building, storage, or parking?

16. *Neighborhood.* What can you and neighborhood property owners do to upgrade or revitalize the community or neighborhood? Contrary to popular perception, you can change the location of a property. You can change the location when you improve the schools, redirect flow-through traffic, beautify properties, or reduce crime.

17. *Neighbors.* Sometimes a disrespectful or callous neighbor can create value-diminishing problems for nearby property owners. What can you and other property owners do to bring that wayward neighbor into line?

18. *Legal.* What laws and regulations (zoning, building codes, homeowners association rules, easements, deed restrictions, environmental standards, health and safety ordinances) control what you can and cannot do with your property? By learning the detailed ins and outs of these dos and don'ts, you can avoid costly blunders and capitalize on seldom-noticed (or recently emerging) opportunities.

By securing a change in zoning, a variance, or a special-use exception, you can dramatically add value to a property. You can also use zoning codes and ordinances to discipline those scalawag property owners (tenants) whose behavior adversely affects neighborhood property values.

As you can see from this list of 18 possibilities, entrepreneurs create value for their properties by systematically examining the house, garage, outbuildings, site, neighborhood, neighbors, and all critical laws, rules, and restrictions that regulate property use and design. In contrast, most buyers (and sellers) remain uninformed about many of these potential areas for profitable change. They typically inspect only for needed repairs and superficial cosmetic improvements. As a result, they miss some of their best opportunities to enhance their returns.

> **Profit from the ignorance and oversight of others.**

Fortunately, such ignorance and oversight will work to your advantage in two ways: First, you may face less competition for good properties. Second, due to the fact that sellers often fail to recognize the true potential of their properties, you can buy great properties for much less than they are really worth. In this sense, I don't mean far less than a property's current as-is market value but rather a market value price that still yields wide room for a large margin of profit.

It's true that you can occasionally find steeply discounted prices offered by those so-called motivated sellers that most real estate authors write about. But your success as an entrepreneurial fixer should not rely on that relatively rare occurrence. By thinking entrepreneurially, you will dramatically expand your profit opportunities.

Multiple Ways to Profit

As you master the art of creating value, you will pleasantly discover that you can earn your gains and build your wealth in multiple ways.

Fix and Quick Flip

Using the fix and flip approach, you buy, renovate, and sell a property all within the shortest period possible. This technique works well to generate fast cash. You can then pyramid these profits to reinvest in larger and higher-profit projects. Suzanne Brangham (the author of *Housewise*) began her fix and quick flip career with an unseemly $40,000 condominium (that she sold six months later for $80,000). Then, over a period of years, Suzanne worked herself through dozens of properties all the way up to multimillion-dollar executive homes.

> **Quickly build up your cash through fix and flip.**

However, under current tax law, multiple quick flips may expose you to onerous personal income tax liabilities. You will need to consult tax counsel to either work these transactions within a corporate structure or a tax-deferred retirement account such as an IRA or 401(k). Nevertheless, for your first several deals, fix and quick flip can put cash in your bank account faster and more surely than any other legal money-making endeavor that I am aware of.

Fix and Flip Slowly (Two Years)

Although current tax law treats the fix and quick flip rehabber less kindly than was possible prior to 1998, it treats the two-year owner-occupant far more favorably. If you live in the property for at least two years, your gain of up to $250,000 ($500,000 for a married couple) will land in your bank account completely tax free! Replicate this technique five or six times over a period of 10 or 12 years and you could easily build up a nice-sized sum of $500,000 or more.[3]

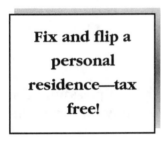

Fix and flip a personal residence—tax free!

Fix, Hold, Refinance

Personally, I have generally preferred to fix and hold properties as rentals. This approach will not only permit you to avoid paying taxes on your gain in equity but also allow you after a year or so to pull tax-free cash out through a refinance. Then you can use that tax-free money as a front-end investment to acquire another property.

In one such transaction I paid $106,000 (appraised at $106,500) for a property and put $26,000 down. Then I creatively improved the property for about $15,000 in renovation costs. After these improvements, the property ap-

Pull out tax-free cash with a refinance.

---

3. For more on this trend, see "Tax Law Is Leading Some to Serial Homebuying," *The New York Times,* March 30, 2003, Bu-8.

praised at $150,000. I then refinanced and pulled out $40,000 in cash. Next, I placed that money as down payments on two other properties. Again, you can see through this single example how creating value with fixers not only can earn big short-term profits but also can help you accelerate your wealth building with leverage (borrowed money).

(Also note that the profits in this example did not derive from a steeply discounted purchase price. I earned these profits because I knew how to recognize and realize the potential of the property, whereas the former owners did not.)

Fix, Hold, Trade Up

Here's another way you can pyramid your real estate profits and wealth while still avoiding income taxes. The Internal Revenue Code Section 1031 permits real estate investors to trade up tax free.

Say you buy a $100,000 property and through profitable improvements boost its market value to $160,000. Now you want to invest the equity you've created into a more expensive property. Moreover, assume that a sale would net you a taxable gain of $40,000. Alas, though, the Internal Revenue Service (IRS) would claim a big chunk of that money. So instead of selling, you or your real estate agent find a larger (more expensive) property you would like to own. Next, you execute a Section 1031 exchange. Your full $40,000 of gain (less trading fees) gets counted toward the purchase price of this more expensive acquisition. You pay the IRS nothing.

> **Use a Section 1031 exchange to pyramid your wealth without paying taxes on your gains.**

Repeat the process until you reach your financial goals. You need never pay tax on your equity gains. Your wealth builds tax free. If along the way you need cash, don't sell. Draw tax-free cash against an equity line of credit.

The Home (or Neighborhood) You Can't Afford

> **Buy a fixer to conquer the problem of affordability.**

Although I'm writing this book primarily for investors, homebuyers can also put this knowledge to good use. With the huge run-up in home values since the late 1990s, some of the most desirable homes and neighborhoods are now priced out of reach for many hopeful homebuyers. If that's the situation you face, apply the creative techniques discussed throughout the following pages. You will find that buying a fixer can move you into the type of home or neighborhood that you otherwise could not afford.

Vanquish Your Fears: You Can Become an Entrepreneurial Fixer

Throughout my career I've talked with hundreds of people who have expressed an interest in buying and improving properties. They know that fixers yield better returns than virtually every other type of investment. Yet, few take the first step. Why? Because they block themselves with a multitude of fears. In reality, none of these fears are warranted. I know because I've been there. Let me recount my own amateurish beginning. . . .

1. *Completely inexperienced.* My entire prior experience with property improvement had consisted of cutting grass at home to earn my high school allowance.
2. *Lack of cash and credit.* As a 21-year-old college student, I scraped together $1,000 and financed my first purchase with a seller-held land contract.
3. *No technical knowledge.* Not only did I not know anything about electrical systems, carpentry, plumbing, painting, or wallpapering, I soon found out that I lacked any ability to skillfully pursue these crafts. (Even today, after having profitably bought, managed, improved, and

sold several score of properties, I wouldn't even try to change a faucet washer or repair a broken window.)

4. *No time.* By age 26 I was carrying a full load of coursework in my doctoral program, teaching at two universities (one full-time, one part-time), and overseeing my portfolio of 32 rental houses and apartments.

5. *Poor economy.* During the early years of my investing, the U.S. economy was in the pits—high unemployment, skyrocketing inflation, a country running out of resources (so we were told), and a supposedly bleak future as we watched our industrial leadership get eclipsed by the land of the rising sun.

Do I relate the facts of my entry into real estate to trumpet my accomplishments in the face of tough circumstances? Not at all.

> **Entrepreneurs build wealth. Most people build a pile of excuses.**

Nearly everyone I know who invests in single-family houses, condos, and small rental properties got started under like conditions. No, not in the precise details, but in the sense that they, too, met head-on many constraints of time, money, credit, job, family, knowledge, and experience.

Nevertheless, they did not erect a wall of excuses. They simply decided that it was now or never and plunged ahead.

Yes, You Do Need Some Skills

By saying that the successful investors I know vanquished their fears and plunged ahead, I don't mean to imply foolishness or random acts. Rather, these investors possessed the eight skills and attributes that really matter:

1. A willingness to learn what they really need to know.
2. A capacity to delegate tasks and manage others who perform the needed work.

3. Self-discipline in their use of their money and time.
4. An open and inquisitive mind that persistently searches for new and better ideas.
5. A high capacity for work and productive activity.
6. The habit of accepting responsibility and reviewing mistakes.
7. Clear personal and financial goals committed to writing with a plan for achievement.
8. A love of real estate and pride of accomplishment.

Experience shows that the first seven of these skills can lead to success in nearly any endeavor. But for true personal and financial success in real estate—and especially in the field of real estate entrepreneurship—you should enjoy your work.

Personally, I love looking at properties, talking about real estate with sales agents, learning the latest trends, and all the while trying to figure out how I might apply something new that I've picked up.

> **Build wealth without "work."**

Every year, I crisscross the United States to look at properties and explore various local markets. When traveling out of the country, I do the same. I read nearly every book that comes out in the field and stay abreast of a dozen or so real estate journals, magazines, and newsletters.

Yet, I don't consider any of these activities "work" in the traditional sense of that word. Although I wouldn't necessarily expect you to develop this level of over-the-top interest and desire, still you should not pursue active real estate investing solely to make money. Unless you can get excited about the process of creating value for your properties, you should choose another row to hoe.

My Promise to You

Unlike so many other books aimed at people who want to earn profits in real estate, this book doesn't feed you pie in the sky. It

> **Real investors focus on realistic, doable deals.**

doesn't send you into the market looking for deals that may occur no more than 1 out of every 50 times. Most importantly, it doesn't pretend to give you a canned, step-by-step approach as to exactly what types of properties, price ranges, and neighborhoods provide the most profitable opportunities. Nor will you learn exactly what to say in your negotiations.

Indeed, authors who peddle such nonsense ought to have someone unplug their keyboard.

Why do such detailed "instruction manuals" fail? For at least eight reasons:

1. *Local markets differ.* What worked best in San Diego or Albuquerque last year may next year prove quite impossible in Peoria or Orlando.
2. *Relative prices change.* Just like stocks, different types of properties, neighborhoods, and price ranges run from hot to lukewarm to cold. To profit most with the least risk, you need to pay attention to these relative strengths and weaknesses.
3. *Target markets differ.* To earn the highest profits and create the most value, you must specifically direct your market strategy toward a well-defined target market. Generic strategies will undoubtedly land off the mark.
4. *Competition differs.* You cannot develop your best strategy without full knowledge of local competing properties, their features, and their price ranges.
5. *Financing differs.* Often, great financing can lift a so-so deal into the highly profitable category. Likewise, adverse terms of financing may kill an otherwise good opportunity.
6. *Improvement costs differ.* Costs vary enormously not only among different locales but also among different contractors for the same improvements at the same property.
7. *Originality pays big dividends.* Through vision and market research, you will discover creative possibilities that

give your strategies the difference that sets up the distinguishing difference for your buyers (tenants).

8. *Ideas not sweat equity.* In this world, the largest rewards go to people who can think for themselves. You can't expect to achieve superior returns if you merely follow someone else's manual of detailed dos and don'ts.

Quite likely, the all-time best-selling business book (over five million copies sold) is *In Search of Excellence* by Tom Peters and Bob Waterman (Harper & Row, 1982). In this book, these authors presumed to give corporate America a detailed prescription for success. To prove their points, Peters and Waterman showcased 20 premier companies. Yet, just two years after this book was published, *Business Week* ran a cover story entitled "Oops."

It turned out that six of these so-called premier companies had hit the skids. The Peters and Waterman prescription no longer seemed to work.

How does this fact relate to real estate? It serves to perfectly illustrate my basic point: To best earn quick (or slow) profits in real estate, throw out the step-by-step instruction manuals. The rules of the game change. You can't create the future you want by thoughtlessly following what worked in the past.

> **Increase your profits. Tailor a strategy to your area.**

Instead, stack the odds for success in your favor. Learn to tailor your strategy to the market conditions that prevail at the time you are investing. Craft your business plan to fulfill the most pressing (and profitable) needs of the day. It is toward that objective that we now turn.

CHAPTER 2

Market Value versus Market Strategy

To naive investors, the concept of market value tells them all they need to know to get a good deal. Buy for less than market value, great! Pay more than market value, you've made a mistake. Even worse, by excessively focusing on market value, these naive investors most often try to meet the competition rather than truly differentiate from and surpass it.

In contrast, the entrepreneurial investor looks at market value as one data point—but only one. Most importantly, real estate entrepreneurs always search to extricate themselves from the tyranny of market value.

Think about it like this. If you own a share of IBM, that share is just like every other IBM share (of the same stock class). When you want to sell, market value rules. There's nothing you can do to secure a price higher than market value. And neither you nor anyone else need sell at a price less than market value. At any given time, that one share of IBM has one and only one price.

Of course, in real estate no entrepreneur would ever think about value in this narrow and passive way. Why? Because even though so-called comparable properties do share some

> **Entrepreneurs find those differences that make the *profitable* difference.**

similar features, it is within the power of the entrepreneurial reno-vator to find or create different features that will enhance the ap-peal and the price of a given property to a selected type of buyer (or tenant). The entrepreneur thinks in terms of strategic improve-ments, not merely repairs and fix-up. To clarify this critical point such that you may eventually achieve what I call the entrepre-neurial advantage, let's go more deeply into the concept of real es-tate market value.

> **Learn the strengths and weaknesses of "market value."**

Market Value Defined

As a starting point, we will look at how real es-tate appraisers define the term *market value.* Although formally written in appraisal jargon, this definition includes these major points:

1. *Most probable selling price.* In this sense, the term *most probable price* reflects the fact that (contrary to com-mon belief) the real estate concept of market value does not assume one and only one "correct" value for a prop-erty. Instead, market value presumes a range of values.
2. *Competitive open market.* Strictly speaking, the term *market value* presumes an active market (similar to shares of stocks) with numerous look-alike houses up for sale. Ideally, the concept works best in cookie-cutter, tract home subdivisions. It works least for properties with unique features (advantages or disadvantages).
3. *Fair sale.* Market value assumes that both buyers and sell-ers enjoy "walkaway" willpower. Neither party feels forced to buy or sell due to pressures of time, money, or super-persuasive sales tactics. (Have you ever attended a free din-ner gathering where you sat face-to-face with a time-share salesman? The property prices that result from these sales

presentations most certainly do not reflect market value. Typically, if you try to resell a time-share, you're lucky to get 50 cents or 60 cents on the dollar.)

4. *Equal knowledge.* Market value presumes that both buyers and sellers know all of the advantages and disadvantages of a subject property as well as the prices and terms of sale for all nearby houses that have recently sold.

5. *Terms of sale.* Market value presumes that the sellers do not offer any desirable terms of financing or unusually favorable concessions (e.g., sellers pay all closing costs, sellers carry back a five percent mortgage, sellers include select pieces of furniture).

With the above definition (conditions of sale) in mind, the appraisal process directs appraisers to three different appraisal techniques: (1) the cost approach, (2) the income approach, and (3) the comparable sales approach. Typically, residential appraisers chiefly rely on the comparable sales approach. They use the cost and income approaches merely to check their results. Accordingly, we will focus here on comparable (comp) sales.

The Comparable Sales Approach

The comp sales approach really seems quite logical. If you want to know the price at which a subject property will sell, simply look at the recent sales prices of similar nearby houses. To complete this technique, appraisers use a form similar to that shown in Figure 2.1.

> **Comp sales inform, but they don't dictate.**

As you can see from this form, the appraiser lists the features of the property to be appraised. Then he selects three look-alike houses (preferably from the same neighborhood). He notes the following information:

Adjustment Process (Selected Features)			
	Comp 1	Comp 2	Comp 3
Sales price	$112,560	$106,720	$105,530
Features			
Sales concessions	0	–5,000	0
Financing concessions	–7,500	0	0
Date of sale	0	+5,000	0
Location	0	0	–10,000
Floor plan	0	+2,500	0
Garage	+5,500	0	+8,500
Pool, patio, deck	–4,500	–6,500	0
Indicated value of subject	$106,060	$102,720	$104,030

Figure 2.1   The Comparable Sales Approach.

1. All property addresses.
2. Where each comp property is located relative to the subject properties.
3. The actual price at which each comp house was sold.
4. The source of information for the comp house data.
5. Any seller financing or concessions.
6. The dates on which each of the comp houses closed.
7. A basic feature-by-feature comparison of each comp house vis-à-vis the subject property. Where differences are found, the appraiser estimates the value of each difference. However, note that positive differences result in a negative adjustment (and vice versa). Why? Because if the subject property lacks this advantage, it will sell for a lower price.
8. Adjusted sales prices for each of the comparable houses according to how they differ in total from the subject property.

In performing this final step, the appraiser asks, What price would the buyers of this similar house have paid *if* the features of this house had precisely matched those of the subject property?

The Market Value Conclusion

Once the appraiser completes this form and makes the required adjustments, the estimated market value of the subject property practically jumps out at you. If three similar nearby houses show adjusted sales prices that range between $140,200 and $146,375, it doesn't take Einstein intelligence to put a $143,500 market value on the subject property. All other things equal, that's the most probable price at which the property can be expected to sell—when that sale meets all of the conditions of a market value sale.

Strengths of the Appraisal Process

At its best, the appraisal process serves two related purposes: (1) It helps us communicate by providing a common denominator for discussions about current property values; and (2) it provides a disinterested third party's informed opinion.

Common Denominator

> **Market value provides a uniform standard for comparison.**

People buy and sell houses under all sorts of terms, conditions, negotiating pressures, and assumptions. To merely know that the house down the block sold for $378,000 is to know very little. Did the sellers offer carryback financing? Did they pay all closing costs? Did they sell by owner? Were they represented by a competent real estate agent? Likewise, we could ask many questions about the buyers' pressures, motives, market knowledge, negotiating skills, and creditworthiness. Any and all of these factors can and do affect selling prices. Therefore, to talk about price without some knowledge or assumptions about the actual transaction can easily lead to confused thinking and substantial error.

In contrast, when we talk about market value, our ability to communicate increases. Since the terms and conditions of sale are set by the definition of the term itself, market value provides a common denominator. Without this standard or benchmark of value, conversations about selling prices per se can easily prove meaningless.

Disinterested Third Party

Buyers, sellers, the guy or gal down the street, the mailman, or the FedEx driver—all may express opinions about whether the price of a property seems too high, too low, or just about right. But where did they get their information? What do they really know about the property? What biases do they hold? Does self-interest or emotional attachment color their judgment?

Can you really place much weight on such opinions? Probably not. On the other hand, when an appraiser *competently* prepares an estimate of market value, you've got an informed, objective, and disinterested opinion that you can reliably count on. Just as importantly, the appraisers clearly display the data and calculations on which they base their value estimates.

> **Comp sales give you objective, market-based information.**

Overall, these two strengths (common denominator, disinterested expertise) explain why most homebuyers, investors, sellers, and mortgage lenders use market value appraisals to inform their decision making. You should do likewise.

Weaknesses of the Appraisal Process

Although you should use market value to inform your buy/sell decisions, never rely on it as your primary guide. Even a competently prepared appraisal does not come close to answering the strategic (entrepreneurial) questions that you need to address. Here's why.

Rearview Mirror

Comp sales never purposely alert you to strategic improvements.

Even at their best, market value appraisals work only as a rearview mirror. They help you see the past. They do nothing to help you see the future. To estimate market value, an appraiser looks only to *past* sales prices. No data in the appraisal report relates to what is happening in the market right now. Nor do any appraisal facts provide clues to help you detect how the market may evolve over the coming 3, 6, or 12 months (or longer).

Indeed, the comp sales included in the appraisal report quite often look further backward than the appraisal report indicates. That's because appraisals cite the date a sale closed, not the date the buyers and sellers actually struck their deal. In some cases, buyers and sellers may have signed their sales contract two to four months prior to the date that settlement eventually occurred.

You Need Data about the Future   If you plan to fix and flip a property within, say, a 3- to 24-month time frame, you need to carefully consider what the market may throw at you in the months to come. You cannot safely assume that the relative balance of supply and demand that prevailed three to six months ago will continue unchanged.

What if you've got short-term financing that will fall due and you're counting on a sale to generate the necessary cash? Or maybe you want to refinance out of a high-cost acquisition and improvement loan into lower-cost, long-term financing? Either way, you must appraise the future, not the past.

Buy, Fix, and Hold   Even when you plan to hold a property as a rental, you still need to concern yourself with changes in the short term. Will the property rent up quickly at a premium rent? Or will you face hot and heavy competition from several new apartment or condo complexes that are scheduled to come to market shortly?

As a buy, fix, and hold investor, you also want to assess the long-term potential for development. Ideally, you would like to buy properties in those areas where shortages of buildable land, high construction costs, and government zoning and environmental restrictions minimize competition from new subdivision, apartment, and condo projects.

Narrow Focus

As an investor, you always want to compare potential appreciation rates among different neighborhoods, communities, and types of properties. But a market value appraisal only gives you a glimpse of the pricing for one type of house in one area of town.

To illustrate: Assume that you must buy and hold for at least five years one of two properties, either:

1. You can buy property A at a price of $10,000 below its market value.
2. Or you can buy property B at a price $10,000 above its market value.

Property A will probably appreciate two percent per year over the next five years. Property B will likely appreciate six percent per year over the next five years. Your purchase price for either property will equal $150,000. Which do you choose?

Nearly all popular books on real estate urge you to search for properties that you can buy for less than market value. Good idea. Unless you plan to hold for perhaps 3, 5, 10 years or longer. In that case, it pays to carefully forecast appreciation potential. In fact, it often turns out that bargain-priced properties show up much more frequently in neighborhoods where values increase at relatively slower rates of appreciation.

Bargain Price or Appreciation Potential?   Now, here's the answer to the above question: Property B gives you the most profit. Assuming a current market value for the property of $140,000 (remember, you paid $10,000 above market) and a six percent per annum rate of appreciation, after five years property B is worth $188,720, whereas A would show a market value of just $176,800. After 10 years, property B's value would shoot up to $254,395, whereas property A's value would have merely edged up to $195,364.

> **Go mainly for appreciation potential, not necessarily a bargain price.**

Smart investors love to buy properties at below-market prices. But before they jump to snag a presumably good deal, they compare relative values across neighborhoods and property types. Smart investors know that over the mid- to long run, strong appreciation potential should outweigh today's immediate discount. Warren Buffet says that he would rather buy a company with great potential at a fair price than buy a mediocre company at a bargain price. You should adopt a similar investment strategy.

Condo or House?   Let me illustrate again through personal example. In the early 1980s, I was buying properties in Dallas, Texas. At the time, condominiums were all the rage. Both home-buyers and investors were snapping them up almost as fast as they came to market. Yet, I thought, something's crazy here.

Within the same neighborhood, condos were selling at $100 per square foot, while perfectly nice single-family houses were selling at $65 per square foot. It seemed obvious to me that relative to condos, houses provided a far better buy. So I decided to go against the trend of the day and bought houses. As I forecasted, within a few years, condomania subsided. Homebuyers and investors came to realize what I had figured out several years earlier. As a result, their buying shifted from condos to houses. Condo prices suffered. House prices shot up.

> **Always compare the prices of competing *types* of properties.**

Even if I had originally bought a new condo at a price 10 percent below market, the houses I bought at market value would still have proved to be the more profitable investment.

The Appraisal Process Shuns Entrepreneurial Vision

As an entrepreneurial fix-up investor, you want to discover those properties that offer (or could offer) unique features that a select target market of buyers (renters) would value very highly. The appraisal process provides clues toward this goal only by chance, not design. Appraisers try to choose only those comparable properties whose existing features closely match those of a subject property. Their appraisals of market value never point out those features that could significantly boost a home's value. To a very limited extent, the price adjustments for slight feature differences may at times provide a glimpse of insight, but typically they do not.

> **Now you know why very few appraisers ever build wealth in real estate.**

In contrast to appraisers, when you survey the sales prices (or rent levels) of competitive properties, look for those striking and unique differences that really give some properties a distinct competitive edge. Remember, when appraisers follow the appraisal process, they hate property differences and love similarities. As an entrepreneur, you want to view the marketplace from a precisely opposite perspective. You want to find or create those differences that will really make a startling, advantageous difference.

Summing Up the Appraisal Process

Far too many homebuyers and investors naively focus on the market value. They view competing properties only to learn current market prices. They then use this market information as a benchmark against which they formulate their purchase offers. Overall, they believe that the bigger their price discount from market value, the better their buy.

Entrepreneurs choose a somewhat different strategy. Yes, they, too, try to buy at a below-market price. But that's not their prime goal. Instead, they evaluate the competitive market to achieve three additional objectives: (1) Entrepreneurs forecast the quantity and quality of competition that may be coming to market; (2) they compare types of properties, neighborhoods, and communities to ferret out the types of properties and locations that offer the best *relative* values and potential for appreciation; and (3) they look at every property to figure the amount of value they can create.

If you will go out and talk with successful investors, you will find that very few have earned their fortunes by picking up properties at prices 30 percent below their current market value. From time to time, all of us do score such fantastic bargains. But over a career, to build wealth, we most want to avoid losses, gain appreciation, create value, and, for rentals, generate positive cash flows.

You Need More Market Data

To achieve rehab and investment profits, you will need to follow the appraisal process and research the past sales prices of houses whose features and locations closely match the properties that you may buy. But to really understand and forecast a changing competitive environment, you need more facts about your area's housing trends. You can boost profits and minimize risks when you also bring other types of supply and demand data into your effort to discover and create your most profitable strategy:

> **You can make far more money as a value creator than you can as a vulture.**

1. *New construction.* Check with your local planning office. Find out the number of subdivision, apartment, and

condo projects that are planned or are under construction. Where are they located? What price (rent) ranges prevail? What features do they include?

2. *Buildable land.* Does the geographic area you're looking at include large tracts of nearby vacant land? Or do land shortages set the norm? How difficult is it for builders and developers to get their building permits approved?

3. *Inventory of homes up for sale.* Your local association of Realtors tracks this number weekly. Is it trending up or down? At the current rate of sales, how many months of inventory remain? Is this number shrinking or lengthening? Ask a Realtor to break the figures down by price range, location, and type of property.

4. *Time on market.* On average, listed houses may sell in a matter of weeks, or sales may take six months or more. Where is your market trending?

5. *Selling price/asking price.* In hot markets, homes may sell for more than their asking price. In slow markets, sellers may eventually come down 10 percent to 20 percent or more. Where does your market stand?

6. *Vacancy rates.* Does the area show an increasing or decreasing trend in vacancies? Check for houses, apartments, and rental condo units. What areas show the most (least) strength?

7. *Rental rates.* Are rents increasing or decreasing? Are the large apartment complexes offering rental concessions such as a free bicycle, no security deposit, or short-term leases? Pay close attention to vacancies and rental rates according to apartment (house) size and location.

8. *Mortgage delinquencies and foreclosures.* When mortgage delinquencies and foreclosures begin to increase, bargain prices become more plentiful. But also, a large number of mortgage defaults signal a market about to worsen.

9. *Types of buyers (renters).* What types of buyers (renters) do you plan to appeal to? What features and amenities

will they value most highly? What differences can you create for your properties that will make the big and deciding differences to your customers?

10. *Pricing and financing.* What price and/or terms can you offer that will generate a good profit for you as well as a great buy for your intended market?

Overall, to maximize your returns, you need detailed knowledge of the features and sales prices of comparable properties, a good forecast of competitive trends, and a deep feeling for the likes, dislikes, turn-ons, and turnoffs of your targeted buyers (tenants). With this informational advantage, you're now positioned to develop a winning renovation strategy. With one eye on the competition and one eye on your potential customers, you will be able to craft your improvement strategy to create a preferred value proposition (PVP).

In other words, your improvement and marketing strategy will explicitly acknowledge that before people choose a place to live, they typically shop and compare a dozen or more competing properties—often in different neighborhoods. They weigh and consider features, location, price, and terms. Then they go for the best value they can find that meets or surpasses their wants, needs, and expectations. In recognizing this fact, when you craft your value-creating efforts, you will persistently ask yourself, How can I best make my property stand above its competitors in the eyes of buyers (renters), yet do so in a way that gives me a wide profit margin? By the time you complete this book, you will be able to answer that critical question.

> **Always focus on building a competitive advantage for your properties.**

CHAPTER 3

Your Formula for Profits

Do you know what distinguishes professional, profit-seeking entrepreneurs from the many amateurs who get involved in remodeling? It's the way they calculate the expected selling prices of their renovated properties. Amateurs buy a property, fix it up, and then try to price it high enough to recoup their rehab expenses plus, say, another $10,000 or $20,000 in profit. In other words, amateurs tend to use a cost-plus-profit figure to arrive at their selling price. Bad idea. This naive way of operating explains why too many homeowners and novice investors lose money on their fix-up work. With after-the-fact, cost-plus pricing, the hoped-for sales price all too frequently grossly exceeds market reality.

> **Calculate how much buyers will pay before you budget your costs of purchase and renovating.**

In contrast, professionals first study the market. They closely inspect competing properties. They evaluate the features, strengths, and weaknesses of these properties. They carefully track asking prices, selling prices, and rent levels. Professionals contrast and compare how a property looks today with how it might look tomorrow. Even more, they imagine a target market of buyers (renters) to whom they would like to appeal. Professionals learn everything that they can about these potential buyers. Then after thinking

Minimum improved value (MIV)	$ _____
Less	
Purchase price	_____
Acquisition costs	_____
Improvement costs	_____
Financing costs	_____
Other holding costs	_____
Selling costs	_____
Opportunity costs	_____
Oops factor	_____
Income taxes	_____
Net profit	$ _____

Figure 3.1   Your Formula for Profits.

through all of their facts, visions, and forecasts, professionals design their improvement strategy and calculate their potential profits according to the profit formula shown in Figure 3.1.

The Pieces of the Puzzle

You might think of the profit formula in Figure 3.1 as a jigsaw puzzle. Each entry forms a piece of this puzzle. You succeed in putting the pieces together when at the end of the game, you generate a bright profit picture.

In most cases, though, the pieces of this puzzle aren't fixed in size. Through your skill, knowledge, and creative efforts, you can make some pieces larger and others smaller. Indeed, the

> **Juggle the pieces until you see a pretty picture of profits.**

careful, entrepreneurial investor typically works through a variety of iterations—or we might call them "what if" calculations.

When the renovation costs or purchase price, for example, seem too high, the entrepreneur looks for ways to slice them down to size. Or maybe the estimated improved value seems too low to make the project come out right. In that case, you take another look at your renovations and overall plan. You try to figure if there are even more or better ways to create value than you've currently come up with. As you read through this chapter and the remaining chapters of this book, you will be given scores of ideas that relate to every piece of this profit formula. All you need do is put together the combination of pieces that will yield a big bottom line that brings a smile to your face and a boost to your bank balance.

Now let's turn to a brief description for each line item in this profit formula.

Minimum Improved Value (MIV)

As Stephen Covey advises, "Begin with the end in mind." So, your profit formula begins with this question: What's the lowest reasonable price at which I know I could sell this property once I've completed the changes that I envision for the property (and its neighborhood)? To determine this end point of your renovation efforts, you combine your knowledge of market prices (the appraisal process) with your insights about how to create a competitive advantage for the property.

> **Keep your MIV well within the price range of the neighborhood.**

Except in unusual circumstances, you should limit the minimum improved values (MIVs) of your properties to no more than 80 percent of the top selling prices in the neighborhood. If you aim higher, you run the risk of overshooting the market. Homes that sit toward the high end of a neighborhood price range tend to sell with more difficulty. On the other hand, properties that sell in the low- to mid-price range for a neighborhood tend to go quickly. When you can acquire and improve at the low end, you gain more upside potential.

Purchase Price

As mentioned before, most fix-it, flip-it books tell you that to make a deal work, you must buy your fix-up property at a price 25 percent to 30 percent below its current as-is market value. Not true. Entrepreneurial renovators do not just fix up or repair properties. They find hidden values. They create value. They turn sow's ears into silk purses. They even revitalize neighborhoods.

> **Try to discover or create hidden value.**

I again emphasize this point for two reasons: First, those investors who insist on 30 percent discounts often blindly pass up properties that offer far higher profit potential—even though the sellers won't give such a large discount. When you evaluate a property for purchase, focus on profit potential. Naturally, a steep discount will help you achieve that end—but it's not a necessary component. Second, by insisting on an outsized (and often unrealistic) price discount, you could spend valuable time chasing deals that you will rarely find.

> **Negotiate bargain prices, but don't limit yourself to those properties that you can buy at a steep discount.**

Don't get me wrong. Do try to negotiate steep discounts and bargain prices whenever possible. And Chapter 10 shows you where and how to increase your odds of doing so. But never confuse the profits earned from purchase discounts with those earned through value-creating improvements. If you lose sight of the difference, you will invest time and money on renovations when you might just as well flip the property and pocket some quick, easy profits.

Acquisition Costs

In addition to the purchase price of your property, you pay for acquisition costs such as title insurance, property inspections, attorney fees, an appraisal, a survey, and other miscellaneous expenses. Quite often you can reduce these costs through negotiation and comparative shopping. But there's no way to eliminate them. Make sure your profit formula includes a realistic figure to cover these costs.

Improvement Costs

Your improvement costs may include amounts for labor, materials, landscaping, design fees, and government permits. When reviewing cost estimates from contractors, break down each of these figures into as many itemized components as possible. Then attack each one. Always search for the most cost-effective means to solve each repair problem or to capitalize on each opportunity to create value. Never accept the first cost estimate you receive. Never accept a contractor's *gross* bid for a job. Always critically review each line item in the cost estimate. Savvy cost management can sometimes turn so-so deals into real moneymakers. (You'll find helpful tips on working with contractors and making improvements later in this chapter.)

> **Persistently look for ways to reduce the costs of your improvements as you also enhance their appeal.**

Financing Costs

During the period you hold a property, you will need to pay interest on any amounts you have borrowed to acquire the property or to fund the costs of improvements. In addition, you may have to pay points, a loan origination fee, and a mortgage application fee. If you raise funds from a partner to help finance your acquisition and improvements, the amount you pay for these monies also counts as a cost of financing.

As with all other costs, savvy planning can help you slash the costs of your financing. Chapter 12 shows you how to effect this result by using short-term mortgage assumptions, lease options, "subject to" purchases, and similar techniques of creative finance. You'll also learn about the FHA 203(k) mortgage, which permits owner-occupant homebuyers to roll nearly all of their costs of purchase, acquisition, closing, and improvement into one mortgage. What's even better, your buyer can assume this mortgage for only a small fee.

Other Holding Costs

Even if you own a property for only three to six months before you resell it, you'll pay property and liability insurance premiums, property taxes, and utility bills. These amounts add another type of cost for you to charge against your potential profits.

Selling Costs

> **Learn how to profitably sell by owner.**

Most investors use real estate agents to sell their properties. Normally, agents charge 4 percent to 7 percent of your property's sales price. However, if you follow the marketing pointers provided in Chapter 9, you will eliminate the Realtor's commission. You still will need to pay some monies for advertising, promotion, and perhaps bird-dog fees. Plus, as is customary, you will pay some portion of the settlement expenses that your buyer incurs.

Opportunity Costs

To buy and renovate properties, you will develop a strategy, look for properties, negotiate deals, supervise contractors, and go through the selling process. All of these activities require time and effort. Even though these personal efforts don't draw down your cash, you should figure them into your profit formula.

How much do you think your time is worth? Given your job skills and education, how much could you earn per hour working in your own field? The more you earn, the more it will pay you to hire other people to perform as much of your work as possible. More importantly, never count as part of your fix-up profits any hands-on renovation work that you yourself perform. If you actually paint, hammer, plumb, cut grass, or finish floors, tally up the value of this labor as an opportunity cost. Don't confuse the wages you should earn for manual work with those profits you earn through entrepreneurship and strategy. You're seeking to build wealth through real estate, not merely secure self-employment as a carpenter or painter.

> **Pay yourself for any labor you perform.**

Oops Factor

I wish I could tell you that perfect planning yields perfect results. But you and I both know that we make mistakes. The people we hire make mistakes. Ballpark estimates grow into cost overruns. A three-month fix and flip time horizon evolves into a five- or six-month project. Interest rates shoot up and shut your target buyers out of the market. Your MIV becomes a maximum. When any or all of these setbacks occur, the oops factor allows you a margin of safety.

How much should you allocate to the oops factor? It all depends. For simple jobs in hot markets, probably 1 percent or 2 percent of your property's MIV will prove adequate. For larger or more complex projects, you may be wise to use 5 percent to 10 percent of MIV.

As another approach to allow for the oops factor, identify those individual cost estimates that present the most uncertainty.

> **Oops! We all make mistakes. Budget for them.**

Then, figure your bottom-line profits under two assumptions. One, assume low-end costs; two, assume high-end costs. When the deal still looks good with the high-end cost estimates, go for it. If not, rethink your strategy. Search out ideas and bids from other contractors. If no solution appears, move on to another property.

Income Taxes

If you plan to fix and flip, as opposed to fix and hold, I again remind you to discuss your sales strategy with a tax advisor. Typically, any time you sell a property within 12 months after you've purchased it, the IRS taxes your gain at ordinary income tax rates. (For most investors, ordinary tax rates range between 25 and 40 percent.) Even worse, should you fix and flip three or four properties within, say, a two-year time frame, the IRS may call you a dealer.

Name-Calling Can Hurt You   As a child you may have recited, "Sticks and stones may break my bones, but names will never hurt me." Well, if the IRS calls you a dealer, it will hurt you. You may lose all right to claim long-term capital gains from real estate on your income tax return. The IRS may classify every property you own (except your home) as inventory. And when you sell inventory, you cannot enjoy those relatively low capital gain rates that run just 10 percent to 20 percent of your gain.

> **Don't let the IRS call you a dealer.**

The IRA Tax-Deferred Option   Popular personal finance magazines and other Wall Street hypesters almost never mention

| You might be able to tap your retirement account to fund real estate investments. |

the fact that you may be able to buy real estate through a self-directed IRA or some types of employer-sponsored, tax-deferred retirement plans such as the 401(k), Keogh, or SEP. You will need to use a third party retirement plan administrator to handle your transactions. But, nevertheless, you call the shots. You decide what properties to buy and what improvements to make.

For more information on this tax-deferred technique, visit Mid-Ohio Securities at www.midoh.com.

How to Escape Income Taxes As noted previously, owner-occupant homeowners can flip their home every two years and pocket up to $250,000 of capital gains tax free ($500,000 for married couples filing jointly).[1] (Also, homeowners typically can obtain financing on better terms and at lower costs than investors.) Without a doubt, tax-free gains for homeowners represent one of the best breaks available under the tax code. If at all possible, take advantage of it.

| Always check with a tax advisor to search for ways to reduce your taxes. |

Fortunately, real estate investors, too, can escape income taxes on the profits they earn from property improvements and appreciation—at least during the time that they're building up their portfolio of properties. To achieve this end, they can use a Section 1031 exchange. With a 1031 exchange, you simultaneously (within a specified period) sell your property and buy another one.[2] Your entire equity counts

---

1. Under the "unforeseen circumstance" (e.g., job change, divorce, ill health) rule, the IRS may permit you to realize a tax-free gain even though you sell your home before two years have elapsed.

2. Generally, you must complete the total transaction within 45 to 180 days. Consult your exchange pro for the details as they would apply to your specific property acquisition and disposition.

toward the down payment for your new purchase. Over a period of 8 to 12 years, some investors have used their Section 1031 rule multiple times to work themselves up from a $100,000 property to a $10,000,000 property—all tax free!

Profit Formula in Action

In later chapters, we'll discuss each item in the profit formula. You'll learn how to arrange financing, how to create value with improvements, how to effectively market the property to its target market, and how to raise the money. If you're like most of the new investors that I meet in my investment seminars, though, right now you're probably most concerned with the difficulties of the renovation process itself. So, before we move on, let's look at some basic pointers on getting the work done.

Getting the Work Done

Even though you may have heard any number of remodeling "horror" stories, rest assured that by following basic precautions, you can keep your projects on schedule and within budget. To transform your entrepreneurial ideas into profits, carefully address the following issues:

- ◆ Know your limits.
- ◆ Clearly distinguish the personal from the profitable.
- ◆ Carefully plan your total project, and then work your project according to plan.
- ◆ Secure bids from competent and dependable contractors and tradespeople.
- ◆ Eliminate the possibility of mechanic's liens.
- ◆ Obtain all necessary permits and comply with all zoning and building codes.

Know Your Limits

Many renovators who get into difficulty do so because they stretch (or go beyond) their actual knowledge, time, money, or capacity to bear risk. This affliction occurs most often at two vulnerable times. As you might expect, the first point of vulnerability occurs with the enthusiastic beginner who rushes into a deal without a full due diligence property inspection and, correspondingly, informed cost estimates for repairs and improvements.

> **Try a few easy jobs first.**

The second major point of vulnerability can occur after your first three or four successes. With first rounds of success comes a tad bit of overconfidence or even arrogance. You may tend to jump into projects for which prior experience has not really prepared you. Or, you may skip some steps in due diligence because you say to yourself, I know what I'm doing, or This won't be a problem.

When I was learning to fly my own plane, I was told to memorize this apothegm:

> There are old pilots. There are bold pilots. But there are no old *and* bold pilots.

I believe the same lesson holds true for real estate renovators. As you approach each project you contemplate, realistically weigh the requirements of the project against your capabilities. Consequently, use your first project or two as a learning experience. Conservatively figure your MIV. Overestimate costs (time and money) as well as your oops factor. Negotiate tough on price. It is better to walk away from five potentially good deals than get in over your head in one disastrous project.

Clearly Distinguish the Personal from the Profitable

Each year, *Remodeling,* an industry trade journal, features an article that presumes to tell homeowners how much "payback" they can expect to receive for various types of home improvement

> **Homeowners often fail to create value because they "personalize" their renovations.**

projects. Apart from the methodological deficiencies of the survey from which this publication derives its figures, you should ignore these results (which are reported widely in newspapers and "home"-type magazines). Why? Because these figures do not distinguish *personal* home improvement projects from those undertaken by *professional profit-seeking* entrepreneurs.

What Difference Does It Make? Let me begin with an example. Recently, I stopped by a "for sale" house that was undergoing renovations. As I spoke with the (amateur) homeowner, she bubbled with enthusiasm over the $25,000 that she had just spent to remodel the kitchen in the house. Will she and her husband get back their money for this kitchen improvement? Not likely. Here's why:

1. *Piecemeal renovation.* The new kitchen no longer fit the old house. In fact, it looked out of place. When professionals remodel, they don't approach tasks piecemeal. They always envision the end result in terms of the total impact. Seldom can you take one part of a house to a level substantially above the rest and expect a profitable payback.
2. *Materials over design.* Although the kitchen looked good with its expensive Wood-Mode cabinets, Mexican tile floor, and upscale appliances, the work triangle was horribly ill designed. The stove top, range, and microwave were located 18 feet away from the kitchen sink across a wide-open expanse of floor area. Any professional knows that all major ingredients of a kitchen (fridge, work counter, ovens, sink, range) should be positioned for no more than a three-step triangle for ease of food preparation.
3. *"We've spent $25,000 . . ."* Amateurs frequently emphasize how much they've spent on renovations as if that amount automatically justifies a corresponding increase in value.

4. *Serious negatives remained uncorrected.* The house still retained its original (and functionally obsolete) awning-type crank windows and the expanse of windows in the family room looked out into an unlandscaped backyard and a neighbor's house located not more than 20 to 25 feet away. Again, in keeping with the principle of "total effect," a professional would allocate renovation dollars such that these negatives were cured. Seldom will pizzazz sell, if serious basic flaws remain.

> **Never view improvements piecemeal. Focus on the total impact the renovated house will have on buyers.**

As so often happens, this renovator appears to have gotten carried away with her *personal* vision for her kitchen. Unfortunately, for purposes of achieving a profitable payback, personal visions that ignore market realities too easily turn into money losers.

Professionals Market Test Their Ideas
Professionals never go forward with their ideas until they have tested them against talks with design experts, a survey of competitive houses and sales prices, and, yes, common sense (i.e., buyers' eyes). Professionals also explore their ideas with top realty agents who frequently list and sell houses in the neighborhood. Before you begin your work, verify that you're allocating your dollars wisely. Discipline your personal enthusiasms with a dose of market reality. Buyers pay for benefits they value. They do not reimburse investors for the costs of their personal preferences or off-the-wall ideas.

> **Your total plan determines your success.**

Plan Your Project, Work Your Plan

In keeping with the principle of integration, before you begin any work whatsoever, create a detailed renovation plan for the entire property. This step will serve you in a number of ways:

1. *Budgeted priorities.* As noted above, you want to allocate your renovation dollars across the total project such that you will receive the biggest bang for the buck. Only after you've planned the total work can you realistically trade off and prioritize. The frequently voiced approach of "we might as well get started on this now and figure out the rest later" lays a sure path to regret.

2. *Sequencing.* When you proceed *without* a complete plan in view, you undoubtedly will waste time and money. Some early work will need to be redone, you will lose potential economies of scale, and you could end up throwing away materials early on that actually could have been put to use later—if only you had thought about it. In other words, a fully developed plan helps you sequence and coordinate your work to achieve optimum results.

3. *Change orders.* Some contractors bid their jobs low and make their profits on change orders. They know that many renovators (especially amateurs) follow the "we can decide that later" approach, and that deciding later means that renovators typically lose their power to negotiate and secure competitive bids. The contractor can price change orders for maximum profit (his or her profit, of course, not yours).

4. *"As long as . . ."* A sketchy plan also brings about the three most costly words in renovation, "as long as . . ."

    You know, "As long as we're now doing this, we might as well . . ." If you want cost overruns, make "as long as" your standard operating procedure.

> **Include your "As long as . . ." improvements into your original plan. Avoid add-ons.**

5. *Avoid trade wars.* If you live in a strongly union area, you should be aware that, on occasion, jurisdictional wars break out on jobs over which trade (plumbing, carpentry, electrical, etc.) is entitled to what type of work—often down to the slightest detail. A fully detailed plan can help ensure that potential disputes are

headed off before they become trade wars. Allocate the work early on.

Naturally, you will never achieve perfection through advance planning. You will always want to modify, omit, or add to. Nevertheless, a comprehensive, upfront, detailed plan will serve you far better than the ad hoc one-step-at-a-time approach. Profitable renovations do not proceed according to the whim and fancy of the moment. They proceed according to thoughtful priorities, sequencing, scheduling, and budgeting.

Secure Bids

When you begin to solicit bids for your jobs, your possible choice of contractors, subcontractors, tradespeople, and handymen will run into the hundreds. (But, of course, the same can be said for nearly every trade or profession.) So, before you secure a bid, set credibility criteria for the people whom you will consider for the job(s). Then, make sure all bids cover the same scope of work, competency, quality of materials, and guarantees. Third, select the best (not necessarily the lowest) bidder.

> **You can achieve top quality with low bids.**

Establish Credibility   It does you little good to secure bids from persons who either can't or won't fulfill your renovation agreement. How might you assure yourself of bidder credibility? Generally, you can try some combination of the following:

◆ Ask around. Obtain referrals from people you know. Since home remodeling has become one of our chief American pastimes, this approach will generally turn up some good candidates. You can also obtain referrals from home supply stores, the yellow pages, and the classified and display ads in newspapers.

◆ Once you've obtained some names, interview the people. Secure additional job references, credit information, and specific work history. You must also determine whether the potential bidder can start and complete your job in a timely manner.

◆ Seek confirming evidence that the person is licensed, bonded, and insured. Except for relatively small cosmetic or cleanup work, you should nearly always avoid those who work "off the books" or in some other ways skirt the basic operating procedures of a reputable business.

Scope of Work   Here's another reason you need detailed plans. To secure comparable bids, you want to make sure that all contractors' bids cover the same scope of work and quality of materials. You certainly don't want to walk around the house with a bidder and say things like, "We're going to want these rooms painted; we'll need new flooring here and over there; and we want the kitchen cabinets replaced, and maybe change that light fixture."

> **Make sure your competitive bids cover precisely the same labor and materials (scope of work).**

In terms of preliminary ballpark discussions, you might rely on this type of discussion to get you thinking about the work you actually want to consider. But to accurately solicit and compare bids—and to prevent later controversy about exactly what work the bid covers—every bidder must understand precisely what they're bidding on.

In those instances where you haven't yet decided on brand, model, and color (or similar types of decisions), investigate typical prices. Then specify an "allowance" factor in the bid. Or alternatively, request the bid with an "owner will provide" exception.

Comparing Bids and Bidders   In addition to making sure that all contractors fully understand the precise scope of work that will fall within their responsibility, ask them to submit their bids in similar line-item detail. Do not accept gross bids, that is, bids that omit a precise listing of itemized costs (e.g., kitchen remodeling—$12,627).

The detailed, line-item bid helps you in four ways:

1. *Verify comparability.* Without detail, you can't know for sure that the bids cover the same scope of work and quality of materials.
2. *Question, question.* Use the bid process to learn what, how, and why. The more you understand, the better you will become at finding and designing the most profitable renovations.
3. *Negotiate, negotiate.* As you compare line items among contractors, you will likely find some wide differences. To a certain degree, you can use low estimates from one contractor to justify a cost reduction from another. "I'm leaning toward you for this job, but you show $2,800 to move that wall and replace the windows. If you were to get the job, do you think you could do it for $1,800? That's the price others have quoted."
4. *Cherry picking.* Some hardball renovators I know "cherry pick" their contractors. They ferret out the itemized low-cost items from several bidders and award multiple jobs accordingly. As you might suspect, some contractors won't stand for this ploy. Try it and you may destroy good will and lose a good contractor. Nevertheless, at times you could give it a go.

Once the bids are in and you've questioned and negotiated, whom do you choose? If you're certain that you've established both credibility and comparability, then I see no reason to choose the mid- to high-cost bidders. In my experience, the adage, "you get what you pay for"—which implies the lower the price, the lower the quality—has not proven true.

> **You get what you *bargain* for.**

That doesn't mean I always select the low bidder. For I also want someone who communicates well, coherently explains answers to my endless questions, and displays a fair sense of give and take. When a bidder combines these attributes with lower costs, he or she has won the job (subject only to memorializing our full agreement in writing).

Secure Lien Releases

Virtually any person or firm who supplies labor or materials for property improvement may file a lien against that property—if that supplier doesn't get paid in full for his or her contribution to the improvement project. Say you pay your contractor 100 percent of all amounts agreed. But your contractor doesn't pay the company where he bought the roofing shingles that are now affixed to the top of your house. As a matter of law in every state, that unpaid supplier of the shingles can look to you for payment.

You can claim, "I paid the contractor, go collect from him." But to no avail. The same principle holds for the painting, electrical, and plumbing subcontractors who worked on your property. If the contractor doesn't pay them, you must—or face a lien on the property and a cloud on the title.

The Solution   To avoid this nasty problem, at the time you pay your prime contractor, request that he complete and sign an unconditional waiver and release form. (To secure an *unconditional* release, you may need to pay with a cashier's check—otherwise the contractor may give you a *conditional* release which will mature into an unconditional release once your personal check is cleared by the bank.) In addition, require your contractor to submit to you copies of unconditional lien releases from each and every subcontractor and supplier.

> **Always secure lien releases.**

Because mechanic's lien laws may vary by county and state, check with a local attorney to find the precise forms and procedures that will protect you in the legal jurisdiction where your property is located. But regardless of where you are located, never pay for work to your property without simultaneously obtaining a binding lien release.

Buyer Beware   Now let's view the lien problem from the buyer's perspective. Say you offer to buy a home that shows off a brand-new exterior paint job. Your lender obliges your request for a fast closing. In just three weeks, the deal's done. Shortly thereafter, you receive notice that a painting contractor has slapped a lien against what is now *your* house.

You complain to the unpaid contractor, "Wait a minute, you can't do that. Go after the previous owner. I didn't have anything to do with that paint job." But again, your complaint falls on deaf ears. To clear the title to the property, you must pay the painter. In turn, you can go after the seller for reimbursement. Maybe you will get your money back, maybe you won't.

> Be wary of houses with recent repairs or improvements. Ask to see the lien releases.

One fact, though, remains. Mechanic's liens are levied against a property, not a person. To protect yourself as a buyer, always ask for copies of the seller's lien releases for any work to the property (just to be safe) that has occurred during the preceding 12 months.

Stay Legal: Obtain All Necessary Permits and Comply with All Zoning and Building Codes

Some foolish renovators take the view, "We don't need no stinking permits." But as I emphasize throughout this book, you do need to secure all required permits and comply with all zoning laws and other applicable ordinances. True, in days gone by, do-it-yourselfers, cheapskate renovators, and bootleg contractors could ignore the law with reckless abandon and yet incur minimal risk.

Today, most governments no longer tolerate this behavior. Just as importantly, most buyers now employ professional home inspectors who will frequently note nonconforming work. If a contractor tells you, "Oh, you don't need to bother with all of that bureaucratic red tape. I can do that work without a permit and save you a serious amount of money. Of course, you will need to pay me in cash for the job. That's not a problem, is it?" Don't fall for this ploy. When a bootleg contractor screws up, who's responsible? You are! So stay legal. It is to that topic that we now turn.

CHAPTER 4

Make Regulations Work for You

Savvy renovators learn the laws and profit from the loopholes.

In today's world of real estate, you can't escape regulation.[1] Whenever you buy, finance, renovate, own, lease, use, manage, convert, or sell property, you will need to learn the rights, remedies, restrictions, and yes, opportunities that such rules create. Inexplicably, nearly all books on fixers, as well as those that deal (more generally) with investing in real estate ignore this vital topic.

In my experience, widespread ignorance in this area leads to five types of serious errors:

1. *Missed advantage.* As an entrepreneur, you want to renovate, manage, and sell your properties to create the highest profits. Yet, without detailed knowledge of what you can and cannot legally do, you can miss profitable possibilities or you might incorrectly assume that you can make some changes that in fact the law prohibits.

---

1. Of course, in today's world, virtually no activity of consequence escapes regulation. In this respect, real estate fits the norm.

2. *Purchase errors.* Prior to purchase, you must learn whether the property conforms to all applicable rules. Without this knowledge, you may find that you must undertake remodeling efforts that catch you by surprise. If that enclosed porch or converted attic doesn't comply with the regulations, it's you who may have to pay to tear out these illegal improvements and rebuild it according to code.

3. *Mistakes in use.* Land-use rules not only create exclusive (and inclusive) zoning districts (commercial, residential, industrial), such regulations may also pertain to occupancy, signage, parking, home occupations, noise, yard care, and even whether you (or your tenants) can put up a basketball hoop or hang clothes on an outdoor clothesline.

4. *Mismanagement of rentals.* Federal, state, and local laws may govern anything from security deposits to discrimination to eviction. Failure to follow lawful rules and procedures can subject you to fines or liability claims and court judgments.

5. *Sales and leasing miscues.* Not only do laws prohibit certain defined types of intentional discrimination, rules may also govern your print advertising, property disclosures, and for sale (for rent) sign size and placement.

To win the game of real estate, you've really got no choice. You must either follow the rules, try to get the rules changed, or seek a lawful exception. All too often, I've heard investors and homebuyers rail against the rules of government or the rules of their homeowners associations (HOAs). Yet the rules complained of were in effect at the time these people bought. They simply failed to investigate.

Can you imagine sitting down for a hand of poker, joining a foursome for a round of golf, or stepping onto a squash court, racquet in hand—without first learning the rules of the game? No. Doesn't make sense, does it? Unless you simply don't care about winning. But if you do want to win, please do what many investors

Learn the rules and you can play a winning hand.	fail to do. First, study the government, private, and contractual rules that govern your property (or the property that you're evaluating to buy). Your superior knowledge will pay off directly in two ways: (1) You will capitalize on profitable opportunities that others miss, and (2) you will steer around those potholes and roadblocks that cause others grief and misfortune.

In this chapter, we will merely highlight the types of rules and restrictions that may apply to the properties you buy because space does not permit a full-bodied presentation. Nevertheless, this introduction will put you on the path to learn the sources and types of rules that you need to look out for in your area.

Sources of Rules and Regulations

As a starting point, let's look at the main sources of restrictions that may govern your properties:

- ◆ Governments (federal, state, county, city)
- ◆ Homeowners associations
    - ◆ Private contracts such as mortgages, insurance policies, and easements

Use the rules to control the neighborhood riffraff.

Note, too, these restrictions don't just govern *your* property. They also govern your neighbors and your tenants. Often, you can enlist various rules to stop others from acting in ways that run down the value of your property.

Governments

Government authority to regulate a property or property owner generally relates to where the property is located. However, locations aren't always what they seem. People sometimes buy a property just outside the city limits to escape high taxes or strict zoning. Then, they find that, in fact, the city still maintains authority over them. In some instances, cities regulate into the county up to a mile or more beyond the city limits.

Likewise for coastal zoning and land use. Logic may tell you that coastal zoning applies only to coastline properties. But the law may say something much broader. Even school districts may not govern where you assume. Some homebuyers have purposely bought homes in a certain area of Highland Park, Texas, only to later learn that their kids must attend Dallas schools rather than those of the preferred Highland Park. One of my previous homes carried a Berkeley, California, address, yet the property was subject to the zoning laws and building codes of Oakland, California.

> **Look closely to learn which governments regulate the property.**

Thus, as a first step to understanding the law, clearly identify what government jurisdictions, departments, and agencies can reign over you and your property. The answer to this question may not be as obvious as it might seem.

Who Really Administers and Enforces the Rules?   Have you ever danced the government runaround? It's not fun. But sometimes you must. "We don't handle that. You'll have to see . . ."

When dealing with regulatory issues, you might have to shuttle back and forth among various agencies and departments of government. What's the answer? Persistence and knowledge. If you encounter this type of runaround, don't give up. Especially when you're trying to enforce a rule against a neighborhood scalawag, government clerks may claim that (1) it's not their responsibility; (2) you must first fill out six pages of forms in triplicate; or maybe, (3) yes, the offense falls within our domain, but "we just don't have the time or the personnel to follow up on these types of complaints."

Don't accept these types of answers. Press persistently (but gently) for the results you want. If still no positive response, write the elected official who ultimately exercises responsibility over that department. Send copies to both the department head and the clerk(s) in question. In severe cases, you can sometimes ask a judge to issue a writ of mandamus. (Do you remember *Marbury vs. Madison*?) In issuing a writ, the judge can order government officials to enforce the law. (Similarly, you can also get a judge to force members of an HOA to comply with the association's declarations, bylaws, and rules. We discuss this possibility in more detail later in this chapter.)

> **You can ask a judge to force neighborhood violators to clean up their properties.**

Back Up Persistence with Knowledge   To learn about land-use laws, you can now access most local, state, and federal laws as well as judicial opinions over the Internet (e.g., www.municode.com or www.lexis.com). As a second possibility, talk with other property owners and investors. Find out their experiences in working with regulatory personnel. Learn how they cut through the red tape. Also, consult a lawyer who specializes in property regulatory issues (not the typical real estate lawyer who primarily drafts contracts and shuffles papers at mortgage closings). A lawyer who routinely works the regulatory beat can provide you with a wealth of valuable information about how the regulatory world works in your area.

> **Use a lawyer with specialized knowledge of local zoning practices.**

Use this insider knowledge to both get what you want and figure out ways to avoid, minimize, or alleviate those regulations that work against your interests. Of course, persistence notwithstanding, it always pays to carefully pick your battles. Insider knowledge can help you choose when to fight and when to move on to more productive and profitable ways to invest your time and money. Most importantly, perhaps, insider knowledge about regulatory issues can steer you away from losing efforts before you buy a property in hopes of combating regulatory compliance, enforcement, change, or exception.

I know of many investors and homebuyers who just assumed that they could get a variance that would permit them to make the improvements they wanted. Alas, that assumption too often proved wrong. Always verify. Never rely on the assertions of a seller or sales agent who says, "Oh, that shouldn't be a problem. You can just get a variance to cover it."

Homeowners Associations

Too many people buy properties without fully investigating the fiscal and regulatory controls levied by their condo, co-op, and subdivision associations. These HOAs tax and regulate just as governments do. As a property owner within an association, you must either pay your assessed fees and abide by all properly enacted rules or you will suffer fines and even a potential foreclosure of your property. Not only can HOAs take these steps against recalcitrant property owners but they can enlist the power of the courts and sheriff to enforce them. And if the association itself does not act, any individual member (property owner) within the association has legal standing to bring suit for enforcement or compliance.

> **Homeowners associations can control more tightly than governments.**

What Types of Regulations? HOAs may regulate everything that government regulations control—but often in greater detail and with less judicial review. In addition, some HOAs limit your right to sell or lease your property. Do not ever agree to buy a house, condo, or co-op that's governed by an HOA until you thoroughly review the association's rules, regulations, and restrictions.

HOA Solvency, Fees, Assessments, and Fines HOAs levy fees and assessments to maintain and enhance the community. However, some associations do mismanage their finances. They don't put aside enough money to pay for repaving the parking lots, replacing the roofs, or repairing the tennis courts, club house, and swimming pool. Then, to cover these fast-approaching financial shortfalls, the association significantly boosts monthly HOA fees and maybe even assesses homeowners special charges that can climb into the thousands of dollars.

If you don't pay these charges, the association can place a lien against your property. If you still don't pay, the association can obtain a court order that permits the sheriff to auction your property to the highest bidder.

> **Some HOAs enjoy the power to fine homeowners who violate the HOA rules.**

Likewise with fines. If you (or your tenant) repeatedly fail to abide by the HOA rules, in many cases, the HOA can fine you. Even worse, sometimes these fines accrue for each day the violation persists. I've seen legal cases where obstinate (and completely foolish) homeowners have ended up paying fines in excess of $50,000.

Inspect the Resale Package   I'm not trying to discourage you from buying a property that's ruled by an HOA. With more than 30 million homeowners and tenants now living in such privately regulated communities, these homes are certainly gaining market share as a way of life. But it's not a way of life that all investors and homeowners appreciate.

Before you commit, closely review the HOA's resale package of governing documents. Do the association CC&Rs blend with your intent for the property.[2] Does the association management budget effectively to cover present and future operating and capital costs? What amount of monthly fees must you pay? Are any special assessments looming over the horizon? Does the HOA tend to

---

2. CC&Rs refer to the covenants, conditions, and restrictions that govern the community's homeowners.

fine homeowners excessive amounts for petty violations? Answer these questions. Then decide whether the property will prove to be a good investment.

Private Contracts Also Restrict Property Owners

Will you finance your property with a mortgage? Are you going to buy an insurance policy? Both of these private contracts will regulate how you use your property. In addition, easements might also limit your use.

Mortgage Restrictions Unknown to most borrowers, lenders typically place several property-use clauses into their loan contracts that require you to:

1. Maintain the property in good repair.
2. Obtain the lender's written permission before remodeling or making other substantive changes to the property.
3. Occupy the home for at least 12 months—or otherwise arrange for higher-cost investor financing (see Chapter 12).
4. Assign all rents from the property (if it's a rental and you've defaulted on your mortgage obligations) to the lender.

As standard operating procedure, lenders do not rigorously enforce any of these clauses except in three types of situations: (1) You're impairing the value of the property because you're letting it run down, (2) you've got a warped idea about how to make improvements, or (3) you fibbed to the lender on your loan application. In these cases, lenders will enforce their right to call your loan due immediately.

> **Before you renovate, check the fine print of your mortgage.**

Property Insurance   Although we can't get into a full discussion of property insurance, at least recognize that insurers do not write their policies to cover a property per se. Instead they cover named risks under certain detailed conditions. Such conditions and risks typically pertain to:

1. *Occupancy.* If you change from owner-occupied to tenant-occupied, you must change your policy accordingly.
2. *Vacant.* If you leave the property unattended or unoccupied for a certain period (check your policy for exactly how long), coverage automatically lapses.
3. *Remodeling and renovation.* If you're going to significantly improve the property (as opposed to merely paint, recarpet, and clean up), notify your insurer. You may need to amend your coverage prior to beginning work.
4. *Safety standards.* Verify that your renovations will not violate the insurer's safety standards (materials, building techniques, inadequate design).
5. *Use.* Never change the use of a property (single-family to additional living units, residential to office) without notifying your insurer.

> **Before you renovate, check the fine print of your insurance policy.**

Prior to buying, fully discuss your intent for the property with an insurance agent. Get rate quotes for all necessary coverages. Then after you close title, always inform your agent of any changes in your plans. Breach a clause, restriction, or condition in your insurance policy and your insurer may lawfully refuse to pay for any loss that your property suffers.

Easements   Many properties are restricted by one or some combination of easements. Generally, these easements may give the city, the county, or a utility company the right to place electrical power lines; gas, water, or sewer pipes; alleys; or sidewalks across your property. Although you basically can still use the property in any lawful way that you choose, you cannot do anything that would interfere with the rights of the easement holder.

Creative design turned an "unbuildable" site into a lot for a new home.	*Easement Creates Opportunity for Profit.* I once bought a potentially valuable residential lot for a pittance because the seller thought the lot was unbuildable. Many years before, the seller had sold the county an easement to place a water runoff pipe lengthways through the center of the property at a depth of five feet. A 10-foot-wide easement gave the county perpetual access to the pipe.

However, sensing opportunity, I looked at the lot differently. I knew that in coastal areas, land-use regulations no longer allow property owners to build houses with living areas at sea level. To get around this restriction, owners build their homes on stilts (pier and beam foundation). If you've visited any coastal areas, you've probably seen the same type of construction technique.

So, prior to buying the lot that was restricted by the ease-ment, I checked to verify that I could use a similar idea to keep the drainage pipe accessible, yet still permit a house to be built. The answer came back affirmative. Rather than leave the first "story" access area open, though, I partially enclosed it for storage and parking. When completed, the exterior looked attractive, but actu-ally consisted of non-load-bearing removable walls that preserved maintenance access to the underground pipes.

Two Lessons. This example illustrates two important themes: (1) Closely verify all property restrictions before you buy, and (2) use entrepreneurial thinking to figure out ways to change, modify, alleviate, or get around restrictions when doing so will in-crease the profitability of the property.

One last point on easements: Many easements do not hinder marketability of title. Therefore, you could (as many people do) settle at closing and never realize that the property you're buying is subject to such a restriction. Don't make this mistake. Prior to purchase, physically inspect the site to determine the exact nature and placement of any and all easements that may impair your use or enjoyment of the property. In most (but not all) cases, easement holders must record their rights in the county courthouse land records office. Your title insurer can provide you with this information.

Zoning and Related Ordinances

> **Zoning laws tailor specific rules to specific districts.**

Since the 1930s, zoning and other related property ordinances have steadily increased their coverage in scope and detail. To adequately understand how such laws may apply to a property that you're looking at, you must consult your local ordinances. Or in looking at this issue from the opposite perspective, you could first consult your area's zoning map and relevant governing rules and regulations. Then, once you locate those neighborhoods that are zoned appropriately, look for properties that legally fit within your entrepreneurial plans.

The District Concept

To set up zoning laws, land-use planners design zoning maps that lay out multiple districts that may range in size from one small parcel of land up to several square miles or more. Sometimes, small zoning districts lie within larger districts—as when a small office complex or convenience retail center is surrounded completely by residences. In a few instances, small elite cities may zone the entire community all one district (typically, large-lot, single-family residential).

As you can see from Figure 4.1, planners have invented all kinds of zoning districts. To see what zoning applies to a specific

Article IV. Use Regulations

Division 1. Generally

Sec. 30–41. Establishment of zoning districts and categories.
Sec. 30–42. Designation of district boundaries.
Sec. 30–43. Rules for interpretation of district boundaries.

Residential Zoning Districts

Sec. 30–51. Single-family residential districts (RSF-1, RSF-2, RSF-2, and RSF-4).
Sec. 30–52. Residential low-density districts (RMF-5, RC, and MH).
Sec. 30–53. Multiple-family medium-density residential districts (RMF-6, RMF-7, and RMF-8).
Sec. 30–54. Residential mixed-use district (RMU).
Sec. 30–55. Residential high-density districts (RH-1 and RH-2).
Sec. 30–56. General provisions for residential districts.
Sec. 30–57. Residential leases; teaching of the fine arts.
Sec. 30–58. Home occupation permits.

Office Zoning Districts

Sec. 30–59. Office districts (OR and OF).
Sec. 30–60. General provisions for office districts.

Business and Mixed-Use Zoning Districts

Sec. 30–61. General business district (BUS).
Sec. 30–62. Automotive-oriented business district (BA).
Sec. 30–63. Tourist-oriented business district (BT).
Sec. 30–64. Mixed-use low-intensity district (MU-1).
Sec. 30–65. Mixed-use medium-intensity district (MU-2).
Sec. 30–66. Central city district (CCD).
Sec. 30–67. General provisions for business and mixed-use districts.

Industrial Zoning Districts

Sec. 30–68. Warehousing and wholesaling district (W).
Sec. 30–69. Limited industrial district (I-1).
Sec. 30–70. General industrial district (I-2).
Sec. 30–71. General provisions for industrial districts.

Special Use Districts

Sec. 30–72. Agriculture district (AGR).
Sec. 30–73. Conservation district (CON).
Sec. 30–74. Medical services district (MD).
Sec. 30–75. Public services and operations district (PS).
Sec. 30–76. Airport facility district (AF).
Sec. 30–77. Educational services district (ED).
Sec. 30–78. Corporate park district (CP).

Overlay Districts

Sec. 30–79. Historic preservation/conservation district.
Sec. 30–80. Special area plan district (SAP).

(continued)

Figure 4.1 Common Types of Rezoning Districts.

(Continued)

Traditional Neighborhood Development (TND) District

Sec. 30-237. Purpose.
Sec. 30-238. Design objectives.
Sec. 30-239. Definitions.
Sec. 30-240. Minimum and maximum size, density of TND.
Sec. 30-241. General development criteria.
Sec. 30-242. Land-use categories.
Sec. 30-243. Review and approval process.
Sec. 30-244. Amendments to approved TND.

Article VI. Requirements for Specially Regulated Uses

Sec. 30-81. Applicability.
Sec. 30-82. Day care centers.
Sec. 30-83. Community residential homes.
Sec. 30-84. Housing for elderly persons.
Sec. 30-85. Temporary mobile homes and temporary sales and leasing offices.
Sec. 30-86. Recreational vehicles.
Sec. 30-87. Outdoor cafes.
Sec. 30-88. Nursing homes and intermediate care facilities (GN-805).
Sec. 30-89. Adult day care homes.
Sec. 30-90. Adult and sexually oriented establishments.
Sec. 30-91. Places of religious assembly.
Sec. 30-92. Funeral service and crematories (GM-726).
Sec. 30-93. Gasoline and alternative fuel service stations (GN-554).
Sec. 30-94. Limited automotive services.
Sec. 30-95. Automated or self-carwashes.
Sec. 30-96. Junkyards and salvage yards.
Sec. 30-97. Outdoor storage.
Sec. 30-98. Transmitter towers; retransmission and microwave transmission towers' antennas.
Sec. 30-99. Veterinary services (GN-074).
Sec. 30-100. Dormitories and roominghouses.
Sec. 30-101. Bed and breakfast establishments.
Sec. 30-102. Public service vehicles.
Sec. 30-103. Private schools.
Sec. 30-104. Model homes.
Sec. 30-105. Alcoholic beverage establishments.
Sec. 30-106. Recycling centers.
Sec. 30-107. Temporary sales for fundraising by nonprofit agencies.
Sec. 30-108. Rehabilitation centers.
Sec. 30-109. Social service homes and halfway houses.
Sec. 30-110. Residences for destitute people.
Sec. 30-111. Food distribution centers for the needy.
Sec. 30-112. Historic preservation/conservation.
Sec. 30-113. Consolidated apartment management offices.
Sec. 30-114. Off-site parking facilities for uses in MU-1 or MU-2 districts.
Sec. 30-115. Farmers markets.
Secs. 30-116–30-150.   Reserved.

Figure 4.1   *(Continued)*

property, you would look up the property on the zoning map. Then, after determining the relevant district category, you would read the corresponding explanatory section within the zoning ordinance to learn the precise regulations.

For example, if a property were located in a city's residential mixed use (RMU) district, you would turn to Section 30–54 of the city's zoning manual. If from the zoning map you see that the property is located in an RSF-4 district, you would consult Section 30–51.

What Kinds of Restrictions?

As Figure 4.2 shows, zoning and other related ordinances can control about anything you do outside of the privacy of your own bed-

◆ Type of property use
◆ Special uses/exceptions
◆ Setback dimensions (front and rear)
◆ Sideyard dimensions
◆ Floor area ratio (FAR)
◆ Lot coverage ratio
◆ Building height
◆ Parking
◆ Noise
◆ Light
◆ View
◆ Trees and shrubbery
◆ Accessory apartments
◆ Swimming pools
◆ Subdivision layout
◆ Animal control

◆ Party walls
◆ Obnoxious behavior
◆ Smoke, dust, pollution
◆ Aesthetics/architectural review boards (ARBs)
◆ Occupancy
◆ Home occupations
◆ Home businesses
◆ Trespass
◆ Fences
◆ Crowds
◆ Historical districts
◆ Yard care, weeds
◆ Health and safety
◆ Solar panels
◆ Signage
◆ Environment and ecology

Figure 4.2   A Sampling of Concerns for Zoning and Other Related Ordinances.

> **With some governments, almost "anything goes." With others, you need permission to put up a new mailbox.**

room. Some cities (such as Palm Beach, Florida, or Mill Valley, California–Marin County) regulate everything that's possible as tightly as possible. Other cities (such as Orlando, Florida) adopt a more eclectic approach. In Gilcrest County, Florida, it seems like you can drop a mobile home about anywhere you want without much fear of legal challenge. Right next door in Alachua County, sites permissible for mobile homes are much tougher to locate.

Although we can't go into the full myriad of regulations that governments use to restrict properties and property owners, the following discussion gives you a good idea of some of the issues of most concern to property investors, renovators, and remodelers.

Setbacks, Sideyards, and Height   Virtually all zoning ordinances tell property owners that they can't put their buildings too close to the street, their adjacent neighbors, or the neighboring site in the rear. What's too close? What buildings? It all depends.

Dimensions.   Look at Figure 4.3. There you can see the varying requirements for four different residential single family (RSF) classifications in one small town. Except for the maximum height requirements of 35 feet, the other dimensional standards *do not* represent "typical." For, in fact, no typical exists. Until the zoning law was recently changed, Vancouver, British Columbia, permitted some lots for RSFs at a lot width of 16 feet, sideyards of 2 feet, and front setbacks of 10 feet. In Barrington Hills, an exclusive suburb of Chicago, minimum lot sizes required five acres. Some planned unit developments (PUDs) permit zero lot lines, as do some big city townhouses and tenements. (Note: The du/a shorthand stands for dwelling units per acre.)

Buildings, Structures, Site Improvements, and So Forth. When you check the requirements for setbacks and sideyards, no-

	Principal Structures			
	RSF-1	RSF-2	RSF-3	RSF-4
Maximum density	3.5 du/a	4.6 du/a	5.8 du/a	8 du/a
Minimum lot area	8,500 sq. ft.	7,500 sq. ft.	6,000 sq. ft.	4,300 sq. ft.
Minimum lot width at minimum front yard setback	85'	75'	60'	50'
Minimum lot depth	90'	90'	90'	80'
Minimum yard setbacks:				
Front	20'	20'	20'	20'
Side (interior)	7.5'	7.5'	7.5'	7.5'
Side (street)	10'	10'	7.5'	7.5'
Rear	20'	20'	15'	10'
Maximum building height	35'	35'	35'	35'

Accessory Structures,[1] Excluding Fences and Walls	
Minimum front and side yard setbacks	Same requirements are for the principal structure.
Minimum yard setback, rear[2]	7.5'
Maximum building height	25'
Transmitter towers	80'

1. Accessory screened enclosure structures whether or not attached to the principal structure may be erected in the rear yard as long as the enclosure has a minimum yard setback of three feet from the rear property line. The maximum height of the enclosure at the setback line shall not exceed eight feet. The roof and all sides of the enclosure not attached to the principal structure must be made of screening material.

2. One preengineered or premanufactured structure of 100 square feet or less may be erected in the rear and side yards as long as the structure has a minimum yard setback of three feet from the rear or side property lines, is properly anchored to the ground, and is separated from neighboring properties by a fence or wall that is at least 75 percent opaque.

Figure 4.3 Dimensional Requirements for Residential Single Family (RSF) Districts.

> **Setbacks do not necessarily apply to all types of structures and improvements.**

tice what buildings or structures must comply. Zoning rules may permit screened porches, free-standing storage sheds, swimming pools, decks, garages, and driveways to sit closer to the property lines. With such exceptions common, you may enjoy more room for improvements than a casual glance at the requirements might imply.

Also, notice whether the ordinance specifies where and how to take dimensional measurements. One statute I've seen measures height from street level. If your site slopes down, your structure could actually exceed 35 feet from ground level (if that were the maximum height). You can face measurement ambiguity, too, when your site boundaries do not form a perfect rectangle. With an angular site, your building could meet the setback rules at one point, but violate them at another.

Floor Area and Lot Coverage Ratios   If you're planning to add living or storage space to the main structure, check to see whether the zoning code sets floor area ratios (FARs) or lot coverage ratios (LCRs) for the property. A FAR expresses the square footage of the structure as a percentage of the square footage of the lot:

$$\text{Floor area ratio (FAR)} = \frac{2,400 \text{ sq. ft. (building size)}}{8,500 \text{ sq. ft. (lot size)}}$$
$$\text{FAR} = 28.2\%$$

If a regulation limited the FAR to, say, 35 percent, you could add up to 575 square feet of building size.

$$\text{Maximum FAR} = .35 \times 8,500$$
$$= 2,975 \text{ sq. ft.}$$

However, your plans might also have to fit within an LCR. To make sure that a structure leaves enough room for parking and yardspace, government site planners may limit the footprint of the building to some specified percentage of the site size. If in the above example, zoning set the maximum LCR at 30 percent, you would have to add your space into a second story, rather than building out:

$$\begin{array}{r} 30\% \text{ (LCR maximum)} \\ \times\ 8,500 \text{ sq. ft. (lot size)} \\ \hline 2,550 \text{ sq. ft. (maximum footprint)} \end{array}$$

Now, we get to another complicating issue. What parts of the structure count in these ratios? Basements, decks, porches, garages, driveways? There's only one way to find out. Read the ordinance. If the ordinance remains silent or seems ambiguous, talk with a land-use lawyer to see whether you might have found a profitable loophole.

> **Never assume you know the law. Quirks and loopholes run everywhere.**

Occupancy Restrictions I recently inquired about a single-family investment property that was up for sale. The seller told me that the house was rented to five college students for $1,500 a month. "Sounds pretty good," I said. Then, hoping to win some negotiating points, I pointed out that the city's occupancy code limited single-family rentals to three unrelated adults. Therefore, I couldn't pay what the seller was asking because I wouldn't risk a code citation that could cost me a substantial part of my income flow.

"No problem," the seller countered. "This house sits in a commercial district. Five students don't violate the code."

Well, he had me. It turns out that on this issue and others, he knew more about the code than I did—at least as it applied to his property. Smart seller. He had anticipated code questions and had prepared factual and accurate responses. A refreshing change from most run-of-the-mill sellers and realty agents who don't bother to learn anything about the land-use codes—until a serious mistake teaches them a hard lesson.

Single-Family Occupancy   I've used this example to show how important it is to know the code regardless of whether you're buying or selling. The code affects use and use greatly influences value. But also I want to emphasize that ordinances can even regulate who and how many tenants you place in your property. Many cities discriminate against individual adults who wish to share housing. Although less now than in the past, single-family zoning has literally meant that single-family zoning limited occupancy to one *family* of persons related closely by blood or marriage.

> **Social policy and modern trends sometimes conflict with zoning rules.**

Modern Exceptions   Due to lobbying by property owners, the changing nature of households, and court decisions, restrictions on occupancy have become less severe—especially with regard to senior adult congregate living facilities, foster care homes, shelter homes for abused spouses and children, and group homes for the emotionally or mentally handicapped. Nevertheless, as a general principle, courts have told planners that they can legally establish districts that exclude residents by age, household size, household composition, and, de facto, by household wealth and income.

Indeed, many communities that attract large populations of immigrants are facing horrific occupancy problems—as seen by the communities' long-established residents. Typical middle-class families are finding that the house next door now provides shelter for three generations, four cousins, and a couple of boarders—for a total of 10 to 15 persons. Should zoning and occupancy codes prevent these high-intensity living arrangements? Can code enforcers circumvent charges of racist and ethnic discrimination? Those are issues the courts will be deciding in coming years.

Parking   "No on-street parking between the hours of 2:00 A.M. to 6:00 A.M." You might think that such neighborhood parking ordinances somehow relate to traffic issues. And sometimes they do. But sometimes restricted parking hours indirectly control the population density of a neighborhood. How can 8, 10, or 15 occupants of a house find adequate parking without on-street parking? Park in the front yard? The zoning rules may outlaw that response, also.

> **Zoning laws may regulate all types of on-street and off-street parking.**

Too Many Cars Whether we're talking residential, retail, or office, local ordinances typically regulate both off-street and on-street parking. Laws can regulate the placement of driveways, curb cuts, and minimum-size parking lots to accompany specific uses (apartments, office buildings, shopping centers). If you're thinking of adding living units to a property (such as an accessory apartment, or perhaps splitting a large house into three or four apartment units), verify that you can satisfy the extra parking that the law will require.

Recreation (and Other) Vehicles In Palo Alto, California, and the surrounding Silicon Valley, homes with legal space for RV parking command a price premium. Not because the RVers, themselves, are bidding up these properties, but because housing's so scarce that someone will pay $600 a month just to live in an RV. Could this strategy work in your area (albeit at probably a lower rental rate)? Just note that cities (and HOAs) do regulate the parking of RVs, boats, trucks, and trailers. In my neighborhood, no resident may park a car or truck in their driveway or in front of their house if it displays a commercial emblem or logo that may be seen by passersby.

Home Businesses/Home Occupations Millions of people now work out of their homes. Without a doubt, this trend will continue to grow. Renovating and remodeling houses to meet this need can truly present an entrepreneurial opportunity. But beware: Zoning rules closely regulate people who want to operate an office or run a business from their residence.

> **Home offices and home businesses offer good opportunities for renovators when they are legal.**

Questions to Answer   Does the zoning district of the property permit work at home as a right? If not, can you fit within a special exception category (see later discussion)? What rules apply to parking, the number of allowable customer visits, hours of operation, signage, business licenses, and dedicated space? To what extent could you legally modify the structure to accommodate the home office or business? Can you rent the office or business portion of the residence to someone who doesn't live there? Precisely what types of occupations or businesses will zoning permit?

Missed Opportunity   My experience tells me that the great majority of fixers and renovators completely miss this market. Depending on the wording of the ordinance, you could target any of the following:

◆ Writers
◆ Artists
◆ Accountants
◆ Lawyers
◆ Insurance agents
◆ Music instruction
◆ Financial planners

◆ Seamstress/tailors
◆ Beauty shop
◆ Network marketers
◆ Child care
◆ Answering service
◆ Auto repair
◆ Web-based business

This list merely samples the unlimited variety of small, independent occupations and businesses that proliferate in our rapidly evolving free-agent nation. Learn what locations and what property features work best for one or more types of these free agents and you may find a lucrative niche of opportunity.

Special Uses   Typically, zoning districts permit certain uses as rights and other named uses as special exceptions. If designated a right, you can proceed with your plans without delay. As long as

> **Even districts zoned single-family typically permit other types of property uses.**

you comply with setbacks, height, and other governing details, zoning administrators must approve your intentions. On the other hand, if the use is classified within the special exception category, zoning officials could deny (or modify) your plans (see Figure 4.4). To do so properly, they would have to object because your use would harm the public interest or create adverse effects for neighboring property owners. Fortunately, you can challenge the planner's objection. And if you end up in court, the judge will reverse the normal legal presumption that planners know best. Instead, the planners must prove through the greater weight of the evidence that their opinion should rule.

District: Single-Family (R-1-AA)

Uses by Right

1. Single family houses
2. Customary accessory uses
3. Boat houses and boat docks
4. Foster homes
5. Adult congregate living facilities

Uses by Special Exception

1. Public or private schools
2. In-home professional offices
3. Churches
4. Tennis clubs
5. Guest cottages
6. Golf courses
7. Public swimming pools
8. Shelter homes

Figure 4.4   Uses by Right or Special Exception as per One City Zoning Ordinance.

Do not conclude that a residential, commercial, or industrial district necessarily excludes other uses. As always, read the ordinances.

> **Unless you want to renovate as an unprofitable hobby, avoid historically designated areas and properties.**

Historical Properties Increasingly, to preserve the heritage and history of their communities, planners designate some properties or some areas of town as "historically significant." Unless you really know what you're doing, avoid historically regulated properties as you would a carrier of bubonic plague.

Quite often, planners force such property owners to pony up thousands of dollars to maintain or restore these properties. They will likely want to approve your choice of colors, building materials, and design.

If you should ever want to demolish all or part of the structure, Heaven forbid! When Ritz-Carlton tried to build a new hotel in Sarasota, Florida, it needed to remove or demolish an old house that stood on the site. Sarasota's Historical Preservation Board put the Ritz through four years of public hearings and legal brawls. Only after spending hundreds of thousands of dollars for the costs of lawyers and delays did the Ritz-Carlton finally receive approval for their plans. (In the end, the company paid to remove the "historically significant" structure to another location.)

> **Is neighbor noise a problem? Use the law to eliminate it.**

Unless you've got the patience and money to fight a historical board, run from any property that falls (or could fall) into its regulatory clutches.

Noise Ordinances Most communities have enacted noise ordinances that restrict the maximum decibel levels that will be permitted in various zoning districts. Sometimes these ordinances specify exact rating systems and the type of equipment that code enforcers will use to measure it. Alternatively, code enforcers may rely on a "plainly audible" standard such as the following:

> Plainly audible means any sound or noise produced by any source . . . that can be clearly heard by a person using normal hearing faculties, at a distance of 200 feet or more from the real property line where the source of the sound or noise is originating.

Specifically with respect to radios, stereos, televisions, and musical instruments, noise ordinances often tighten their restrictive standard:

> No person shall operate, play, or permit the operation or playing of any radio, tape player, television, electronic audio equipment, musical instrument, sound amplifier, or other mechanical or electronic soundmaking device that produces, reproduces, or amplifies sound in such a manner as to create a noise disturbance *across a real property boundary.* (italics added)

If a noisy neighbor makes it difficult for you to sell or rent one of your properties, don't start a personal neighbor war. Instead, insist that the code enforcer emphatically tell the offender to cease and desist.

Sunlight and Views   As sunlight and views have become more important to property owners and tenants, some cities have retreated from their historical hands-off policies. With the advent of solar energy and $50,000 (or more) price premiums for view properties, owners have begun to demand protection for these amenities. Nevertheless, far more often than not, when it comes to views and sunlight, the general rule remains: You're on your own.

If your neighbor can legally build a second story that will shade your property's backyard and block its spectacular view of the

> **Make sure your view properties enjoy *protected* views.**

mountains, you will probably lack legal standing to complain. If sunlight or views contribute to the value of a property that you're planning to buy, do not assume that those features will continue to serve your buyers or tenants. Verify, verify, verify!

When Tiger Woods recently bought a home with great views of the Pacific Ocean, the realty agent involved stressed to a reporter of the *Los Angeles Times* the fact that Tiger received a *protected view.* Like Tiger, if you're expecting sunlight or a view, make sure that it's either legally or physically protected from loss.

Be Wary of Nonconforming Uses

> **Nonconforming properties present an additional risk. Verify before you buy.**

Quite often, properties within their respective districts do not meet all current zoning and building codes. Are these properties legal? Maybe, maybe not. If the property and its current use legally predate the code's pertinent restrictions, the property has probably been grandfathered. It's now classified as legal and noncomforming. In contrast, if the property has been altered or operated in ways that were never legal, that property is classified as nonconforming and illegal.

Legal and Nonconforming Here are four reasons why you should pay less for a legal property that does not conform to current zoning and building ordinances.

No Right to Expand the Use With legal and conforming properties, you can add on to the building up to the full extent of the current regulations. With nonconforming properties, the law typically does not permit you such liberty.

Say you own a legal, nonconforming combination retail store with a residence upstairs. Business is so brisk at the store that you want to complete a 500-square-feet addition. Currently the zoning district prohibits retail use. You're probably out of luck. Zoning rarely allows property owners to expand a nonconforming use. In one legal case, the owner of a legal, nonconforming single-wide mobile home wanted to replace it with a double-wide. The planners and the courts said no.

No Right to Extend the Life   You tell the zoning officials, "Okay, I won't expand, but I want to completely modernize the store (or mobile home) both inside and out." Sorry. You're probably out of luck again. The officials want nonconforming uses to die as soon as possible. They don't want you to rejuvenate it.

No Right to Renew the Use   Assume that for some reason or other, you close the store for 90 days. You then want to reopen. Unfortunately, you may have erred. Under most zoning laws, you cannot renew a nonconforming use after it has been discontinued for some period of time (as specified in the ordinance). The shortest period I've seen is 30 days. The longest is two years.

True Story: As a rehabber or renovator, you must attend closely to the way local ordinances and court decisions regulate legal, nonconforming uses and nonconforming properties. I know of an investor who owned a legal, nonconforming duplex that was located in a single-family district. When coincidentally the tenants of both units moved out within one week of each other, the investor decided to renovate the entire property. Working part-time, he completed the job in four months.

Then within two weeks of reletting both sides, the code enforcer cited him for violating the current single-family district zoning. (Almost certainly a disgruntled neighbor had filed a complaint.) When the investor appealed, the zoning board of adjustment turned a deaf ear. The statute was plain: "A nonconforming use

Don't "abandon" a nonconforming use.

that is discontinued or abandoned for more than 90 days shall be terminated permanently." I would like to end this story here, but it actually gets worse.

A single-family home is allowed only one kitchen. But this property now proudly displayed two newly remodeled kitchens. What happens now? The zoning authority forced the investor to rip out one of the kitchens and convert the building into a single-family house.

The Moral: Please, do not misinterpret the lesson this tale teaches. When I relate this example in my investment seminars, attendees nearly always launch into their own war stories about petty, overzealous zoning bureaucrats. But that's not the point. In this case, as in so many others that provoke investor chagrin, the statute clearly states the law. You can't justly condemn a zoning official for enforcing plain English language. Had this duplex investor read the law before he acted, he could have easily worked his renovation plans into compliance. *Learn the law, then work the law to maximum advantage.* That's the true moral of this story.

> **Don't blame others for your failure to learn the law.**

Note: This investor also violated code by performing his renovation work without permits. Had he sought the required permits, the officials may have warned him about the risk he was taking. As to illegally extending the life of a nonconforming use, that issue never surfaced in this case. Nevertheless, I would bet $100 that when the code enforcer saw the unpermitted renovation of a nonconforming use, he became one unhappy camper. At that point, the enforcer probably targeted this investor for a fall.

No Right to Repair or Rebuild   Okay, I was pretty hard on the foolhardy duplex investor. So I'll balance that indictment with a lesson about legal, nonconforming properties that I learned from my own hard experience.

I owned a 60-year-old, small apartment building that was wired with an outdated (legal, nonconforming) 60-amp fuse box. The property suffered an electrical fire that would have required a $200 repair. However, the building code inspector would not permit a repair to below-code wiring. He required me to rewire the entire building with a 100-amp electrical system with circuit breakers, which at that time cost me $2,000.

My property insurance did not pay any portion of this electrical upgrade. Why not? Because unless you buy special coverage (which is often not available at a reasonable cost), insurance policies only promise to reimburse for actual losses. They won't pay the extra costs necessary to repair, reconstruct, or rebuild your property to comply with the latest applicable building or zoning code.

> **Property insurance doesn't cover updating a damaged property to code.**

Illegal, Nonconforming Use   Technically, I suspect that the United States and Canada have at least 50 million houses, apartments, and commercial buildings that *illegally* fail to conform to various zoning and building codes. Bootlegged renovations, makeshift repairs, unpermitted remodeling, excessive occupancy, outlaw home businesses, and incompetent, lazy, or dishonest building inspectors all contribute to this shocking epidemic of crime. Just in the city of Vancouver, British Columbia, for example, more than 100,000 homeowners rent out illegal basement suites.

Calculate the Risks   I would not advise you to avoid buying an illegal, nonconforming property per se. I have owned many such properties and have never suffered serious loss because of it. However, do not buy without knowledge. Calculate the risks. Then factor those risks into your purchase price negotiations. Tell the seller, "Look, the ceiling in your add-on rec room stands at just 7 feet 6 inches. Code says the height should go up to at least 8 feet.

If the building inspectors should ever discover this code violation, they could force me to tear out the entire roof and rebuild it to comply."

"They Never Enforce Those Laws"   The seller's likely response:"How are they gonna find out? Besides, they never enforce those laws." But, of course, they can find out in many different ways.

- ◆ What if you have a small fire or storm damage that requires a permitted repair?
- ◆ What if a spiteful neighbor or tenant turns you in?
- ◆ What if you plan other permitted renovations that bring an inspector into your property?

Code enforcers can learn about illegal properties or uses in a dozen different ways. Is the rec room roof visible from the street? Maybe it will catch the eye of a zealous inspector who's just passing by. As to enforcement, do not rely on the past as prologue. The political winds can change directions—especially when the infractions generate neighborhood ill will (occupancy, parking, appearance, noise, blocked views).

> **Code enforcers can discover violations anytime they're called to inspect a property or approve permitted work.**

Historically, code enforcers have not typically gone out looking for trouble. Unless forced to act by complaint or politics, most inspectors don't go after property owners who aren't causing any noticeable harm to others. In my community, landlords get cited for violating occupancy codes only when their tenants or properties incite the ire of the neighborhood.

As to your final decision to buy an illegal, nonconforming property, you must balance the potential risks and benefits against the seller's bottom-line price. But be wary. Should your renovations and fix-up work require a code permit and in-spection, stay financially prepared to remedy all code deficien-cies (or at the least those violations that fall within the authority of that inspector).

How to Challenge the Zoning Rules

If you feel that zoning rules impact your property too harshly, you can seek change or attack the zoning law itself. Generally stated, you can pursue a remedy in some combination of the following:

- ◆ Seek a variance.
- ◆ Petition for rezoning.
- ◆ Go to court.

> **You can sometimes exempt yourself from the rules.**

Seek a Variance As a matter of right, property owners may request a variance when a zoning rule creates undue hardship. Typically, "I want to make more money," doesn't qualify as hardship. From the planner's perspective, that "hardship" qualifies as tough luck.

When planners speak of hardship, they mean some unique feature of your property that renders it difficult to use in what would otherwise be a legal man-ner. For example, say sideyard setbacks require 10 feet. Your lot line cuts at an angle. At the front part of your planned addition, you've got 12 feet of width, but at the back part, only 8 feet of width. Ab-sent some serious objection by the adjacent property owner, you would probably get your variance.

Not Your Fault Planners, though, do not typically grant hardship exceptions if you've previously created or contributed to the problem. You cannot murder your parents and then beg for mercy from the court because you're now an orphan. This rule particularly holds when you knowingly buy a property that will not legally accommodate your plans. Then you request a hardship variance. Don't expect sympathy from the folks at zoning. To combat this potential problem, place a zoning variance contingency clause into your purchase contract. Most sellers won't like it. But if the variance stands critical to your plans, avoid the risk of refusal unless the seller offers you a sufficiently attractive price or terms.

> **Who you know still counts in zoning decisions.**

No Precise Rules   In the days when the good ole boys lorded over the planning department, the politically connected and financially generous could get variances (and zoning changes) almost at will. Such practices still remain in some cities and counties. More commonly, today, though, variances (and rezoning) must not conflict with the governing district norms and the overall comprehensive plan for the community. Today, variances do not generally create special privileges.

Nevertheless, those "who, when, and why" issues still render the variance process somewhat arbitrary, personal, and situation specific. No precise rules apply. If a variance will help you make more money, seek insider knowledge before you submit your request. How you ask for a variance may rank as more important than what you ask.

Petition for Rezoning   If your property is uniquely situated to benefit from a more profitable use, you can petition the planners to rezone your site. Say that due to a new nearby office development, increased traffic flows, or the evolving nature of the neighborhood, you could make the case that your building merits another zoning classification. Surely professional offices would now better fit this location.

Unlike a variance, which according to contemporary zoning theory should pertain only to adjusting a regulatory detail or two, rezoning puts you in another league with a new set of rules. Much like a variance, though, planners won't rezone your property unless you show how such a rezoning will not harm neighboring properties or the integrity of the overall community plan.

Enlist help to get the laws changed.

Power in Numbers   If you can enlist other nearby property owners to join with you to register a joint request that covers multiple properties, you will increase your chance for success. You would make the same types of community-need arguments. But you would enjoy the power of numbers to back up your case. Most often, property owners push for upzoning. Though in cases of community revitalization, residents may adopt a "Let's take back the neighborhood" approach. If more, not fewer, restrictions could enhance property values, you might push for downzoning.

Boundary Dominoes   What if your single-family residential property sits on a zoning district boundary line? Say you're situated right in back of a Safeway parking lot. You think that you should at least get an R-1-C classification so that you could convert the house to an office for lease to an accountant, lawyer, or maybe a veterinarian. More than likely, the planners will refuse. They will cite the domino effect.

Anticipate and prepare to rebut objections.

"If we shift the zoning on your property, then your neighbor, too, will deserve a change. Where will it all end?" Again, the power of numbers may assist your case. Also, again argue for why the unique location of your property not only justifies the shift in zoning classifications, but also why (absent the power of numbers) your property's location and use doesn't adversely impact neighboring properties. Perhaps your closest residential neighbor sits on the other side of an alley behind a thick hedgerow that stands 14 to 18 feet tall. "As to the property across the street," you point out, "that's a small neighborhood park where people walk their dogs. So, you see, my property would make a great location for a veterinary clinic."

Go to Court   Nearly all zoning laws give property owners and citizens several levels of appeal within the system. If you strike out with front line personnel, you might next go to the department head, then to a zoning board of adjustment, and eventually perhaps to a city or county council. Should you fail at all of these levels, you alone (or with the power of numbers) can file suit.

Typically, you might sue to force government to treat you and your property in a way that better serves your interests. Or you might sue to block the rezoning or planned use of nearby land that will bear adversely on the value of your property as well as the health, safety, morals, or general welfare of the community. (Remember, whenever possible, work the community-needs angle into your argument. Ayn Rand notwithstanding, neither planners nor judges typically appreciate the virtue of pure selfishness.)

> **Position your request in terms of the public interest.**

High Cost   If you do file suit, you must employ an attorney who specializes in land-use litigation. Zoning and land-use cases involve too much complexity for self-help law. As such, given the enormous expense of lawyers and litigation, small investors (by themselves) can rarely afford to use the judicial system to fight zoning battles.

Avoid Trouble   Because "I'll see you in court" doesn't really offer small investors a practical response to planners, I again urge you to learn the law before you act. To avoid trouble with the code enforcers, read your local ordinances; gain insider knowledge; and press your case with tact, diplomacy, and perseverance.

Building Codes

Up to this point, I haven't clearly distinguished zoning and other types of land-use and occupancy codes from building codes. Partly that's because no clear distinction applies. A rule that falls under zoning in one local area may fall under the building codes in another. In addition, sometimes these various types of government control overlap to a degree.

> **Property owners who do their own work must still comply with permits and codes.**

For your purposes, you will primarily meet up with *building code* inspectors when you perform (or contract for) major plumbing, electrical, remodeling, or roofing work. These building codes may force you to use construction techniques, design, or materials that can add to your costs (generally for reasons of safety). But they will seldom seriously restrict basic plans for renovation and market strategy (as can zoning and other land-use ordinances).

Environmental Laws

Small investors and renovators may run into six types of environmental issues:

- ◆ Lead paint
- ◆ Asbestos
- ◆ Underground home heating oil tanks
- ◆ Septic systems and wastewater disposal
- ◆ Tree ordinances
- ◆ Mold

Let me deal with the easiest one first. Tree ordinances may prohibit you from cutting down a tree on your property to make way for a room addition or maybe to enhance a view of the mountains or bay.

As to the serious and costly issues of lead paint, asbestos, mold, heating oil tanks, and waste disposal (if your property's not connected to a city or county sewer line), get copies of the pertinent brochures published by local, state, and federal environmental agencies. If you locate a property that requires removal or abatement of any of these types of environmental problems, get back into your car and look for another investment.

Beginning renovators should never try to carry out an environmental cleanup. Too much risk for too little payback. Instead, focus on value-enhancing opportunities. It's to that topic that we now turn.

CHAPTER 5

Discover Your Possibilities

When single father James Young discovered a termite-infested, Washington Village row house with a charred interior and shaky foundation, he knew he had found the property he was looking for. Priced at $32,000, homes didn't come any cheaper. But James's two kids, Adam and Tenea, definitely weren't impressed. "When they looked at the house," says James, "they said 'No way.' But I could see the possibilities. The house had three stories and I knew I could do a lot with it. I told the kids to just be patient. They'd see."

James's prophecy proved right. Their home is now beautiful, functional, and displays special character. It includes a spiral stair-case, exposed brick firewalls, large matched triangular clerestory windows, a new oak floor, a double-tiered Corinthian column on each side of the living room fireplace, a completely equipped contemporary-style kitchen, and a third-floor master-bedroom suite with skylight, fireplace, and roof deck. As for the kids, they have the complete second floor to themselves with private bedrooms at each end of the hall. Total cost of the property plus rehab expenses came to $77,000 (not including James's labor). Total rehabbed value now exceeds $135,000.

> **Big profits from a destroyed property.**

The Copleys Make Half a Million

"As my husband pulled up in front of that confused amalgam of materials and architectural styles that had once been a proud and stately Edward Durrell Stone–designed home, I told him he was not even going to get me out of the car—let along walk inside. That place was a bastardized disaster," remembers Virginia Copley. But Virginia's husband Carl persuaded Virginia to change her mind.

> **Before you reject, look for possibilities.**

"That's why Carl and I complement each other so well," says Virginia. "He has the better eye for turning a sow's ear into a silk purse." The Copleys bought this house that had sat on the market unsold for nearly five years with a listing price of $3.25 million. The Copleys paid $1.35 million. And with another $400,000, they restored the home to its original splendor and boosted its market value to around $2.5 million.

The Baglivis Discover a Bargain

Christine and Kevin Baglivi recently bought their first home. "The hardwood floors," says Christine, "were encrusted with chewing gum . . . [the previous owner's children] had smashed the bathroom tiles and practiced their artwork on the walls. . . . Every window sash was broken, kitchen drawers were missing, and the bathtub looked as if it had served as a storage bin for used auto parts.

> **Fixers boost your chance for home ownership.**

"Why would two presumably sane adults purchase such a nightmare?" Christine asks rhetorically. "Because like many Californians priced out of the housing market, investing in a fixer-upper helped us break into Southland real estate at a time when we didn't think we could afford to buy. Our three-bedroom Craftsman bungalow cost $40,000 less than similar homes in the neighborhood that were in good condition. To Kevin and myself, this savings gave us our chance to own a home."

Put on Your Rose-Colored Glasses

Do you see the common theme in each of the above success stories? With each property, the buyers put on their rose-colored glasses. They could see possibilities where other lookers only saw problems. As an entrepreneurial fixer, you've got to put on a pair of these rose-colored glasses. Instead of focusing exclusively on what's wrong with a property, ask yourself, What could I make right? What can I imagine for this property that others remain too dull to see?

> **Entrepreneurs must keep a pair of rose-colored glasses handy.**

Don't Quickly Reject a "Fixer"—You Could Mistakenly Pass Up a True Bargain

Far too many investors and homebuyers reject properties too quickly. They walk in, do a quick take on the house with a pass-through tour, and then say something like, "Let's get out of here. It's way too dark; and did you notice that awful burnt orange carpeting in the bedroom?"

"Yes," the spouse replies, "and how about those ugly kitchen appliances and that green linoleum floor—not to mention the garbled floor plan and water stains on the ceiling. This house needs too much work. Anybody would be crazy to buy this nightmare."

Well, yes, anybody would be crazy to buy that home—unless, of course, they could buy it at a steep discount, rehab, redecorate, and sell it for a profit of $10,000 to $40,000. Or perhaps, if in buying a discounted fixer, they were able to move into a higher-priced neighborhood that they otherwise could not have been able to afford. Then these buyers wouldn't be called crazy. They'd be called smart.

As I travel throughout the country and talk to investors and homebuyers, I'm amazed at the number of people I meet who

> **You can turn many negatives into positives.**

have bought properties that had sat on the market for months, if not years. Yet, after buying these houses that were rejected by dozens of other shoppers, these buyers were able to convert the sow's ear into a silk purse and earn profits of tens (sometimes hundreds) of thousands of dollars.

Your Second Set of Glasses (Buyer's Eyes)

Of course, just because a property sits unsold for months or years doesn't mean that it offers undiscovered promise. Many properties remain unsold because they're overpriced money traps. And that brings us to the next question: How can you weed out the money traps without rejecting the moneymakers? For that task you need to bring along a second set of glasses. These glasses give you buyer's eyes. While wearing them, no flaw, shortcoming, or defect escapes your attention. You see every property detail inside and out.

The Critical Balance

> **Use Ben Franklin's approach. List negatives and positives side by side.**

As an entrepreneur, your rose-colored glasses help you to search for profit potential. Your buyer's eyes alert you to risks. To succeed as an entrepreneurial renovator, you must consistently switch from one set of glasses to the other. Then, as Ben Franklin suggested, at the end of the day you tally up the positives and the negatives. At that point, you can make a fully informed, rational decision.

Uncommon Sense   This advice may seem like common sense. But in practice, it's not common at all. Unless you've got ice-water running through your arteries, I guarantee that you're going to react emotionally to the neighborhoods and properties you look at. The human animal tends to pick up on some features of a property (good or bad) and then interprets everything else to fit that first impression.

My Approach   As we go through the process of evaluating properties, sometimes you will put on your rose-colored glasses and look for profit potential. At other moments, you will take off the rose-colored glasses and put on those specs that force you to see with buyer's eyes. By balancing perspectives, you'll learn to recognize those lumps of coal that you can transform into diamonds.

Inspecting the Site

To thoroughly inspect and evaluate possibilities for the site, think of it in four different ways:

1. Site size and configuration
2. Site quality (topography, landscaping, soil conditions)
3. Fencing, driveway, sidewalks
4. Curb appeal

Site Size and Configuration

As a first step, walk the boundaries of the property and measure each leg. Ideally, you'll follow the outline of a plat or survey that the seller provides you. If no plat or survey is available, ask the sellers to point specifically to where they believe the lot lines run. Use this site description in your preliminary measures. But verify it before you irrevocably commit to buy.

> **Much of a property's value lies in the land.**

You might wonder why you need to go to this much trouble. What difference does it make whether you know the exact size of the site and precisely where the boundaries lay?

What You See Isn't Necessarily What You Get   Surprising as it may seem, site size and configuration aren't always as they appear. Friends of mine who bought a home loved their big backyard that ran from the house 200 feet back toward a row of trees. In fact, the property's rear lot line didn't correspond with the tree row, as they had assumed. It actually lay 82 feet closer in. Their backyard was half the size they had originally believed it was. They never checked the site's plat. They simply assumed that what they saw was what they got.

Walking the site's boundaries also can yield two other related benefits:

1. *Discover easements.* Remember, easements will restrict your use of the property. An ill-placed easement may prevent you from building on an addition, erecting a fence, or putting up a storage shed.
2. *Discover encroachments.* Does the neighbor's garage or driveway overlap the property line? Do any trees, shrubs, or fences appear to violate site boundaries?

> **Your site size partially determines what *legal* improvements you can make.**

Should you discover these potential problems, clear them up in some satisfactory manner long before you start spending time and money for professional property inspections, repair estimates, mortgage application fees, an appraisal, or other property acquisition costs.

Improvement Plans: Regulatory Issues Remember those government regulations from Chapter 4 such as FARs (floor area ratios) and setbacks (sideyard, front yard, rear yard). When you measure the site size and locate boundary lines, you're then able to tell whether you can legally add space, build a deck, or move a driveway. I know of too many people who bought properties with grand plans only to belatedly learn that their plans pushed beyond the legal limits of their site.

Does the Site Give You an Extra Buildable Lot? "Where else but in Santa Fe," Realtor Dee Treadwell asks, "could you buy a home for $285,000, later subdivide the property, sell the house for $550,000, and still have a lot to sell?" Now, that's the kind of deal every investor wants to find. Yet, even though this Realtor seems not to realize it, you can find similar sites in every city throughout North America. Granted, Santa Fe's prices rank toward the high end. But whenever a house sits across two or more lots, you can tear the house down and sell the vacant lots individually. This means that if you buy a house that sits on several buildable lots, you might be looking at big *future* profits.

The key words here, though, are *legally buildable.* Just because a house sits on a lot that's large enough to accommodate two or more newly constructed houses doesn't mean you can realize the site's profit potential. To reap the rewards, government building regulations must permit additional subdivision and development.

> **Sites with extra buildable land give you "hidden value."**

Combine Lots with a Neighbor On occasion, a property's lot may include extra side-yard space but not quite enough to form a legally buildable site. In that case, look to the neighboring site. What if you could persuade the owner of that property to sell you a 10-foot strip? You could then assemble enough plottage. Or with extra sideyard square footage, maybe you could put together enough land to create a duplex or triplex—if zoning allows it.

Keep Searching for More Profitable Uses for the Site With accurate knowledge of site size and allowable (or at least tolerated) uses, you can run all types of ideas through a cost-benefit study. What types of added space would appeal to a target market? More living space? Covered parking? RV parking? A workshop? Tennis courts or swimming pool? Storage shed? Community garden? Decks or patios? A gazebo? A combination card room, computer facility, or study area? A guest cottage or accessory apartment? A pet kennel? The list is endless.

In a world where land remains scarce, you can almost always figure out a way to convert unused lot capacity into bigger profits.

> **Upgrade the use of the site.**

You don't even have to target the same people for the "extra" as you do for the main house. If you're holding the property as a rental, you could rent out the added RV spaces or storage areas to those apartment dwellers down the block. Or if you fix and flip, accent the extra rental income as an affordability helper to financially tight homebuyers.

Hidden Value in the Land   Not far from where I live, some homeowners with large lots pick up an extra $3,000 to $5,000 a year in parking fees. How? They rent parking spaces to people attending football games and other special events at the nearby university. Thirty cars at $15 per car for 10 events each year totals $4,500 (tax free, I suspect).

Never think of site size as mere yard space. Think how you can put that land to work making money. Smart investors don't just shop for houses to renovate; they also shop for houses with hidden value in the land.

Site Quality

In addition to views (pleasant or unpleasant), the quality of a site refers to these features:

- ◆ Topography
- ◆ Soil condition
- ◆ Landscaping

Topography   I once owned a property that was sited slightly below grade. After every hard rain, water flowed into the garage as if it were trans-ported there by an aqueduct. In addition to drainage, topography will affect the slope and positioning of the driveway (ingress/egress). Even moderate inclines can make navigation up or down difficult during snow and ice storms. Topography also can increase construction costs and expose a site to greater risk from mudslide or earthquake.

> **Site value relates to quality as well as size.**

As an advantage, though, a downward sloping lot often opens up opportunities for finishing off or enhancing the lower level of a house. As with every feature of a property, thoughtfully anticipate both the problems and possibilities that site topography might play into.

Soil Condition   Would you like to grow a lush yard of grass? Would your buyers or tenants like to harvest vegetables from a garden? What types of flower and shrubs do you intend to plant? Amazingly, people always notice the quality of the yard and landscaping, but few realize that the composition of the soil can enhance or frustrate your green thumb.

The composition of the soil also can create foundation prob-lems. For example, soil with a high content of clay tends to expand and contract. I've seen houses built improperly on clay actually split apart. If the property lacks city water and sewage disposal, you'll want to verify adequate water for a well and percolation tests to determine whether the soil will safely diffuse waste.

Landscaping   Here's where you can really add value to a property. People love a manicured lawn, flower-lined walkways, mulched shrubs, and flower gardens. With landscaping, you can turn an ugly duckling house into a showcase property. With land-scaping you can create privacy, manufacture a gorgeous view look-ing out from inside the house, or eliminate an ugly view. Especially if you're looking at a three- to five-year holding period (or longer), put in those small plants, shrubs, and hedges now. When you sell, you can easily earn a return of at least 10:1.

The rear boundary of one of my properties is lined with a row of hedges 12 to 16 feet tall. Since this home's major living areas and master bedroom include large expanses of glass and windows that look out to the back, these hedges (and other landscaping) create both privacy and pleasant views. In stark contrast, the views from the house of a nearby property owner also are oriented toward the backyard rather than the street, but even though this house is more than 40 years old, no one has ever planted a rear hedgerow or otherwise landscaped the backyard. As a result, each day these homeowners gaze out at a barren yard, and each evening as they turn on the lights, they must draw their blinds. Otherwise, their rear yard neighbors could see directly into their house—for they, too, have never invested in privacy fencing or landscaping. In comparison to these homes, I am sure that the privacy/view advantage of my property boosts its value by $10,000 to $20,000 and probably adds more than $50 per month to its rental income.

> **Think long term.
> Add value-
> enhancing plants
> and trees now.**

As a minimum, to create value with landscaping, you can spruce up the yard in these ways:

- ◆ Remove all litter and debris from the yard and streetscape.
- ◆ Prune, cut back, or remove all out-of-control or straggly bushes.
- ◆ Edge walks and driveways. Apply weed killer to stop growth between the cracks.
- ◆ Trim unsightly trees and remove dead branches.
- ◆ Fertilize the grass and plant or create some type of attractive ground cover to eliminate those bare spots in the yard.

You need to inspect the yard as closely as a mother inspects her two-year-old's first haircut. Make sure every blade of grass is in place and all cowlicks and bald spots aesthetically neutralized. And please, too, remove the bubblegum.

Fences, Driveway, and Sidewalks

As the next part of your inspection, note the quality of the property's fences, driveway, sidewalks, patios, lampposts, and mailbox. After you fix up the property, none of these site features should show any wear or disrepair. Get rid of those driveway oil stains; patch unsightly cracks; paint the lamppost, clean its light fixture, and replace any broken glass plates. If a public sidewalk crosses the property, call the city to request (insist on) needed maintenance. Splurge. Invest $35 to buy a premium mailbox. No single small expense so clearly states pride of ownership.

> **Ill-repaired site features destroy curb appeal.**

For reasons of aesthetics, privacy, and security, quality fences can really lift the value of a property—especially when combined with well-selected, eye-pleasing landscaping. Just as certainly, though, a rusted, rotted, or half-falling-down fence clearly signals that the property suffers from poor maintenance.

Curb Appeal: Attending to the Details

As a buyer-fixer, I love to find good houses with rundown yards, landscaping, and fencing. Taken together—even more than the exterior of the house itself—these deteriorated features lock a negative impression into the minds of most buyers. These negatives heavily discount the property's curb appeal and its market value. Among all of the improvements that you can make to a property, creating dazzling curb (and backyard) appeal will pay back your investment many times over. But you must attend to details.

The Well-Dressed Man or Woman   Think of the well-dressed man or woman. Both achieve that spectacular look by paying attention to a dozen or more details. Hair, makeup, jewelry, color, style, fit, freshly cleaned and pressed—everything works together. Now, place a stain on a blouse or tie and what do you get? A negative impression. That's what people will remember.

How to Achieve That Dazzling Curb Appeal Unless you're creatively gifted, *great* ideas for improving the site may not come to you easily. They certainly don't come easily to me. I rank high among the artistically challenged. Here's how I overcame this obstacle.

> **Lack artistic flair? Look for model properties you can copy.**

I carry a camera in the glovebox of my car. Often when I see a house and yard that display eye-catching features, I snap a picture. Over time, I've put together a large collection of photos. Then, as I'm trying to figure out how to best improve a fixer property, I pull out some of these photos and compare the features of model properties with the fixer property I'm improving. This method always brings forth a rush of value-creating ideas. Try it, you'll like it.

I'll also point out that you don't necessarily have to rely on your own snapshots. Dozens of "house and home" types of books and magazines fill the shelves of bookstores. I regularly buy these publications. Their articles and photos will always juice up your creative thinking and aesthetic sensibilities.

The Outside of the House

After you've thoroughly inspected the site, turn your attention to the exterior of the house. You're about to get into the ring for the main event. To evaluate the home's exterior and generate ideas for improvements, focus on these four criteria:

- ◆ Appearance
- ◆ Condition

◆ Building materials and maintenance expense
◆ Site placement (how the house is oriented on the site)

Appearance

As you begin to inspect the exterior of a house, stand back at least 50 to 100 feet. Place the building in perspective with the site and with other properties in the neighborhood. Does it fit in? Is it too large or too small? Does the architectural style give the house an appealing uniqueness? Or is it a simple box design with no windows on either side? Have a half-dozen other houses in the neighborhood been built with the same design?

> **View the property from across the street. Gain perspective.**

The Roof Pay special attention to the roof. Is it discolored? Are leaves piling up? Are plants growing on the roof or out of the gutters? Roofs scare most buyers because they're costly to replace. Clean it up such that it shows as little wear as possible.

If your remedial efforts can't improve the appearance—and you're planning to quickly flip the property—go ahead and replace it. As Bob Bruss points out, a new roof probably won't give you a dollar-for-dollar payback, but it will enhance the home's marketability.

> **A few loss-leader repairs can pay off by bolstering the total impact of the property.**

Here's how Robert Bruss describes the sound principle behind this advice:

Last week I was in Walgreens where they had a special on 24 cans of Coors beer for $11. That's a VERY good bargain! When I asked the manager how he can make any profit at that price, he claimed that was his cost for the beer. But, as he looked at my full shopping cart of other more profitable items which I bought during the same visit, he pointed to them and said, "That's where we make our profits." The same principle applies to fixer-upper houses. Some items you install won't add to the value of the house at all, yet they are necessary and enable you to sell or rent the house at an overall profit.

To illustrate, at the house I am currently remodeling I am having a new roof installed even though (1) it won't add any market value to the house and (2) the old roof doesn't leak—yet! Why am I so foolish? *That roof is like Walgreens' loss-leader beer special.* I know from experience one of the first questions prospective home buyers ask is "How old is the roof?" If they are reassured the roof is brand new, that makes the sale possible. But if they are told "It doesn't leak but is about 15 years old" that creates a negative rather than a positive buying situation. If your fixer-upper house obviously needs some work, such as a new roof, but you know that item won't be profitable, do it anyway if it will be a big incentive for the buyer to buy.

I must hasten to add it doesn't pay to acquire houses which need lots of unprofitable work. Examples of costly unprofitable but usually necessary work include new roof, foundation repairs or replacement, replumbing, rewiring, and a new furnace or air conditioning system. When you inspect a fixer-upper house which needs all or most of these unprofitable improvements, just walk away *unless* you can get a very low purchase price and extremely attractive purchase terms.[1]

Bob Bruss is right. A new roof can prove to be your most profitable loss leader. But like Amazon.com, if all you sell are loss leaders, you're not likely to make much money.

---

1. Quoted from the *Robert Bruss Real Estate Newsletter,* #92215. You can order past and current issues of this information-packed newsletter by phone at (800) 736-1736, fax (650) 348-6916, mail (Robert J. Bruss, 251 Park Road, Burlingame, CA 94010) or by visiting www.bobbruss.com.

Sharpen the Appeal Can you imagine ways to enhance the property's value with window shutters, flower boxes, a dramatic front door and entryway, new or additional windows, fresh paint, a contrasting color for trim, or accenting the design with architectural details? How well does (or could) the property's exterior distinguish it from other comparably priced properties? Do you rate its appeal as great, so-so, or awful? List possibilities for profitable improvements.

Start poring over your photo collection. Look for features that will really set your property apart from its competitors. Look for those features that will wow your target market.

Exterior Condition: The Professional Inspection

To avoid too many profit-draining, loss-leader repairs, you will hire a professional home inspector to detect potential problems. Generally, though, you won't order a formal report until after you've signed a purchase contract that includes an inspection contingency clause. Nevertheless, prior to that step you should perform a close preprofessional inspection. Your personal scrutiny of the exterior (and interior) will serve three purposes.

1. *Purchase negotiations.* To achieve the best price and terms, you must justify your offer. When the seller says, "What!? You're offering me $115,000!? The house three doors down sold two months ago for $145,000." "Yes," you respond. "But that house was in near perfect condition. As we discussed, this property is going to need. . . ."
2. *Weed out losers.* When your preinspection clearly identifies problems, yet the seller won't accommodate you with concessions (price, terms), stop wasting time. Say sayonara. Move on to your next possibility.
3. *Education and understanding.* When you do bring a professional inspector in, don't settle for a mere inspec-

tion. Go for an education. Ask detailed questions. Use notes from your personal inspection to quiz the pro. Learn all you can about spotting problems, understanding their cause, remedial alternatives, and, most importantly, cost-effective means of prevention.

Materials and Maintenance

Each area of the country has its own types of construction materials that are popular and effective for that locale. Wood, brick, brick veneer, adobe, concrete block, stucco, and steel are possibilities. In addition, some houses are built on a pier-and-beam foundation; others sit on concrete slabs. Windows and roofs differ, too. Crank-style aluminum awning windows are popular in some warmer climates but seldom found up north. In California, you see tile roofs; in Maine, that type of roof is rare.

Evaluate the Quality of Construction and Building Materials   Regardless of the specific types of construction materials used in your area, you can bet that they vary widely in costs, function, and desirability. Before buying, talk to knowledgeable builders, contractors, or building supply companies to learn the differences between high-end, mid-range, and low-cost building materials. Talk with anyone you know who has recently built a new house. They've probably spent months shopping for materials. To compare houses effectively, you've got to move beyond appearance. Savvy investors don't merely judge the quality of a house by its paint job.

Maintenance: Time, Effort, and Costs   Apart from the quality of construction materials, consider how much time, effort, and money it's going to cost to maintain the house. Growing up, I recall that every three or four years we had to scrape peeling paint with a wire brush to prepare our home for its next coat of paint.

> **Always use low-maintenance materials—even when they cost more.**

Now, today's durable paints, stains, and materials often last 10 years or longer.

Whenever you repair or renovate, go with low- or no-maintenance improvements, even if they cost more. Neither you, your buyers, nor your tenants want to fool around with home maintenance. I guarantee you that low- or no-maintenance features sell properties.

For lower- to moderate-priced homes, I strongly favor vinyl siding and eaves. In the South, I like concrete block. Slap on a coat of paint every 15 to 20 years and that's it for exterior maintenance. As to gutters, old-timers love them. I hate them. The best way to deal with rusty, leaf-filled gutters—rip them off and don't replace them. Place a rain diverter on the roof above the front porch or above other exterior entryways.

As I have said before, I possess no talent, no inclination, and no time to personally take on the chores of property repair and property maintenance. With today's materials, that distaste erects no barriers to owning properties.

Site Placement

In looking at a house from the outside, note how the building is situated on the site. Are the windows positioned to bring in beacons of natural light? How about privacy from neighbors? Can residents sunbathe in the backyard without prying eyes to invade their privacy? Are the sleeping areas of the house protected from street noise? How will prevailing winter winds (or summer breezes) strike the house? How will these affect resident comfort and energy bills? In North America, a southern exposure with large windows will bring in the winter sunshine and reduce heating costs.

> **Site placement affects views, privacy, and energy efficiency.**

Does the site placement conform to the standards of feng shui? If your target market of buyers or tenants includes Asians, get up to speed on feng shui by reading one of many books published on the topic. In California, some homebuilders and renovators specifically design their houses to conform to feng shui principles to give their properties a competitive edge with Asian buyers.

After you have thoroughly evaluated the site and the exterior of the property, you next want to carefully inspect the interior for problems and possibilities. For that task, we now turn to Chapter 6.

6

Enhance the Interior

As you inspect the inside of the house, you again balance the critical with the entrepreneurial. Detailing what's wrong helps you negotiate better price and terms. Detailing what's right helps you turn property potential into money-making improvements.

Scrutinize Square Footages

> **Do not count all square footage equally.**

Real estate agents and appraisers frequently quote home values with price per square foot figures. (A 1,500-square-foot house listed at $150,000 would show a price of $100 per square foot). The agent or the seller of a property might say something like, "We got this house bargain priced at just $85 per square foot. Nothing else in the neighborhood has sold for anything under $95 per square foot."

Okay, sounds good so far. But before you bite, check the facts.

Watch Out for Errors of Measurement

Appraisers, sales agents, sellers, and property tax assessors mis-measure properties all the time. In fact, sellers or realty agents often pull their square footage figures from property tax records. Yet in many areas of the country, property tax records are notoriously inaccurate. That's one reason why the fine print on the Realtor's property description flyers says, "Data believed to be from reliable sources, but not warranted."

> **Verify who has measured what.**

Recently, an appraiser reported the square footage of one of my properties at 1,370 square feet, when it actually comes close to 1,750 square feet. The property tax records of one house I owned showed 2,460 square feet. But the house actually totaled over 3,200 square feet because the tax assessor had never adjusted his figures to reflect an 800-square-foot addition.

Of course, errors may also plague the reported square footages of comparable properties. The comp price per square foot could exceed or fall below the figures quoted.

All Space Doesn't Count Equally

The square footage of an attic that's been converted into a spare bedroom isn't worth as much as the square footage of the main house. A finished basement of 800 square feet isn't the equivalent of an 800-square-foot second story that's fully integrated into the house. Don't compare houses or apartment units only in size; also compare the quality and livability of the finished space.

Remember this point not only when you're bidding on a property but also when you're making improvements. Too many amateur renovators create space through bastardized conversions that feature low ceilings, rooms without windows, weird hallways, and no ductwork for heat or air conditioning. To add the most value to a property, integrate the new space within the existing

<table>
<tr><td>

Avoid bastardized conversions and remodelings.

</td><td>

house in such a way that it blends smoothly and harmoniously. Poorly planned conversions and additions often leave buyers with an overpowering negative impression of the property.

On the other hand, when you do run across those bastardized conversions and additions, put on your rose-colored glasses. Can you remedy the oddball appearance? Can you re-

</td></tr>
</table>

design and enhance its functional utility? I often find that by investing a few thousand dollars along with some creative insights, I can transform awkward space arrangements into open, smoothly flowing areas.

Make Sure All Like Space Does Count Equally

Some sellers count all space with a roof over it. Others count only the basic living areas. The sellers of one house may describe its size as 1,980 square feet and include in that square-footage figure a garage that's now a den conversion. An owner of a similar home may describe that house as 1,600 square feet and simply footnote a similarly converted makeshift den as an extra, but not include its size in the square footage quoted for the house.

In appraising the market value of one of my properties, the appraiser listed a comp property at a size of 2,200 square feet. Yet, I had visited that property during an open house when it was available for sale. I knew that its square footage didn't come close to the size the appraiser had reported.

What accounted for the difference? The appraiser believed that the comp property's garage had been converted to living space because the property owners had constructed one of those awning-type carports over the driveway. The appraiser had carelessly counted the comp house garage as living area (when in fact it was being used as storage for a home business), whereas he counted the garage of my property as a garage. Like spaces weren't counted equally.

Appraisers Seldom Inspect Comp Houses   How could the appraiser make this mistake? Easy. As noted previously, appraisers seldom inspect their comp houses. They'll probably drive by and snap a photo or two. But they won't walk the property or go inside. In addition, during hot housing markets (sales and refis), appraisers try to complete 8 to 12 appraisal assignments per day. At that breakneck pace, no appraiser takes the time to truly weigh and consider. The superficial and impressionistic kicks aside care and reason.

> **Appraisers adhere to slipshod practices.**

Fixer Profits Require Detailed and Accurate Property Inspections and Comparisons   All too often, appraisers, sales agents, sellers, and even investors accept and repeat inappropriate price per square foot figures. It's such a widely quoted rule-of-thumb measure that buyers often overlook its complexity and inconsistencies. You, though, must avoid this casual approach. When someone quotes you a price per square foot number, critically question its accuracy and applicability.

To earn fixer profits, you must (1) accurately value a property in its as-is condition and (2) accurately estimate the minimum (reasonable) improved value (MIV). When employed carefully, square footage comparisons can give you a good idea of relative home values in a neighborhood. Used naively, they can mislead you into believing you're getting a bargain when you're actually overpaying. Or, you could overestimate the real market value of that basement or attic conversion that you're planning. Thus, your actual payback would fall far short of your profit goals.

> **Quality adjust all per square foot figures.**

I always use price per square foot figures, but only after I've adjusted them for quality, consistency, and accuracy. How do you gain this ability? Go to open houses. Thoroughly inspect the neighborhood properties that come up for sale. Judge for yourself the size, quality, and condition of these houses. Personally track selling prices. Then when a seller, realty agent, or appraiser throws out a per square foot figure, you'll know whether that figure makes sense.

Floor Plan: Does the Layout of the House Work?

Once you have moved beyond the size of a house, next evaluate its floor plan. Does the layout of the house offer convenience and privacy? Does it work efficiently?

When you first approach the main entry of the house, do you have to climb steep steps? Is there a covered porch area so visitors can avoid standing in the rain or snow while waiting for someone in the house to answer their knock? If the main entrance lies below grade, does it appear that water may build up in the entrance area? As you walk in the front door, notice whether you're dropped immediately into a living area or does the house have a foyer? Is there an adequate-sized coat closet nearby? Relative to the main entrance, where is the kitchen located? Can you walk from the entry door to other rooms of the house without passing through a third room? How are the location and size of bedrooms, baths, and closets?

Livability

Now, imagine people living in the house. Where will their kids play—both indoors and outdoors? Will the parents be able to keep an eye on them? Does the house have a "Grand Central Station" living room? Or is it pleasantly isolated from other house activity areas?

> **Square footage doesn't necessarily create livability.**

Go into the kitchen. How long does it take the faucet to draw hot water? For purposes of work efficiency, can someone step conveniently between the refrigerator, oven, stovetop, and sink? Do you see adequate counter and cabinet space? Is there an eat-in kitchen area that separates the family members who are eating from those who are working (preparing meals, cleaning up)? Is there easy access to the kitchen from the garage or carport? Can someone conveniently enter the kitchen from the parking area while carrying several bags of groceries?

On this tour to evaluate floor plan, make back-and-forth trips throughout the house as if you were living there. Perhaps the long walk from the kitchen to the master bedroom wouldn't faze an investor on a quick walk-through. But how would you like to make that trip a dozen times a day or more? Would it then get tiresome? Where's the laundry located? Is the floor plan open or closed? Does the house live to the front or the rear? Catalogue your detailed observations. Think target market.

Target Market

Will the layout of the house appeal to your target market? Alternatively, can you think of certain types of buyers or tenants who would find the floor plan especially appealing? For example, residents with small children typically prefer to have the master bedroom close to the kids' bedrooms. Seniors typically prefer single-story houses with few steps. Rental roommates generally like separate privacy areas, especially split floor plans. How about a home office? Is there a large, private room that could serve the person who works at home?

> **Imagine people living in the house.**

Investors frequently focus too heavily on the physical condition and appearance of a property and fail to imagine its actual livability. In contrast, think how most buyers (or tenants) evaluate a property. As they move through the house, they begin to visualize people, activities, and furniture in various rooms and areas. They ask themselves and imagine:

- Where will the kids play, sleep, and entertain friends?
- Where will we place our furniture?
- Where will we eat family dinners?
- How conveniently can we work in the kitchen?
- Where's a good place for the workshop?
- Does the kitchen include enough cabinets and storage space?
- Where will we entertain our friends?
- Will we have enough room for guests when they visit?
- Will we have enough closet space?
- Will members of the household be able to enjoy privacy and quiet zones?

As you get to know your target market, you will anticipate their concerns and needs. You will soon understand what features light up their eyes and what features close their minds to the property. You will learn these features by talking with potential buyers (tenants), visiting open houses, touring model new homes, conferring with real estate agents, and through any and all other methods of discovery that you can think of.

> **Anticipate the needs and wants of your buyers and tenants.**

Savvy renovators don't just "fix and repair ugly houses." More importantly, through their property improvements, they make living easier for their buyers and tenants.

Rightsize Rooms and Room Counts   Some houses include bedrooms that seem no larger than a closet and bathrooms that seem no larger than a phone booth. Can you figure out a way to either increase their size or change their use to better match buyer needs? Or could you subdivide that cavernous great room into smaller living areas? As you judge the room sizes and room counts (number of bedrooms, bathrooms, living areas, kitchens, home office) within a house, try to generate ideas about how you could employ the space more effectively.

Ill-Designed Houses Dominate the Market   Many older and even newer houses were ill de-signed at the time they were built. Others were okay for the 1930s, 1940s, or 1950s, but no longer reflect modern tastes. Personally, I like to find houses with those old-fashioned closed floor plans (each room separate and distinct from all others) and open them up with a living space that flows through the kitchen, dining, and living areas.

> **Modernize a floor plan for big profits.**

Make the Kitchen Work Better   When kitchens are too large, I tighten up the work triangle and add either a small office/bill-paying type of workstation or an eat-in area if none previously existed. Or maybe I'll do both. A center island with a counter overhang and stools tucked underneath can serve double duty as a food preparation area and an informal sit-down, in-kitchen eating area. And you can still create a household office area.

Closets and Bedrooms   In some older houses, the bedrooms are large, but the closets won't hold much more than a navy trunk. When you find a house that fits this description, do as I have done. Trade two feet of bedroom for a wall-length closet. If you buy a house with one or two small bedrooms, you could install a Murphy bed. This tactic will permit the residents of the house to make more effective use of the floor space. You could also build in a loft bed, which will free up floor space.

Install Pocket Doors   Sometimes the way a door swings can chew up livable space. Again, as to my personal preferences, I like to put in pocket doors if the studs permit. These can work espe-cially well to make better use of the off-bedroom bath. Because pocket doors cost more to install, few people use them. But I think that many buyers consider pocket doors a nice special touch. On occasion, you might also add space to a room by reversing the swing of an existing door.

Increase Storage Areas   You can think about storage space in at least three ways:

◆ Bring dead space to life.
◆ Rightsize existing storage space.
◆ Create new space.

Bring Dead Space to Life.   Let me illustrate with what seems trivial, but in fact always creates a lasting favorable impression. Look

> **Everyone wants more storage. Give it to them.**

in the cabinet under your kitchen sink. You will see a small gap between the front panel of the cabinet above the door and the sink. In other words, dead space. How might you use that space? Install a small pull-down compartment to stow away soap, sponge, and Brillo pad. No more sink clutter. Whenever I show this little innova-tion to other people, I always get a "Wow, isn't that neat" response.

Okay, I admit it's trivial. But it illustrates the point. All houses include generous amounts of large and small dead spaces that with creativity you can bring to life:

◆ Under stairs and stairwells
◆ On the tops of kitchen cabinets
◆ Under porches
◆ Dead-end cabinets
◆ Walls suitable for shelving
◆ Interior access to an under-the-house crawl space
◆ Recessed storage between studs (as with an in-wall medi-cine chest)
◆ Kitchen hanging bars for pots and pans

These ideas represent just a sampling of possibilities. If you go through any house and ask, "Where are the dead spaces that I can bring to life for purposes of storage?" I guarantee that you will find them.

Rightsize Existing Storage Space   My favorite examples to illustrate this point come from the California Closet Company (CCC). As this innovative firm has proven, you can double (or triple) your storage capacity without adding even one square inch of new space. Simply reorganize and redesign the raw space that already exists. Although founded as a closet company, CCC now redesigns garages, offices, workshops, and kitchens. Put these same organizing principles to work and you'll truly enhance the appeal of your properties.

> **Take a cue from the California Closet Company.**

Create New Space   My father ran out of space in his garage to store all of his lawn and garden equipment. But through creative design, he added about 100 square feet of space to the end of the garage for a cost of just $1,000—a mere $10 per square foot. Plus, because much of the "shed" is glass with a southern exposure, he's able to also use it as a makeshift greenhouse to hang his tomato plants and get a head start on the Indiana growing season.

As you evaluate properties, first look for dead spaces and functionally deficient existing storage areas. But if these improvements still don't wow your buyers, build new space—with multipurposes, when possible.

Aesthetics: How Does the House Look, Feel, and Sound?

"I was once in a house," recalls real estate appraiser Dodge Woodson, "that made me feel as if there should have been a coffin sitting in the living room. The drapes were dark and heavy—a ghastly green that gave me an eerie feeling. I don't spook easily, and I'm used to seeing a lot of houses in a lot of different conditions, but

> **Homes sell with emotional appeal.**

this house made me uncomfortable. If I had been a prospective buyer, I would not have been able to focus on anything but the drapes."

Woodson's reaction to this house with the eerie dark green drapes wouldn't have surprised Professor Mary Jasmosli of George Washington University. Jasmosli has developed an expertise she calls environmental sensitivity. Through her research she has found that people react emotionally to the interiors (and exteriors) of homes in ways that they themselves can neither explain nor understand. "Home features such as number of windows, window treatments, color schemes, views, placement of walls and doorways, room size, ceiling height, and amount of light all hold special meaning," reports Jasmosli.

Now, we'll turn to Dodge Woodson. "The next time I entered that house, I couldn't believe the difference," he remarks. "The owners had replaced the dark green drapes with flowing white window treatments. . . . Not only was the house pretty, it appeared much larger. . . . I noticed features that I had never seen before. The house was alive with light. This experience convinced me of the power that window treatments have."

Create Emotional Appeal

It's not just window treatments that can change the emotional appeal of a home. You can dramatically improve the look and feel of any home by changing, replacing, or removing any of its negatives. If you are looking at a house that doesn't generate the warmth, brightness, or romance you think your buyers or tenants would pay extra for, don't rush out and get back in your car. Linger a while. Isolate the sources of your discomfort. Mull over ideas. How would the house (or apartment units) look, feel, sound, or smell if you . . .

- ◆ Put in skylights.
- ◆ Remove a wall.

- ◆ Eliminate the litter box and pet odors.
- ◆ Replace the worn, ugly carpeting.
- ◆ Increase the size or number of windows or add brighter, more modern window treatments.
- ◆ Create a view with a flower garden or arrangement of plants, shrubs, or hedges.
- ◆ Paint and wallpaper with different colors and textures.
- ◆ Install new cabinets or appliances.
- ◆ Pull out that dropped-ceiling acoustical tile and create a vaulted ceiling.
- ◆ Soundproof the home with insulated windows, shrubs, or an earth berm.

Put your imagination to work. With good ideas you can transform any property, making it more comfortable, appealing, and valuable. In some cases, emotional appeal will even trump function and floor plan. I learned this from my own experience.

> **Strong emotional appeal can even overwhelm cool-headed negatives.**

In buying one of my previous homes, I was so taken with its wooded views, expansive windows, beamed ceilings, hardwood floors, skylights, and Jacuzzi in the master bedroom, I didn't think carefully about floor plan, internal traffic patterns, and functional efficiency. After moving in, I began to recognize many serious flaws in the home's design and function. For example, the master bedroom was located directly above the den, and sounds from the television came right up; the hot water heater lacked enough capacity to fill the Jacuzzi; and access to the kitchen from the garage was quite cumbersome for carrying in bags of groceries. (I might add that this house was only three years old!)

Check Noise Levels

Noise is a potential problem within households. Will sound from a television or stereo carry into other rooms? Bring along a portable radio on your house inspections. Place it in various rooms. Turn up the volume. Do the walls give you enough soundproofing? Families and roommate tenants want privacy and quiet. If your property fails to offer these essentials, your property will lose its appeal.

Just as important, will residents hear neighbors or neighborhood noise from inside the house? Again, people pay for quiet. They discount heavily for noise.

Although potential neighbors and neighborhood noise are especially important to note in townhouses and condominiums, single-family developments are no strangers to loud stereos, barking dogs, and Indy 500 engine revving. Does the drum corps of the nearby high school practice outside three or four hours a day? When possible, visit the property during periods of high traffic or peak noise. Don't assume that a neighborhood offers peace and quiet. Verify.

> **Buyers (renters) will pay a premium for quiet.**

Seek written disclosures from the sellers and talk with neighbors. Determine whether anyone has tried to enforce quiet by complaining to city government, the homeowners association, or by filing a nuisance suit. If you buy the property, could you effectively invoke any of these remedies? Could the house, itself, incorporate more features to reduce noise that emanates from either the outside or the inside of the house? When you suppress noise into quiet, you create value.

Clean Thoroughly

Perhaps more than any other common problem, dirt turns buyers (and tenants) off. Dirty windows; accumulated dirt and debris on porches, patios, and entryways; and even old and dirty doormats seem to build a wall of emotional resistance. Dirt signals that a house has not been well cared for. Most tenants and buyers want to steer clear of dirty houses.

Now, imagine the home's appeal if it were given a top-to-bottom cleaning. Because houses with dirty exteriors frequently have unkempt yards, you may have to picture the home as if the grass were neatly cut, the shrubs trimmed, and the flowers blooming. Close your eyes. Now what does the house look like?

> **Clean pays back many times over.**

In their idea-generating book *Dress Your House for Success* (Three Rivers Press, 1997), Martha Webb and Sarah Zackhem write:

> The uncomfortable feeling an of unclean house causes apprehension, and the buyer will start to disengage . . . when she finds accumulated dust, dirt, grime, mildew, or soap scum, she mentally disengages because she's slightly embarrassed of what else she might find. For the rest of the house tour, she will become remote, hesitant, and will proceed with a detached attitude. And guaranteed, when later she thinks of your house—if she thinks of it at all—she will most remember the dirt. (pp. 73-74)

After this introduction, Webb and Zackhem continue for eight pages of specific cleaning details. When they say clean, they really mean *clean*.

- ◆ Spotless windows and mirrors.
- ◆ High-luster interior wood.
- ◆ Crumbless kitchen drawers and cabinets.
- ◆ Fresh paint wherever walls or other painted surfaces refuse to give up their previous scuffs and marks.
- ◆ No dust or dead insects inside light fixtures.
- ◆ No collected dirt or dust in corners or along baseboards.
- ◆ Scrub down to perfection all faucets, sinks, showers, toilets, and bathtubs.
- ◆ Replace or refinish wherever stains persist.

Their list goes on. But you see their point. Clean means perfection. To achieve this goal, here's a trick that I've used. Hire an 8- or 10-year-old. Tell the child that you will pay him or her five dollars base pay to seek out flaws in your house preparation plus a dollar for each flaw discovered. After cleaning inside and out, you still need fresh eyes to give the house another detailed inspection. No one gets a second chance to create a stunning first impression.

Condition: How Much Time, Effort, and Money Will the Property Require?

Before closing on a property, hire a professional to inspect it. Place an inspection contingency in your written offer to the sellers. Then, depending on what the inspector turns up, you can go ahead with your purchase, renegotiate price and repair credits, or withdraw from the agreement. Prior to hiring a professional, though, remember to closely check the condition of the house yourself.

As noted earlier, you'll need to get a general idea about the home's condition so that you can compare various properties to each other. Second, you can use any shortcomings you do discover to persuade sellers to offer a lower price, better terms, or an escrow credit for repairs. And third, you'll want to weed out some houses because they clearly require too many money-losing repairs and replacements (the wrong things wrong).

> **Homes that need repairs scare away many buyers.**

To go through an interior preprofessional inspection for a property, here are six items to consider: (1) plumbing; (2) heating, ventilating, and air conditioning; (3) electrical; (4) ceilings, walls, and floors; (5) appearance and floor plan; and (6) quality of materials.

1. *Plumbing.* To check the condition of the plumbing, first test the water pressure. Turn on a couple of baths or showers, then flush the toilets. What happens? Is the water pressure sufficient to maintain the water flows? Check all the water faucets for drips. Determine whether the water heater is large enough to allow all members of a household to take hot showers when everybody is trying to get ready at the same time. Inspect all the pipes and shutoff valves under sinks and cabinets. Is there any sign of leaking, rust, or corrosion? If the house has a basement or accessible crawl space, inspect the plumbing from that vantage point. What type of piping has been used—plastic, copper, galvanized steel, lead, or something else? Each of these materials has its own advantages and disadvantages, installation procedures, and building code standards. Discuss these points with a professional inspector.

2. *Heating, ventilating, and air conditioning (HVAC).* Depending on the season of the year, you may not be able to adequately test the HVAC system of a house. Nevertheless, at least note the placement and size of the duct vents. Do any rooms lack outlets? Are the vents positioned to evenly and efficiently distribute heat throughout a house? If the house (or specific rooms) lacks central heat or air (e.g., it has floor furnaces, wall furnaces, or window heat and air units), residents may experience hot and cool spots throughout the house. Because most HVAC equipment has a limited life, ask the ages of various components. An age of more than 8 or 10 years may point to coming problems. Check with an expert.

3. *Electrical.* As with plumbing and HVAC systems, judge the condition of an electrical system by how well it will serve the household needs and whether it meets modern standards of performance and safety. Reserve this latter

question for your expert. But you can evaluate the home's amperage (60, 100, or 200) and voltage (115 or 230); whether it has circuit breakers or an old-fashioned fuse box; and the number, location, and convenience of electrical outlets, switches, and built-in light fixtures.

4. *Ceilings, walls, and floors.* As you walk through a house, examine the ceilings, walls, floors, and floor coverings. Note their condition, but also note any related problems. Water stains may indicate roof or plumbing leaks. Cracks may point to foundation problems. Check floors to see whether they are level. Would a marble placed in the center of the room roll swiftly to one side or the other? Don't feel as if you're out of line to pull back rugs, peek behind pictures, and look under furniture. More than a few sellers have been known to selectively place wall hangings, rugs, and furniture to hide stains, cracks, or other defects. I once pulled back a room-sized Oriental rug and discovered the underlying floor was particleboard.

5. *Appearance and floor plan.* A home may not *require* any redecorating, repairs, or remodeling. Yet it still may not look good. If that green shag carpeting or a closed-in kitchen doesn't meet contemporary tastes and preferences, you're going to have to spend some time and money to bring the house up to higher standards. But if you redecorate or remodel simply to suit your own preferences (as opposed to those of your buyers or tenants), you may not be able to make money from your improvements. If you plan to own the house for the long term or rank tenant satisfaction above profit, then you still may want to change the home to match your tastes. Just keep in mind the difference between profitable and personal improvements. (Of course, in this instance you might profit from quicker renting, lower vacancies, and less tenant turnover.)

6. *Quality of materials.* Note the quality of the materials used throughout the home's interior. The cost of carpeting, for example, may range from $10 per square yard up to $50 or more. Some interior flat-paneled, hollow-core doors can be bought for $15 to $25 each. Other doors, solid wood, stained, and decorative paneled, can cost upward of $500 each. You can buy a set of kitchen cabinets for $1,500 or $15,000. Low-grade vinyl floor coverings run $5 per square yard. Top-of-the-line can cost $25 per square yard or more.

You can find similarly large differences in quality and costs for light fixtures, wood paneling, paints, wallpapers, sinks, bathtubs, faucets, and nearly all other interior building materials. Although cost seldom correlates one-to-one with value, buyers do expect to pay something extra for a property that includes better-grade materials. Just evaluate with caution. Make sure your study of buyer preferences and realistic pricing shows that you will earn a good return on your improvement dollars.

Legal Compliance

As you go through the property, I again urge you to look for problems of illegal or nonconforming use. Ask the sellers for written disclosures. Tell your professional inspector to alert you to any areas of noncompliance that he spots. Although inspectors don't specifically give legal opinions, most that I have dealt with will voice their concerns—especially if the violations pertain to matters of health or safety. If any part of your compliance discovery does point to code infractions, conform (or refute) your suspicions with the city regulators. Determine whether code enforcers deem the problem major, minor, or of no real concern.

> **Again, know the code. Watch for possible violations.**

(I also remind you to verify that your planned work will conform to code. Never spend any nonnegligible sums for unpermitted or noncompliant repairs or improvements.)

Estimating Costs of Repairs and Improvements

As a neophyte fixer, you will rely primarily on experts for your cost estimates. But be forewarned. You will need to educate yourself as you go along.

Recently, I secured bids from a recommended plumbing contractor to completely replumb a house. When the house was built 50 years ago, the pipes were laid in the concrete slab foundation but were now springing leaks. Rather than suffer repeated repairs, I decided to replace. This contractor bid $5,500 and explained how the work would require large amounts of cutting through walls and ceilings.

I know very little about the technical fine points of plumbing, but I could see that this estimate of costs and plan of repair did not seem to make sense. Time for a second opinion.

The Second Opinion   The next contractor who bid gave an estimate of $2,800 (same quality of materials). He said that his workmen could thread

> **Contractors manage and design their work much differently.**

the pipe through just a few small exterior wall cuts and one small cut through a closet wall. After getting one more bid ($3,300), I awarded the job to the "second opinion" contractor. True to his word, his firm completed the job as promised, on time, and for the amount bid.

(Note: When you replumb a house built on concrete slab, you run the new pipe around the exterior of the house. However, when you repair slab pipe, you must jackhammer the concrete in the area where you think you hear or feel the pipe leaking.)

Learn by Doing   How did I sense that the first cost estimate and plan of repair was way out of line? Because I always listen closely and try to follow the reasoning.

Even though someone else wears the mantle of expert, you should not suspend your critical faculties. Whenever you secure estimates, obtain multiple bids. Ask the contractors to explain their method and plan of attack. Consult with floor personnel at lumberyards, hardware stores, and home supply companies. Talk with other property owners who have completed similar work. By following this approach, you will quickly learn to distinguish reasonable from unreasonable estimates of costs and work plans.

> **Learn from experts. Don't let them bamboozle you.**

Published Cost Estimates   Often you will see estimates of repair and improvement costs published in magazine articles and books. Read these with casual interest, but never accept them as necessarily close to accurate or reasonable.

Costs vary far too much for any general statement. As you saw with my plumbing contractors, the highest estimate almost doubled the lowest estimate. Estimates vary by the time of the year, the area of the country, the job backlog of the contractor, and the detailed repairs that the job will require—some of which may not even be known until the job begins. (That's why your cost estimates must include an oops factor.)

Search Out Bargain-Priced Materials   Also, you may be able to buy excellent quality used items. I once bought a complete high-quality kitchen—I mean the entire kitchen stripped to bare walls—from some wealthy homebuyers who simply did not like the color of the kitchen in the house they had just bought. They decided to tear out the old and install another kitchen that met their precise tastes. You can sometimes gain from the extravagant waste of other property owners.

> **Never pay retail.**

Also, you can sometimes find great bargains in closeout sales, scratched and dented merchandise, and inventory overstocks. I sometimes talk with contractors on large commercial jobs to learn whether they're going to have any leftover materials that I can buy cheaply. Buildings that are scheduled to be moved or torn down can also yield treasures (such as light fixtures, wood flooring, doors, wood paneling, cabinets, shelving, carpeting, or maybe even an antique Victorian claw-footed bathtub).

As a savvy, entrepreneurial renovator you can find bargain-priced contractors and materials. Forget that old saw "You get what you pay for."When renovating, you can spend a lot for a little, or a little for a lot. Shop to always try for the latter. As an absolute minimum, always ask your merchants for contractor discounts when you buy materials and supplies for your repairs and renovations.

Utility Bills (Energy Efficiency)

In some parts of the country, utility bills rank as the second- or third-largest expense in the budgets of many families. During months of peak usage, utility bills of $200 to $500 a month are common. As you compare properties, find out (1) which utilities are available to a house, (2) how much they will cost each month, and (3 what you can do to reduce utility expenses. Lower utility bills mean a higher selling price or higher rents and less tenant turnover. Excessively high bills will create a tenant revolt.

What Utilities Are Available?

A friend of mine owns a rental house near Lakeland, Florida. He recently complained that he had to install a new sewage-disposal drain field at the property. He expected the cost to run around $1,400. As we talked about this repair, this friend admitted that when he bought the house he hadn't even realized that its sewage-disposal system wasn't connected to the city sewer. As an inexperienced investor, he hadn't even thought to ask. Don't make a similar mistake. Before you offer to buy a house, ask what utilities are available (sewage, disposal, water, electricity, natural gas, cable TV, digital high-speed cable, telephone, etc.). Many investors are surprised to learn that even properties located within a city may lack one or more of the utilities that they previously had taken for granted. For investors in properties located in suburban or rural areas, the need to identify available utilities is even more pressing.

Identify Ways to Reduce the Utility Bills

> **Energy efficiency pays off.**

Once you've checked a property's utility bills (obtained from either the sellers or the utility companies), look for ways to reduce these expenses. For example:

1. Would more insulation, caulking, or storm doors and windows significantly lower the costs of heating and cooling?
2. Has the water heater been wrapped with insulation?
3. Can you profitably switch from higher-cost energy (electric) to lower-cost (natural gas)?
4. Do utility companies offer special incentives to make the house more efficient? In some cities, natural gas companies will replace electric water heaters with gas water heaters at no charge to the homeowner. Utility companies frequently give reduced rates to property owners or residents who agree to accept energy cutbacks during peak usage times. Many companies also will perform an energy audit on a property at little or no cost.
5. From time to time, the government, at the local, state, and federal levels, offers various tax credits, low-cost loans, and direct grants to property owners who upgrade to

conserve energy. Are any of these benefits available for the properties that you're comparing?

Over a 10-year period, utility bill savings of just $100 a month will add up to nearly $18,000 (assuming interest compounded at 8 percent). Numbers like these will certainly give your properties a competitive edge and enhance your value proposition.

Save on Property Taxes

Prior to beginning your renovations, you might want to learn the ins and outs of the property tax laws that apply to the property.

> **You can lower the property taxes on a property.**

Each tax jurisdiction sets rules and procedures that govern how property improvements are assessed and taxed. For example, built-in cabinets and wall-to-wall carpeting will likely add to the assessed value of the property, whereas cabinets that do not attach permanently to the walls and carpeting that does not get tacked down may not count.

These examples merely illustrate the types of quirks that tax laws frequently include. To find the quirks that can work to your favor in your area, talk to the folks at the property tax assessor's office. If in learning the ins and outs you slice your tax bill by just 5 percent to 10 percent, you've probably saved yourself or your buyers $100 to $400 (or more) per year.

Save on Property Insurance

Facing low investment returns and heavy casualty losses, property insurers have hit hard times. In response, they're raising rates, cutting back coverages, and tightening their underwriting standards.

Before you buy a property, check with several insurance agents to make sure you can obtain adequate insurance protection at an affordable price. Also learn the types of improvements you can make that will get a rate break for you or your buyers. How about smoke alarms, earthquake retrofit, hurricane shutters, safety glass, burglary alarm, heavier locks, fencing, upgraded electrical system, what else? Thoroughly review the rating criteria the insurer will use. Then, where economical, make the necessary changes.

Enhance the Safety and Security of Residents

Your improvements to obtain lower insurance rates will help make the property safe and secure. Other hazards of concern include the following:

- ◆ Environmental (lead paint, asbestos, mold, radon, improper discharge of wastes)
- ◆ Electrical fires
- ◆ Electrical shock
- ◆ Falls (bathtub, stairs)
- ◆ Sharp corners on countertops or other places that children can run into
- ◆ Insecure locks on windows
- ◆ Swimming pools
- ◆ Cracked sidewalks
- ◆ Dead trees or branches that overhang the house

> **You owe your buyers (tenants) a safe and secure home.**

Depending on the ages and household composition of your target market (as well as the neighborhood in which the property is located), an emphasis on special features that enhance safety and security might add to your value proposition. Apart, though, from your target market per se, safety check the property to eliminate all obvious dangers to life or limb.

Special-Purpose Uses

Don't forget, you may find that renovating toward some special-purpose use might secure you a premium price or rental rate. Most renovators go generic. In return, they receive a generic profit. But when you renovate toward the specific needs of a bull's eye segment of seniors, the disabled, children, home businesses, college students, or any other specialized target of customers, you favorably differentiate your product.

> **Tailor unique features of a property to a niche segment of buyers (tenants).**

To discover a profitable niche, talk with people at social service agencies, hospitals, and local colleges. Imagine the special needs of single parents, multigenerational households, hobbyists, roommates, group homes, and shelters. Always stay alert to markets where demand runs strong and supply falls short. Whereas most run-of-the-mill renovators know how to fix up a property, entrepreneurs perpetually search for a special niche of customers. Then they tailor the features of the property to perfectly fit that target market.

CHAPTER 7

Add More Living Space

You will almost certainly make money with a property if you can create *quality* living space. As discussed in Chapter 6, to value properties, investors, homebuyers, and sellers routinely use price per square foot. If you know that 1,300 to 1,600 square feet, three-bedroom, two-bath homes in a given neighborhood typically sell for $80 to $90 per square foot, then you can figure that a decent three–two, 1,400-square-foot house should sell for at least $112,000 and perhaps go for as much as $133,000.

> **Match the features of the house to the zoning laws. More quality space adds value.**

Now, say that you find a two-bedroom, one-bath, cosmetic fixer with just 1,100 square feet. Because of its rough condition and undesirable room count, you can buy this house for $80,000 ($72.72 per square foot). If you dress the house for success and add another bedroom and bath (300 square feet), your minimum improved value (MIV) should climb to around $125,000 ($89.28 per square foot). Your only question becomes, can you complete these improvements for less than, say, $20,000 to $25,000?

Work the Numbers

In my area of the country, these numbers look quite reasonable. In your area, the numbers may look too low or too high. But the method still works. Just plug in the per square foot selling prices and compare them to the renovation costs that prevail in the neighborhood where you plan to buy. Generally, this strategy for improvement works best when you find fix-up houses that are relatively small compared to other nearby houses. It typically does not work well when you try to add living space to a house whose size already dwarfs neighboring properties.

Attic, Garage, and Basement Conversions

When shopping properties, look for homes with an attic, garage, or basement that you can convert to *quality* living space. Again, I emphasize the words *quality space* because amateur home remodelers often convert as inexpensively as possible. Consequently, their finished spaces not only look cheap, they may lack natural light; the ceilings may hang too low; or the newly created traffic patterns or floor plans seem weird, convoluted, or garbled.

> **Add quality space, not space that looks weird.**

In contrast, renovators who design and finish their conversions to wow potential buyers can and do make serious money for their efforts. Remember, to earn good profits, your conversion should strive to meet the following objectives:

- ◆ Needs of target market
- ◆ Aesthetically pleasing
- ◆ Well integrated within the overall plan and design of the property

Target Market Needs

When remodeling only for personal use, it's okay to convert your basement into a rec room that mimics the look of your favorite tavern. For profitable remodeling, though, aim to please your target market. What type of highly valued space can you offer that competing houses lack? A dynamite home office, a study, a playroom for the kids, a workout area, a library, an entertainment center, a seductive master bedroom and bath? Put on your creative thinking cap.

Aesthetics

Basement conversions often fail because they lack windows and give off that damp, musty odor so common to below-ground living areas. To overcome these problems, use window wells and carve outs to bring in natural light. To eliminate the musty smell and dampness, use high-quality sealants and fresh air ventilation. Follow the same general ideas for attic and garage conversions. You want these finished areas to look, live, feel, and smell as good as the rest of the house. You want light, height, warmth, and color. You do not want to merely tack up cheap four-foot-by-eight-foot paneling, hang acoustical tile ceilings, or lay down a roll of indoor-outdoor carpeting. Romance the home. Think pizzazz!

> **Can you make a basement seem homey?**

Integrate the Conversion into the House

When you evaluate properties for their conversion potential, don't just think of added living space as an independent area. Think of your work as expanding the total integrated living area of the house. The best conversions flow smoothly to and from the original living areas. Think access and flow. How well can you blend the conversion into a natural traffic pattern?

As much as possible, you want to avoid signaling to your prospects, "Now entering a converted garage (basement or attic)." Or "Watch your head. The ceiling's a little low in here." Look for properties that are currently designed with potential for an integrated addition. A well-planned conversion can easily pay back two dollars (or more) for every dollar invested.

Create an Accessory Apartment

> **Accessory apartments pay back huge returns.**

Variously called in-law suites, basement suites, garage apartments, mortgage helpers, or accessory apartments, these separate living units can easily pay back their cost many times over. Depending on the city and neighborhood, an accessory apartment can bring in rents that range anywhere from $250 to $750 per month. Yet, unless you build from scratch, you can usually create a quite desirable unit for as little as $5,000 and certainly no more than $15,000.

In other words, viewed in terms of return on investment, $10,000 in renovation costs can often generate a rental income of $4,000 to $6,000 per year. You can search the world over and never find as much return for so little risk.

The Zoning Obstacle

Unfortunately, absurdly restrictive zoning ordinances exclude accessory apartments from many single-family neighborhoods. According to these ordinances, it's okay for two parents, four teenage kids, three SUVs, and two dogs and a cat to occupy a 2,200-square-foot, four-bedroom, three-bath house. But if the 75-year-old widow who lives next door to this all-American family wants to convert two spare bedrooms and a bath into an efficiency apartment to house a grad student from the local college, she's breaking the law.

Lax Standards of Enforcement   Fortunately, such law-breakers seldom get hauled to court for this egregious offense to the health, safety, and morals of the community. Except in elite communities with Dick Tracy investigators, most illegal accessory apartments fall into the "don't ask, don't tell," category. While I typically advise renovators to stay within the law, I back off from this advice as it pertains to accessory apartments.

Our nation now has 30 million single-person households. Many younger (and older) single persons need high-quality affordable housing. Many other households (including singles and seniors) need an extra source of income to help make mortgage payments or even to help pay living expenses. Accessory apartments benefit all concerned with virtually no harm to anyone else.

Request a Variance or a Change in the Law   To try to stay legal, you could request a zoning variance from the code enforcers. Although technically, accessory apartments don't normally qualify as a bona fide issue for variance, if the neighbors don't complain, you might prevail. Similarly, you could seek a change in the zoning law. Many public policy and social service agencies strongly support rules that permit accessory units. Enlist the power of numbers, as well as the power of persuasive reasoning, and you might prevail.

Threaten a Lawsuit   If you don't win your appeal to reason, threaten a lawsuit. To pass constitutional scrutiny, zoning laws must not prove arbitrary. They must bear a close rational relationship to the objective sought. Wholesale bans on accessory apartments clearly violate this constitutional standard. Since families can fill up a neighborhood with kids, cars, and barking dogs, why can't Mrs. Widow or those nice, newly married schoolteachers bring another person into their households? If the law related objectively to noise, parking, or condition of the property, then it could reasonably regulate accessory units but not prohibit them outright.

The (arguably) unconstitutionality of ordinances that ban accessory units is prompting many jurisdictions to review these laws. (Similarly, many jurisdictions are reviewing their hostile laws that govern or prohibit home offices and home businesses.)

> **No objective reasons stand against accessory apartments per se.**

As our society continues to age, we will experience more and more widows and widowers living alone in their now too large, longtime family homes. Yet they do not want to move. We also see many hopeful first-time homebuyers who are now priced out of the homes or neighborhoods where they would like to live. In each of these situations, an accessory apartment could serve to promote social and personal goals.

Moreover, fewer than 50 percent of U.S. households now consist of the traditional family of mother, father, and children. Given all of these demographic realities, the political winds are blowing stronger toward change. With more lobbying, maybe you won't need a lawsuit.

Technical Compliance As another alternative, closely read the fine print of the ordinance that prohibits or restricts accessory apartments. Often you can find loopholes. For example, most such ordinances pertain to separate, fully-contained living units that include a kitchen. But note carefully how the law defines "kitchen." If you forego a full-size range in favor of a microwave, a countertop convection oven, and a hotplate, you may technically comply with the law.

> **Look for loopholes.**

If you do skirt the law, don't flaunt your civil disobedience. Do not construct an obvious direct entrance to the unit, set up an unsightly second or third parking space in the sideyard, or nail up a second mailbox. To truly stay incognito, ask the tenant to receive all mail at a post office box. And as advised before, if you're converting a garage, blend the conversion into the design of the house—and get rid of that dead-end driveway.

Other Zoning Districts   Keep in mind that the legal obstacles that I've set forth pertain to districts zoned single family.[1] If you buy a house that's located in a district zoned for higher density residential, professional offices, or commercial use, no unreasonable restrictions may apply. Of course, if you buy a single-family house in a district that permits two to four units (or more), you might renovate the property into multiple units. (This possibility goes beyond our present discussion. For more on this topic, see my book *Make Money with Small Income Properties* [Wiley, 2003].)

The Family Exception   Some single-family zoning districts permit accessory apartments, but only if two conditions are met: (1) The owners of the property live in the home; and (2) the person(s) who lives in the unit must be related to the property owners. Again, this type of ordinance displays an arbitrary and irrational standard. To the extent such ordinances regulate at all, they should regulate behavior, not family status. Indeed, many fair housing laws prohibit discrimination by family status, yet zoning laws, themselves, frequently discriminate along these lines.

> **Should "families" receive preference in the zoning laws?**

(As an aside, note that federal law and the great majority of state and local fair housing laws throughout the country do not

---

1. Remember, too, that most communities establish at least three or four distinct single-family zoning categories. Some single-family districts may permit accessory units while others do not.

apply to owner-occupied dwellings of four units or less. Consult an attorney or a local fair housing office to learn the rules in your area.)

The Mortgage Helper

I want to elaborate on the idea of an accessory unit as a mortgage helper. You can use this technique personally or to expand the market for a property that you're renovating to sell or rent. Consider the experience of freelance artist Andrea McKenna.

Andrea McKenna's Fixer   Andrea bought a three-story fixer and converted the lowest floor into an accessory apartment that she rented to two sisters for $350 a month. But once Andrea fully realized the income potential of her house, she carried her idea one step further. After the tenant sisters moved out, Andrea relocated herself to the third floor of her home. Next, she renovated both lower floors into two private units that she then rented for $550 a month each.

> **An accessory apartment expands the market for your property.**

"I don't earn much," says Andrea, "and I doubt that I'll ever become another Andy Warhol and make a fortune. So it's great to have the security of rent checks coming in. I'm now receiving $1,100 a month. That's enough to pay my mortgage and cover part of my property taxes and homeowners insurance."

Buy the *Biggest* House on the Block   You've probably heard the old saw, "Never *buy* the *biggest* or most expensive house in the neighborhood." For the renovator who plans to build an accessory apartment, though, that advice doesn't hold. When you think income potential, the biggest house often proves to offer the lowest price per square foot of living space.

Say you look at an 1,800-square-foot, three-bedroom, two-bath house that's typical for the neighborhood. It's priced at $115,000.

The biggest house on the block can make you money.

If you put 10 percent down, your mortgage payment will run $654 per month (6.5 percent, 30 years). You're interested but you decide to drive around the area and see what else you can discover. You then find a 2,200-square-foot, five-bedroom, three-bath house priced at $135,000. With 10 percent down, payments for this house would cost you $768 a month.

Given that you now realize the profit potential of accessory apartments, you buy the larger house. Next, you obtain a home equity loan for $5,000 and use that money to remodel two bedrooms and a bath into an efficiency apartment. After deducting the monthly payment on your home equity loan, you clear $300 a month from the rental of the efficiency apartment. You apply that amount to your $768 mortgage payment, which brings your monthly outlay down to just $468. You're still able to enjoy three bedrooms and two baths, but they're costing you much less per month. As a bonus, you will build more equity with the larger house. This technique can work especially well to enhance your affordability in markets with high-priced housing. By splitting a larger house, you might boost your affordability from say, $350,000 up to as much as $500,000.

Renovate for Sale   You can use this same principle when you're renovating a property for sale. Choose an outsized property for a given neighborhood. Then renovate with an accessory unit. The rental income will increase the number of homebuyers who can afford the property. The house will cost the buyers less per month and at the same time they're able to afford a larger house and possibly a better neighborhood than would otherwise be available to them. Yet, even though your buyers receive a great deal, you can still command a premium price. A true win-win transaction.

Renovate to Lease   Say you find an 1,800-square-foot, three-bedroom, two-bath house that after renovation will rent for $1,500 per month. But rather than leave it as a single-family residence, you slice off 400 square feet to remodel as an efficiency

> **Smaller rental units typically bring higher total rental revenues.**

apartment along with a newly built 100-square-foot bathroom. This efficiency will rent for $650 per month. The remaining living area of 1,400 square feet with two bedrooms and two baths will now rent for $1,250 a month. By renting two smaller living areas instead of one larger area, you've boosted your income by $400 per month.

Naturally, you will need to look at comparable rentals to actually determine the most profitable-sized units to aim for. But as a rule, for the same level of quality, smaller living spaces bring in more rent per square foot than do larger areas. Look for large houses or even houses with large oversized garages. Then rightsize the number, type, and square footages of the rental units to maximize rental revenue. That's why I always try to buy the biggest house in the neighborhood. You often get what amounts to a quantity discount. Or you might say that you're buying space wholesale and renting it out retail.

What Type of House Works Best?

In my experience, I've found that five types of housing designs lend themselves particularly well to efficiency conversions:

1. Split level
2. Two story with new separate exterior stair access
3. Ranch house with split floor plan
4. House or townhouse with a basement or lower level that opens at ground level to the backyard (usually the house front entry is at street level on a lot that slopes downhill)
5. House with an attached garage or carport

Please, though, don't let these examples dampen your imagination. You can find houses in an infinite range of shapes, sizes, styles, and designs. With thought and creativity, your possibilities multiply. For example, an inverted L-shaped house as shown here can also work well:

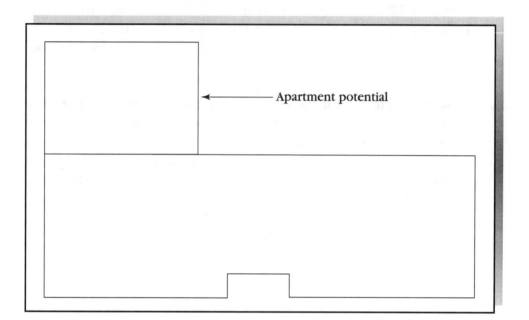

I once owned a house where a large additional unit had been built in the attic, but it lacked a fully equipped kitchen. Because putting a kitchen into an attic often entails considerable expense, attic conversions typically work best as areas for sleeping, studying, or playing. Depending on the configuration of the plumbing, an attic bathroom may or may not prove financially feasible.

The attic apartment in my property consisted of a bedroom, a large living area with a makeshift kitchen (counter appliances, dorm fridge), and a bathroom. Two dormers had been added to bring in more natural light. Heat was baseboard electric and a large window unit provided air conditioning. An entry stairwell to the attic was built just inside the main front entry to the house. Originally, the previous owners of the property had built this apartment for an adult child (pun intended) who was living in the home.

Today, with boomerang kids becoming more prevalent, apartments of this nature could see increased popularity for this purpose.

Any way you look at it, add quality living space to a house and you will increase its value. Check zoning, check comps, check costs, and run the numbers. In most cases, you will find that your extra living space will give you a great margin of profit. (For excellent and much more detailed illustrations of how to add extra rentable apartments to single-family houses, see Patrick Hall and Jolene Ostler, *Creating an Accessory Apartment* [McGraw-Hill, 1987].)

CHAPTER 8

Revitalize the Neighborhood

You've probably heard it said 100 times: Buy in the best location you can afford. You can change anything about a house except its location. At first glance, this advice sounds plausible. But rethink what the term *location* actually refers to:

- Convenience
- Aesthetics
- People: attitudes, lifestyles
- Legal restrictions
- Schools
- Taxes/services
- Microclimate (weather)
- Safety and security
- Image/reputation
- Affordability

Now, what's your answer? I trust you can see that with the lone exception of weather, you most certainly can work to improve a property's location in dozens of specific ways.

Neighborhoods Can Get Better

The past 5 to 15 years have seen many previously "marginal" neighborhoods revitalized and gentrified—but now priced beyond the

> **You can profitably improve the neighborhood.**

means of many first-time buyers: the Wrigley section of Long Beach, South of Market in San Francisco, South of Houston in Manhattan, Lincoln Park-De Paul in Chicago, and Capitol Hill in Washington, D.C., are just a few examples. "Boy, I wish I had gotten into Rockridge (Oakland, California) ten years ago," someone recently said to me. And on my last trip to Chicago, I talked with a now not-so-young couple who complained, "In the early '80s, we could have bought a house on a decent block in Hyde Park for $62,000. But we eventually decided against it. Now we can't find anything like it for less than $250,000."

Ten to 15 years ago, every one of the above-mentioned neighborhoods was experiencing its share of the urban problems typical of larger cities everywhere. And none of these neighborhoods is free of problems today. But each of these neighborhoods has enjoyed renewed popularity and price increases of 100 percent or more.

What's more important for your future, though, is that hundreds of somewhat similar neighborhoods are positioned for turnaround during the next 10 years. As good people are priced out of

> **Everyone has to live somewhere.**

"highly desirable" neighborhoods, they move into "less desirable" neighborhoods. But that's not where the story ends. As home-buying counselor Mary Ortez tells her clients, "You have to realize you can make almost any area nicer."

Neighborhoods aren't inherently good or bad. It's the people in them and the standards and values they enforce that determine a neighborhood's future. No one would encourage you to invest in a neighborhood where kids dodge gunfire as they walk to school or a neighborhood where residents post signs in the car windows, "Please don't break in. Radio already stolen." But standing in between the "worst" and "best" neighborhoods are many areas that are improving because the people who own properties there are working to make better lives for themselves and their families.

Wilma Haynes, former chairman of the Watts Property Owners Association, says, "People who come to Watts are very surprised at what they see. All around me people are fixing up their houses, buying lots that have sat vacant for years, taking pride in their neighborhood again."

Fred Greer, codeveloper of the Santa Ana Pines subdivision in Watts, has explained this view as follows:

> We'd like to bring back to Watts those people who have moved out to rent in Gardenia and Inglewood, people who are tired of driving back in from Palmdale and Rialto, people who want to move back to the neighborhood where their mama still lives. We're trying to build nice enough homes to give them a reason to come back to Watts. There's no reason you can't put up nice homes here. Watts deserves decent homes as much as any other place.

> **High home prices are forcing buyers to expand their alternatives.**

The problems of Watts have been well publicized; the advantages have not. "It's the only affordable area close in," says Realtor board president Leslie Bellamy. Other Realtors point out that the neighborhood sits right next to the University of Southern California. And when home and lot prices have stalled in much of Los Angeles, lot prices in Watts continued to go up and its home sales outpaced other parts of the city.

In one of its articles on home buying, *Money Magazine* advised its readers, "With interest rates sinking, it's a great time to shop for your dream house. . . . You'll need to seek out the neighborhoods where property values are rising faster than your community average." Surprising to many investors, though, is the fact that the neighborhoods where prices are positioned to rise fastest may not be the most prestigious or well-established neighborhoods. Often, the largest price increases can be expected in areas that are poised for turnaround or renewed popularity.

Entrepreneurs Improve Thorton Park (and Make a Killing)

"Florida's new urban entrepreneurs have the vision to see a bustling district of sushi bars, loft apartments and boutiques on a glass-strewn lot or rat-infested warehouse," writes Cynthia Barnett in the August 2001 issue of *Florida Trend*.

Phil Rampy is proud to have been one of those early entrepreneurs. Twelve years ago, Rampy bought a house in the then-shunned Thorton Park neighborhood near trash-strewn Lake Eola (or as they used to call it, Lake Erie-ola). Today, Thorton Park has climbed up the status ladder to rank among "the trendiest addresses" in Orlando. That $60,000 bungalow that Rampy renovated is now valued at more than $200,000. Although the Thorton Park neighborhood still sits on this Earth in the same place as it did 10 years ago, nearly everything else about this location has changed.

> **Which neighborhoods do you believe will gentrify within the next decade?**

Every Neighborhood Has Potential

When you compare neighborhoods, don't just look at the present. Imagine potential. List all of a neighborhood's good points. How could you and other property owners join together to highlight and improve these features? List the neighborhood's weak points. How can you and others eliminate negative influences? Who can you enlist to promote your cause? Can you mobilize mortgage lenders, other investors, homeowners, Realtors, not-for-profit housing groups, church leaders, builders, contractors, preservationists, police, local employers, retail businesses, schoolteachers, principals, community redevelopment agencies, elected officials, civic groups, and perhaps students, professors, and administrators of a nearby college or university?

Throughout the United States, people like you have joined with other property owners and tenants to revitalize and reinvigo-rate hundreds of neighborhoods. From South of Market in San Francisco, to the Madison Valley in Seattle, Lakeview in Chicago, Boston's North End, Manhat-tan's Bowery, So-Ho, Miami's South Beach, and the "M Street" neighborhoods in Dallas, in all of these locations neigh-bors, merchants, investors, and home-buyers have organized campaigns to make living, working, and shopping in these areas much more desirable. "We liked the community," says recent homebuyer Roy Owens of Cum-berland (Atlanta), "but we felt the community association was too passive. It needed some *oomph,* so we incorporated and worked hard to get to know people and inspire them to get involved."

> Learn what people are saying about different neighborhoods.

In speaking of a San Diego neighborhood that's poised for turnaround and redevelopment, Lori Weisberg says, "To the out-sider, there's very little here that seems inviting. . . . Yet, where most people see a shabby area . . . visionaries see an exciting new downtown neighborhood adorned with a grand, tree-lined boule-vard, a central plaza, artisans' studios, loft housing, and crowned with a sports and entertainment center. . . . [Already] there are pockets of gentrification—a budding arts district, scattered loft conversions, and . . . structures well-suited for preservation. . . . But [the total revitalization and redevelopment] does have to be imagined."

"There's no doubt," says Pam Hamilton, an executive with San Diego's Centre City Development Corporation, "this project will happen—it's just a question of when."

How can Pam express such certainty that this revitalization will occur? Because when people join together to bring about positive change, neighborhoods improve. Everybody wins with a better quality of life and increased property values.

Community Action and Community Spirit Make a Difference

Community action can conquer crime and criminals.

In his review of the book *Safe Homes, Safe Neighborhoods* (NOLO, 1993), real estate investor, attorney, columnist, and book reviewer Robert Bruss, says, "This is an action book. . . . This is a welcome and long-overdue book for activists who want to learn how to improve their neighborhood." This book illustrates perfectly how through community action and community spirit people can improve the quality of their neighborhoods and their lives. Without a doubt, many city and suburban neighborhoods must tackle problems of one sort or another. Besides crime, these problems may range from barking dogs to speeding high schoolers to a lack of parks, sidewalks, or storm sewers. Yet, regardless of the specific problems to be solved (or prevented), as urban entrepreneur Tony Goldman proved with Miami's South Beach, people acting together can make a difference.

Fix broken windows.

"While it may seem that everywhere crime is on the rise," write Stephanie Mann and M.C. Blakeman *(Safe Homes, Safe Neighborhoods),* "in many neighborhoods the opposite is true. In cities and towns across the country, local crime prevention groups have reduced burglaries and car break-ins; helped catch muggers, rapists, and kidnappers; established Block Parents and other child-safety projects; driven out drug dealers; eliminated graffiti; and, in general, made their homes and streets safer. All it takes is a few people to get things started. By identifying and focusing on a neighborhood's main concerns—and working with police and each other—neighbors can make a difference."

Become a Neighborhood *Entrepreneur*

You don't have to live in a big-trouble, inner-city location to become an urban entrepreneur. You can do it anywhere. No neighborhood is perfect. I suspect that even Beverly Hills and Scarsdale could stand improvement in at least a few ways.

> **Values jump with neighborhood improvements.**

Since neighborhood quality drives up property values and rent levels, keep yourself alert for ideas to initiate (or join in) to make the neighborhood a better place to live. When you simultaneously improve your property(ies) *and* its location, you more than double your profit potential. Would any of the following suggestions work for the areas that you're considering?

Add to Neighborhood Convenience

Would a stoplight, wider road, or new highway interchange improve accessibility to the neighborhood? Where are the to and fro traffic logjams? How can they be alleviated? Is the neighborhood served as well as it could be by buses and commuter trains? How about social service transportation? Could you get the vans that pick up seniors or the disabled to place this neighborhood on their route? What about the traveling bus for the library? Does it stop in the neighborhood?

> **Try to attract new retailers, coffee houses, and restaurants.**

On the other hand, maybe the neighborhood could work to pull more employers, health care services, restaurants, or coffee houses into the neighborhood. Could that old warehouse or industrial building be converted for use as professional offices? Remember, you can add convenience to a neighborhood in two ways: (1) Make travel to and from the neighborhood easier, cheaper, or more timely; or (2) bring more shops, services, nightlife, culture, jobs, and recreational facilities into the neighborhood.

Improve Appearances and Aesthetics

Put together a civic pride organization. Organize a cleanup and fix-up campaign. Plant trees, shrubs, and flowers in yards and in pub-

> **Fix-up becomes contagious.**

lic areas. Lobby the city to tear down or eliminate eyesore buildings, graffiti, or trashy areas. Try to reduce on-street parking. Get immobile or abandoned vehicles towed. Enforce environmental regulations against property owners and businesses that pollute (noise, smoke, odors). Walk the neighborhood. Closely observe and note any value-diminishing negatives. Then, do what's necessary to change, remove, or alleviate them.

In fact, just by fixing up your properties, you can motivate other owners to enhance their own properties.

Here's what nationally syndicated columnist and longtime real estate investor Robert Bruss reports:

> Fixing up houses spurs a contagious effect. You will be amazed at how, within a few months after you fix up your house the neighborhood owners will begin fixing up their properties. To illustrate, recently I completed fixing up a foreclosure property I acquired a few months ago. Before I was even finished, the next door neighbor (who has lived there over 20 years!) began painting and landscaping his house. "You shamed me into doing it," Manuel told me. He also owns a rental house across the street which he cleaned and painted. Another neighbor tells me he plans to paint his run-down house because now he noticed how bad it looks. All it takes is one or two owners fixing up their houses and the neighbors

catch the fix-up fever! As a result, the whole neighborhood increases in market value.[1]

Amen!

Zoning and Building Regulations

Are too many property owners in the neighborhood splitting up
single-family houses and converting them into
apartments? Do too many residents run businesses out of their homes and garages? Are high-
or midrise buildings planned that will diminish
livability? Are too many commercial properties
encroaching on the area? Then lobby for tighter
zoning and building regulations. On the other
hand, do areas within the neighborhood and
those nearby make more intense use of properties desirable? Then
lobby the city to rezone the area to apartments or commercial.

> **Enlist the help of
> the code
> enforcers.**

Because zoning and building regulations affect property use,
they can dramatically affect property values. When value-creating
changes are warranted, pressure the politicians and planners to accommodate you.

Eliminate Neighborhood Nuisances

Do one or more households in the neighborhood make a nuisance
of themselves? Junk cars in the driveway, barking dogs, loud

---

1. Quoted from the *Robert Bruss Real Estate Newsletter,* #92215 (p. 2). You can order back issues of
this information-packed newsletter or subscribe to current issues by telephoning (800) 736–1736 or
by visiting www.bobbruss.com.

stereos, constant yelling and shouting, out-of-control yards littered with debris—you and other property owners can force them to clean up their act or suffer severe and continuing penalties.

Invoke Your Local Ordinances, Deed Restrictions, or HOA Rules

Pore over your local ordinances and any pertinent private rules and restrictions. Sift through the regulations for zoning, aesthetics, occupancy, use, parking, noise, disturbing the peace, health, safety, loitering, drug-dealing or possession, extortion, and assault. You can almost certainly find some regulatory violations under which you can file a complaint.

> **Rules seldom permit nuisances to continue if complaints are registered.**

If after receiving a citation the people continue to offend common decency, a judge can issue an order to cease and desist (or something similar). Further violations would then bring a citation for contempt of court. They've now angered the judge. Each day the breach persists could rack up multiple fines and possibly jail time. Or in some cases, the government will remedy the problem—cut the weeds, haul off a junk car—and bill the offenders.

Sue in Small Claims Court

Although you can get a judge to force inconsiderate neighbors to comply with local ordinances, you don't necessarily have to rely on this approach. The common law (except in Louisiana) provides another type of recourse. It's called the tort (legal wrong) of nuisance. With or without a specific ordinance, you can sue your offensive neighbor(s) in small claims court (no lawyer, low filing fees) for committing a nuisance.

> **Judges can force people to comply with the law.**

The great jurist Blackstone defined a nuisance as "Any thing that unlawfully worketh hurt, inconvenience, or damage." In modern times, an Illinois court has said that nuisance includes "everything that endangers life or health, gives offense to the senses, violates the laws of decency, or obstructs reasonable and comfortable use of a property."

Reasonable   To sue for nuisance, you need only show that: (1) The neighbor's conduct *unreasonably* offends you or your tenants and/or harms the value of your property; and (2) your complaint does not run afoul of common sense or community standards. In other words, if a neighboring property owner's children play loudly, scream, and carry on as kids do, you won't stand much chance of winning your case. Nevertheless, whenever you can persuade a jury of your peers that you're not merely oversensitive, you will likely prevail. (Unless the defendant can claim some constitutional or statutory protection. For example, absent some type of aesthetics ordinance or HOA rule, the rights of property permit people to paint—or not paint—their house any way they choose.)

Dollar Damages   Although most small claims court judges can't issue "clean up your act" orders, they will award the plaintiff damages. If the offender (defendant) still fails to follow the straight and narrow, you can continue to go back into court and sue repeatedly for as many times as necessary. Each case you win means more damages that the offender must pay.

> **People who refuse to clean up violations can suffer multiple fines or claims for damages.**

Also, in your nuisance suit, you can name a property owner whose tenants are creating the problem. As you probably know, many short-sighted landlords care only about collecting rent—not protecting the interests of the neighborhood. I guarantee you, though, a court judgment will sober them up. Plus, if the wayward landlords don't pay the court-ordered damages, you can place a lien against their property.

Moreover, your suit does not preclude other neighborhood property owners or tenants who suffer harm from also suing those inconsiderate tortfeasors. A perpetual sequence of nuisance suits will almost always bring deviant landlords and tenants into line.[2]

Upgrade the Schools

The *Wall Street Journal* (August 23, 2001) reports that all across the country "parents and property owners have become increasingly aggressive about trying to improve their public schools." When you think that in many areas parents spend $3,000 to $10,000 a year to send their kids to private schools, why not rechannel those monies and support into the neighborhood schools?

> **Improve school performance and watch property values set new highs.**

In some cases, too, neighborhood schools may not deserve their dismal reputations. Or perhaps a strong-performing school (at least in some area of specialization) isn't receiving the favorable notice it deserves. Improvement in these instances might focus more on publicity and press releases. Let potential homebuyers, tenants, and realty agents know the positive facts. Because better schools and better school reputations boost property values, neighborhood improvement can easily begin with upgrading the schools.

---

2. For a comprehensive discussion of neighbor law, see Mark Warda, *Neighbor vs. Neighbor* (Sphinx Publishing, 1991).

Safety and Security

In addition to reducing crime (see *Safe Home, Safe Neighborhoods*), you can bolster the safety within the neighborhood (especially for children and seniors) by slowing down or rerouting traffic. In fact, if you can get the city to lay down speed bumps, you achieve both objectives at the same time. Speed bumps not only force motorists to let up on the gas pedal, they tell drivers who want to speed that they better travel a different street.

You might also try lower posted speed limits and more intense enforcement. In Berkeley, California, several neighborhoods lobbied the city to erect traffic barriers at residential intersections. This effort converted many formerly through streets into cul-de-sacs.

Lobby the Politicians

> **Insist on the government services for which you and other property owners pay taxes.**

Property owners pay taxes. Now insist that you get what you pay for. As the Berkeley experience proves, when property owners and neighborhood residents join together to form a political force, they can push the city politicos to alleviate traffic problems, clean the streets, enforce ordinances, upgrade the schools, beef up police patrols, create parks, and provide other services that neighborhoods should expect.

Of course, the politicos can't achieve neighborhood goals without the continued input and assistance of community groups. City assistance works most effectively when combined with self-help. If no neighborhood action groups now exist, spearhead their formation or revival.

Add Luster to Your Image

Some good friends of mine used to live in Miami, Florida, but now they live in the upscale Village of Pinecrest, Florida. Did they move? No. They and their neighbors persuaded the post office to give them a new address so they could distinguish themselves from that diverse agglomeration known as Miami. As part of their efforts to create an improved neighborhood, some residents of Sepulveda have formed a new community and renamed it North Hill. In Maryland, Gaithersburg has changed its name to North Potomac, attempting to capitalize on the prestige of its nearby neighbor. Some residents of North Hollywood got the official name of part of their community changed to Valley Village. "With the name change," says Realtor Jerry Burns, "residents take more pride in their neighborhood."

> **Give your neighborhood or community a new name.**

Accent Something Special

As another idea to shine up the image of a neighborhood, accent or create something special. This "something special" can be as simple as the sincere friendliness of St. Johns or Brentwood. It can be sophisticated, such as the art deco architecture of South Beach. Or it could be the rural feeling— "It's like an oasis in the big city. We have owls living in our trees and all kinds of animals"— like Montecito Heights or Rogers Point. It can be the waterfront of Marina Bay, the ethnic diversity of Richmond Annex, the American heritage of the historical district in Annapolis, or the Victorians of Hyde Park.

> **Publicize neighborhood strengths.**

Create and accent a "something special" theme for the neighborhood. You will boost property values.

Talk Up the Neighborhood

Most people learn about various neighborhoods through word of mouth and articles they read in their local newspapers. As all good publicists know, you can influence these methods of "getting the word out." Talk up the neighborhood to opinion leaders. Comment to friends, coworkers, relatives, and acquaintances about the great improvements (or underappreciated assets) of the community.

Convince a reporter to play up the neighborhood's potential for turnaround, quality of life, convenience, or affordability. Let everyone know that the area deserves a better reputation.

Get the Banks Involved (Affordability)

To meet their obligations under the Community Reinvestment Act, many mortgage lenders are now working hard to revitalize urban areas. One could say that instead of "redlining," lenders are now "greenlining." They're targeting some communities and neighborhoods for easier-qualifying home mortgages and home improvement loans. Instead of pulling out of these areas, many mortgage lenders are pouring money into them.

> **Banks are required by law to invest in neighborhoods where they accept branch deposits.**

Homes for Dallas

In Dallas, city council member Charlotte Mayes has exclaimed, "I'm so excited, I'm so enthusiastic. . . . It's really exciting news for renters of low-income status to be able to have an opportunity for once . . . I could just kiss Fannie Mae." The object of Charlotte's excitement was the "Homes for Dallas" home-ownership initiative struck by the city of Dallas, a group of participating mortgage lenders, and Fannie Mae.

Under this Homes for Dallas initiative, 15,000 renters who buy a home within the city limits of Dallas—and in some instances, within certain targeted neighborhoods—will become eligible for a variety of special financing programs, which include grants and loans for down payments and closing costs, lease-purchase programs, flexible underwriting standards, home improvement loans, and homebuyer counseling (to be offered in both English and Spanish).

Easier Financing Means Appreciation Potential

Naturally, as home financing becomes easier, many neighborhoods are positioned for turnaround. With mortgage money more widely

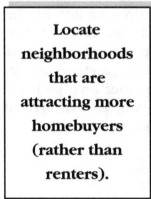

Locate neighborhoods that are attracting more homebuyers (rather than renters).

available, residents who are renting today will become homeowners tomorrow. Then, as these homeowners renovate and remodel their properties, the character of their neighborhoods will improve. To help identify turnaround potential, discover those neighborhoods where community redevelopment or community reinvestment monies are targeted to flow. As investors, homeowners, tenants, and community groups revitalize their neighborhoods, property values will appreciate.

Buy on the Bad News

There's an old saying in the stock market: "Buy on the bad news, sell on the good news." (Or stated more colorfully, "Buy with the sound of the canons, sell with the triumph of the trumpets.") When bad news or a pessimistic mood prevails, bargains are ripe for the pickings. With bad news all around, sellers outnumber buyers.

This same advice holds for neighborhood "stigma" or other types of "bad news." If a neighborhood is poised for turnaround but hasn't yet lost its "reputation," you can look forward to strong price gains as improvements take hold and the good word begins to spread.

Baron de Rothchild urged investors to buy when you see "blood running in the streets." When it comes to investing in neighborhoods, I wouldn't follow that advice literally. But I am absolutely convinced that the most recent escalation of housing prices has shut many first-time homebuyers out of those neighborhoods and communities that seemed affordable prior to, say, 1998.

> **The echo boomers will flock to affordable neighborhoods.**

Four million echo boomers are scheduled to continually pour into the housing market every year for at least another 15 years. Fixing up neighborhoods will become a national pastime. Property owners, citizen groups, not-for-profits, businesses, and city government now recognize that community improvement pays big dividends for everyone. To gain these sure-to-be profits, certainly fix up your own property. But don't stop there. Also work to revitalize and renovate the neighborhood.

CHAPTER 9

Market Your Property for Top Dollar

Now's the time to pocket your reward. You've renovated your property to wow your potential buyers or tenants. You've revitalized the neighborhood. You know that the property will virtually sell itself. Your value proposition easily beats the competition. All you need to do is:

1. Go to Kmart and pick up a small $1.98 cardboard for sale (or for rent) sign.
2. Write your telephone number on the sign with a no. 3 pencil or light blue ball-point pen.
3. Stick the sign in the front yard of the house.
4. Run a classified ad in your city's major newspaper.

Presto! A line of prospects will show up with each one carrying a checkbook in one hand and a mortgage preapproval letter in the other. You merely select the lucky buyer (tenant)—or maybe you put the property up for bid. The prospects fight each other for the privilege of owning (or leasing) this property. You end up with a sales price $15,000 higher than you were asking (or much higher rents).

* * * * *

If you think this scenario sounds like fantasy, you're right. Yet too many sellers or landlords think they can sell (rent) a property with such woefully inadequate marketing techniques. In truth, even when you do renovate a property to dazzle your prospects, you can't put marketing on auto pilot. To earn the highest profits, you must think through and plan your marketing just as you have planned your property improvements.

> **Properties rarely sell themselves for top dollar.**

Later in this chapter, you'll see the pros and cons of using a real estate agent to sell (or rent) your properties. For now, assume that you're going to sell by owner. Even if you do decide to employ a real estate sales agent (or property management company), these marketing pointers will help you guide and evaluate the work of your agent.

Whom Do You Want to Reach?

In crafting your renovations, you chose a bull's eye target market of buyers or tenants. Who are these buyers? Where do they work? Where do they shop? What publications do they read? What clubs, organizations, and trade or professional associations do they belong to? What churches do they attend? In what colleges are they enrolled? Do they have friends, coworkers, or relatives who currently live in the neighborhood? What social service agencies cater to their needs? What do their demographics and psychographics look like?

Why So Many Questions?

You answer these and similar questions because you do not want to waste time, money, and effort shotgunning your promotions and sales messages. You want to rent or sell this property as quickly as

> **Publicize your property where you can most effectively reach your target market.**

possible. And you want to achieve this result with the least amount of time, effort, and expense. To keep from working harder, you must work smarter. The more you know about your potential prospects, the better you can figure out where to spread the word about your property and what to say. Why spend good money for ineffective advertising in a major newspaper if a well-written notice on a bulletin board will immediately make your telephone ring?

Sell Benefits, Not Just the Property

As you think about who you're trying to reach, remember the marketing maxim "People don't buy features, they buy benefits." Yet many property owners never thoroughly plan their message. They just take five minutes to jot down the usual features of their property. Then they phone an ad in to their major newspaper. What results is nothing more than a generic, unexciting property description such as the following:

> Park Terrace: Split plan, 3-br, 2-bth, den, 2-car garage, 1650 sq. ft., large lot, close to schools and shopping. For more information, call (555)123 – 4567 after 5:00 P.M. No realtors!

Standing by itself, this ad may seem okay. But standing in the classified section of a newspaper surrounded by hundreds of other ads, it does nothing to grab the target buyer's attention and shout, "Here's the home you've been looking for. Here's why you will want to phone about this property right now."

> **Sell the sizzle *and* the steak.**

To draw targeted buyers into the ad and motivate them to call, you must emphasize benefits. Don't trust the buyer's imagination. Even worse, don't think that if prospects want more information they will call. There's too much advertising competition. Prospects seldom call just to get more info. They will call only when out of all the ads they looked through, your ad excited them enough to make the final cut.

Advertising pros tell sellers to organize and write their ads to "sell the sizzle, not just the steak." To the extent possible, always describe a property's features in a way that presses your prospect's hot buttons. Sergeant Friday may be pleased with a "Just the facts, Ma'am" approach. But you need to sell the sizzle.

Sell the Sizzle

So that brings us back to the questions:

1. Who are your prospects?
2. What benefits do you offer that distinguishes your property from other competing properties?

Are your prospects looking for one or more of these benefits?

- Bright with natural light
- Spacious open floor plan, wonderful for entertaining
- Quiet street
- Home warranty, no repair costs for at least two years
- Top-rated school district
- Unlimited storage space
- Bargain price
- Mortgage helper in-suite
- Warranted new roof
- Great appreciation potential
- Low cost of upkeep
- Choose your own cabinets, carpets, and colors
- Owner will carry financing.
- Safe and secure neighborhood
- Prestigious address/community
- Energy-saving, low utility bills
- Lowest price in neighborhood
- Low down payment
- Seller pays closing costs
- Walk to shops, cafes, and restaurants
- Easy-qualifying assumable financing

- ◆ Drop-dead gorgeous kitchen and bathrooms
- ◆ Totally private setting
- ◆ Serene views
- ◆ Immaculate condition, pride of ownership

Go through your property and carefully list every feature and benefit that will excite your buyers (tenants). Which of these features and benefits will best motivate your prospects to call? Which of these features and benefits are your prospects least likely to find in competitive properties? If you've strategically crafted your improvements, you will also be able to strategically craft a sales message that will get your property sold (or rented).

Crafting a Newspaper Ad

To save money, many sellers cut their classified ads too short. They list a few cold property facts and then expect prospects to call for more information. Don't waste your time and money with such meager efforts. If you do choose to advertise in a newspaper, make sure you include the following information:

- ◆ Sizzling hot buttons
- ◆ Square footage
- ◆ Room count
- ◆ Street address
- ◆ Price
- ◆ Terms, if any
- ◆ Amenities
- ◆ Open house hours
- ◆ Lot size/landscaping
- ◆ Telephone number/web site

> **The better you tell, the more you sell.**

As an owner-seller, you cannot use the same tactics that many real estate agencies follow. Contrary to what most people believe, real estate firms do not run house-for-sale ads to sell specific houses. They run ads to generate prospects for agents. Then once the agent hooks the prospect, they set off to tour a number of properties. Eventually, the agent hopes to sell some property, but they don't particularly care which one (except they do prefer to sell their own listings).

Since you only have one property to sell, you can't play this numbers game. If you do not hit your targeted buyers with the information they're looking for, your ad won't get circled. On the other hand, with a misdirected or sparsely worded ad, you may very well get lots of calls from tire kickers, looky loos, and people who want something other than what you're selling. Poor advertising (especially when linked with overpricing) goes a long way to explain why most for sale by owners fail to sell their properties and end up listing with a real estate firm. For example, compare and contrast these actual ads.

1. **LAKE FOREST Lease Option/ Owner Financing.** Gated community 4BR/3.5BR, fplc. Luxury pool. Home built in 2000. 2600 sf home on child-safe cul-de-sac. Move-in now! Call to pre-qualify. 1-987-654-3210.

2. **ORLANDO**—4br/2.5ba 2572sf, 2 car garage, owner will finance. $219,950. Call 1-987-654-3210.

3. **OCOEE HILLS**—3/1.5. CHA. Large corner lot, must sell. $84,500. Please call 1-987-654-3210.

4. **DELAND**—4 br ba brick hm, firepl, 2 car gar. Scrn pool & patio. Excel area. Call 1-987-654-3210.

5. **CLERMONT/GREATER PINES**—3/2 w/den. New schools. Call owner for more info. 1-987-654-3210.

6. **ALTAMONTE SPRINGS/LAKE ORIENTA**—FSBO, 3/2, 5, 2, 2300sf, scrn pool/Jacuzzi, $299,995. 1-987-654-3210.

7. **LONGWOOD/MARKHAM WOODS**—Private 5/3.5, 3620sf + 600sf office/apt., 1.6 acre, pool/spa, 2700sf scrnd lanai, gourmet kit, huge master, best schls. $425K. 1-987-654-3210.

8. **DR. PHILLIPS/TURTLE CREEK**— Gated. Corner Lot, 3/2.5 w/Loft, gorgeous landscaped 1 acre. Master Down, Pool, Model Condition, Fabulous Kitchen w/Island, Courtyard. Lowest Price in Turtle Creek, $288,900. 1-987-654-3210.

9. **THE VILLAGES**—2/2, corner lot, 1990 site built, sun porch, W/D, new carpet, paint, across from pool. Survey, termite/ house inspections & treatments include. $99,500. Open House, 808 St. Andrews Blvd. 1-987-654-3210.

10. **CLERMONT**—Lake view, Fl living at its affordable best. Saw Mill Subdiv, 1,836 sf, 3br/2ba, walk-in closets, Jacuzzi tub/mstr bath, blt 1997. 3/4 corner lot. Beautiful established lawn, priv. fence, spacious liv rm w/vaulted ceiling, dining rm, fam/great rm. You'll love the kitchen, breakfast rm, ofc area. 2 car gar, attic storage. New school to be constructed nearby. Gated, security patrolled. $174,900. 1-987-654-3210.

The ads in the right-hand column entice their prospective buyers far better than the ads on the left. Ad no. 1 does try to score with hot button owner financing but omits essential pricing and qualifying information in favor of "call to qualify." Ad no. 2 again goes for the "owner finance" benefit but omits the amount of the down payment, monthly payments, qualifying standards, and enticing information to sell the sizzle of the property itself. Ads nos. 3 through 6 illustrate the Joe Friday "just the facts" minimalist approach. Little in any of these sales messages attempts to excite or motivate targeted buyers. In fact, ad no. 5 wastes a full line by stating the obvious, "Call owner for more info."

Rather than merely telling people to call for more info, spark their enthusiasm to call with feature/benefit enticements. This ad further illustrates how to draft an effective sales message:

Affordable—Spacious—Stunning
Mint condition. 3/2, 1840 sq. ft. $6000 d.p., $830 per mo., romantic 400 sq. ft. Mstr. BR suite with fplc., open living area, flower garden views, light and bright kitchen delight, unlimited storage. $160,000—compare at $175,000! 210 Pecan. Open Sat. & Sun. 12-5.

Rare find, please call. 987-555-1234.

You see how this ad blends facts and benefits. It conveys comparative advantage (a value proposition that beats competitors) and it emphasizes the need to "jump on this one" before it's gone. This approach follows the well-known format of AIDA:

- ◆ Attention (headlined benefits)
- ◆ Interest (condition and affordability)
- ◆ Desire (prized features and benefits)
- ◆ Action (open house, rare bargain, please call)

This ad will make the phone ring with motivated buyers. If you deliver as promised, you'll sell the first weekend.

A Word about Price This ad prices the property at $160,000, yet it invites the prospect to compare with homes priced at $175,000. Does this mean that you're giving the property away? No.

Think of it like this. Except in super hot markets, sellers who have listed their property with a real estate firm

> **Advertise a good price.**

at $175,000 will likely accept an offer of, say, $162,500 to $167,500. Subtract a 6 percent sales commission and the seller nets somewhere around $155,000. So you will net about the same amount (or more) while making a quicker sale and still giving your buyer a good deal on the stunning home that you've created from a lump of coal.

Recheck the Market You toured comp homes and scoured the for sale ads before you bought and renovated your

> **Update your comp price data.**

property. But that was probably three to six months ago. Now before you write your ad and settle on an asking price, recheck the market. Go through some of the open houses in competitive neighborhoods. Read the ads for these properties. Note strengths and weaknesses vis-à-vis your property. Then craft your ad and your asking price to accent your property's advantages. Never forget. Houses sell within an intensely competitive market. Always know what your competitors are offering, what prices they're asking, and the sizzle of their sales message.

Prepare a Property Brochure or Flyer

Although well-crafted newspaper ads can prove effective, you should also prepare an advertising brochure or flyer like those you see hanging in tubes beneath for sale signs. Again, though, give your sales message some sizzle. Avoid the bland random lists of features as shown in Figures 9.1, 9.2, and 9.3. These actual flyers illustrate how not to write a sales message.

Lazy Agent's Flyer   Figure 9.1 shows the lazy agent's way of preparing a flyer. Simply photocopy the Multiple Listing Service (MLS) property description form. This flyer recites sterile facts and then gratuitously throws in a few benefits without elaboration. In fact, I looked at this house. It was immaculate inside and provided drop-dead gorgeous views from the living area and the master bedroom (full glass exterior wall) to a beautifully landscaped backyard. Yet the agent does not even mention this unique and highly desirable selling point.

> **Brochures and flyers provide a highly effective, low-cost way to motivate your prospects.**

The flyer also fails to include any information about the neighborhood. We learn that the roof is shingle, but nothing about its age or condition. The buyers will receive a warranty, but what will it cover, for how long, and for what amounts? As for selling points that distinguish this house from competitors, again nothing. Not even a photo. Interior and exterior photos should always play a starring role in your flyers for two reasons: (1) to show the property in a favorable pose, and (2) to provide a memory jog to prospects.

Potential buyers often will grab a flyer from the for sale sign tube but then not look at it again for several days. By then they may have also collected a half-dozen other flyers (or more). Unless the prospects already know the property and the neighborhood, their recollections will fade. And with no strong selling message, the buyers will likely place this property at the bottom of their priorities.

The Agent-Designed Flyer   Figure 9.2 shows an agent-designed flyer. Rather than photocopy the MLS form, at least this agent took 10 minutes to design and write his own flyer. What's interesting here is that the owner is also the agent. You would think that an owner-agent could do a better job than this boring property flyer. Except for the last paragraph, the listing of the property's basic description and features could just as well have been taken from the MLS form.

MLS # 213655 ADDRESS: 1212 NW 18th Terr			**BEDROOMS: 4 BATHS: 2 PRICE: $164,900**		
SUBDIVISION: Brywood			**TAXES: $3,219 ZONING: SFRI**		
TAX PARCEL #: 06426-100-012			**HOMESTEAD EXEMPTION: 2001**		
OWNER'S NAME: M.M. Jones as Agent			**LOT SIZE: 164 X 123**		
LISTING REALTOR: Shirley Saleslady			**SQ. FOOTAGE: 1932 (including utility room)**		

		EXISTING MORTGAGE	%	BALANCE	P&I
FOYER: Yes	**CONST: Brick & Concrete Block**	EXISTING MORTGAGE		**BALANCE**	**P&I**
LIVING RM: Yes	**YR BUILT: 1973**	1.			
DINING RM: Yes	**ROOF: Shingle**	2.			
FAMILY RM: Yes	**FIREPLACE: Yes**	3.			
GREAT RM:	**WALLS: Paneling & Hardcote**			**ESCROW:**	
OTHER: Extra Storage & Work Shop in Garage	**FLOORS: W/W Carpet, Cerramic Tile, Vinyl**	VA: ☐ FHA: ☐ CONV: ☐ ARM: ☐ TOTAL:			
	HEAT: Gas				
PARKING: 2-Car Garage	**AIR: Electric**	**TERMS:**			
UTILITY: Inside	**H/W TYPE: Gas**				
PORCH: Open Patio	**ELEC: City**	**COMMENTS: Home Warranty Provided to Buyer, Window Coverings Stay**			
TERMITE CONT. No	**WATER: Metered**				
	SEWER/SEPTIC: Sewer				

EQUIPMENT: Oven/range, dishwasher, disposal, microwave, refrigerator, paddle fans, washer, dryer, automatic garage door opener, sprinkler system.

Personal Photo

SHIRLEY S. SALESLADY, GRI
REALTOR

(800) 123-4567, (987)456-7890 BUS.
(987) 654-3210 FAX
(987) 456-1234 RESIDENCE

**COLDWELL
BANKER**
M.M. JONES REALTORS

1305 Knox St.
Holly Hills, FL 33333

PRIVACY IN BACK!

CONVENIENT

LOCATION!

HOME WARRANTY

This information although believed to be accurate is not guaranteed or warranted to be so by listing office.

Figure 9.1 MLS Property Flyer.

3814 NW 21ST AVENUE, CAPITOL CITY, FL

Photo

$184,900

Style of Home: DET
Bedrooms: 4
Half Baths: 1

Apx Year Built: 1967
Full Baths: 2
Square Ft: 2221

Features

Interior
Window Coverings
Crown Molding
Fireplace
Ceiling Fan

Exterior
Open Patio
Screened Porch/Room
Swim Pool-In Ground
Sprinkler System

Remarks: BEAUTIFUL BRICK HOME IN KINGSMILL FOR THE ACTIVE FAMILY. NICE YARD WITH POOL. CONVERTED GARAGE HOUSES REC RM, OFFICE W/2 PHONE LINES & STORAGE RM. $2500 CARPET/WALLPAPER ALLOWANCE. AHS SELECT HOME WARRANTY. 2 MILES TO COLLEGE. JJ FINLEY, WESTWOOD, GHS. OWNER/AGENT.

Listed By:
JOHNSON REALTY CORP
ALVA BEMER
(456) 789-1234

Info Deemed Reliable but not Guaranteed

Figure 9.2   Agent-Designed Flyer.

Omits Important Features   As to the most important home features such as style (DET stands for detached single-family house, which is not really an architectural style), floor plan, kitchen quality and design, ceiling height, natural light, and quality of bathrooms, this promo piece falls short. Indeed, look at the bland list under Interior and Exterior. Facts, boring and mainly trivial facts. Not one feature translated into a benefit or a selling message and theme.

Confuses with Classified Adspeak   Now look at that last paragraph. What's the first thing you notice about this feeble attempt to create an enticing description of the property? It's written in run-together all caps, classified adspeak. It's very close to unreadable.

When you write your flyer, you're not paying by the word or the line. Forget the choppy, abbreviated classified adspeak. Spell out your words and write in short descriptive phrases that relate to specific benefits. And definitely never write using all capital letters. Not only do capitals make reading more difficult, they look amateurish.

Deceptive Description   As a final point that the flyer only hints at ($2,500 carpet/wallpaper allowance), the house, itself, contradicts its description as "beautiful." In fact, the interior was a wreck with a garbled floor plan and 20-year-old appliances. The postage stamp swimming pool lacked a screen cover and seemed much more a liability than an amenity. As to that "converted garage rec room," I wish you could have seen it.

Do you recall our discussion about the quality of conversions dramatically affecting their value? To "convert" this garage, the owner had done nothing more than lay down indoor/outdoor carpet, tack up thin, cheap wall paneling, and install a suspended tile ceiling. Even worse, the owner/agent included this space in the 2,221-square-foot figure shown on the flyer and on the property listing sheet. When I looked at this property, it had already been on the market for more than four months. At that time, most houses in that neighborhood were selling in less than 30 days.

Overpriced Lemon   Let's go back to price per square foot as a guide to value. Most comp houses in this area were selling at around $80 per square foot. Using this measure and the 2,221-square-foot figure, you can come up with a value of $177,680 for this property. Since most comp houses didn't have pools and the owner here was willing to pay a $2,500 decorating allowance, the asking price might *appear* reasonable to some buyers.

> **Your flyer won't sell if the property doesn't deliver.**

I hope you never fall for this type of overrationalization. Remember, price per square foot gives you a guide. It does not compensate for the true quality of the living space. That's your job. And that's why you will always need to inspect comp houses before you apply their per square foots to a property that you're valuing. The quality of space in this property was so poor (condition and design) that no one should have paid more than $60 to $65 p.s.f. or a purchase price somewhere around $140,000. At $180,000 the property stands as an overpriced lemon.

By-Owner Flyer   After reviewing the two agent-prepared flyers, you can easily see that this by-owner sales sheet (Figure 9.3) also fails to provide persuasive copy. But here are several more points:

1. *Never give "For Sale by Owner" such a dominating position.* Use an attention-grabbing headline that conveys a strong benefit to the targeted buyers.
2. *Place one or more photos of the property on the flyer.* As noted, photos help jog the prospect's memory, and if done well, can accent the sales message. Use a digital camera and print color flyers from your computer. Black and white photocopies cheapen the property.
3. *Organize your information in related sections.* Make sure you emphasize the strongest features and benefits.
4. *Explain possibilities.* Notice that this property is zoned commercial. What does that mean for the value and uses

FOR SALE or RENT

BY OWNER

4000 NW 6th Street

---

4 Bedroom / 2 Bath

approx. **1550 sq. ft.**

Large corner lot with 6 ft. wood privacy fence in backyard

Central Heat and A/C (one bedroom has separate wall mount A/C)

Appliances: Washer, Dryer, Refrigerator, Stove

Ceiling fans in each room

Zoned: Office/Residential (currently residential)

FOR SALE
$85,000

FOR RENT
$975 / month

Available 11-15
(First, Last and $500 Security deposit required)

Call **(789) 123-4567** for more information
or to schedule a visit.

Figure 9.3   By-Owner Flyer.

of the property? Do not leave property potential to the buyer's imagination. (Of course, as an entrepreneurial renovator, you will actively search for properties that offer potential that sellers either do not recognize or undervalue.)

To consistently earn your highest returns, you must clearly extol the advantages of your property. Otherwise, your sales message can zip right past those people who would value your property most highly. How many sales messages hit you and everyone else every day? At least hundreds, and maybe thousands. To persuasively motivate your prospects, your sales message must cut through the advertising glut that engulfs us.

> **Your sales message must cut through the clutter.**

Rewrite of the By-Owner Flyer   Now read through my rewrite (Figure 9.4) of the by-owner flyer (Figure 9.3). You might first notice that I raised the price. Why? Because the owner thought that he was trying to sell a rundown property. In contrast, I'm selling the promise of making money. When the present lacks obvious appeal, sell the future.

> **Emphasize the facts and benefits that will most appeal to your market.**

You will also notice that I've packed my flyer with facts and benefits. Experience proves that the more you tell, the more you sell. Look at any successful immediate response sales message. Whether it's a TV infomercial, or an 800 number, magazine ad, advertisers load their sales messages with features and benefits. They try to prove that their sales proposition offers customers the best value available.

Where to Distribute Your Flyers   Place the flyers in a waterproof tube or pouch and hang them on the for sale sign that you place in the front yard of the property. In addition, distribute copies wherever you might reach your targeted buyers:

Cosmetic Fixer ◆ Bargain Price
◆ Loaded with Profit Potential

4000 NW 6th St. — 4/2/1550 sq. ft.
$95,000 — Terms Possible

Photo	Photo	Photo

Zoned Office/Residential – Great Income Property
with Rehab/Conversion Upside

Location

- Growing high-traffic corridor
- 5 minutes or less to downtown, the university, major retail
- 3% office vacancy rate in area
- Neighborhood revitalization in progress

Exterior and Site

- Low maintenance concrete block
- 4-year-old roof
- 1/2 acre lot with up to 12-car parking
- Building expansion possible

Interior

- Easy office conversion
- In-suite possibility
- Plaster soundproof walls
- Nearly new energy-efficient heat/AC

My Loss, Your Gain:

Owner relocation.
Lowest price per sq. ft. in area.
Will sell, lease, or lease option.

Make offer.

Cosmetic fix-up will net you a high return.

Will show at your convenience

(789) 123-4567

Realtor coop @ 3%–$250 Bird-dog Reward

Figure 9.4   Rewrite of By-Owner Flyer.

- Neighborhood bulletin boards (such as those in grocery stores, libraries, and coffee shops)
- Neighborhood residents
- People you know at work, church, and clubs
- Neighborhood churches
- Mortgage companies and real estate firms
- Schools, colleges, and employers
- Homebuyer counseling agencies
- Apartment complexes (if you don't get thrown off the property)

Don't wait for buyers to find you. Bring your opportunity to them. At any given moment, many prospects for your property aren't actively searching. Rather, they're procrastinating. They're waiting for your sales message to push them off the dime. So hand out your flyers to anyone and everyone who might know of a potential buyer (or tenant).

Emphasize your $250 bird-dog fee.[1] I have bought and sold many properties through word of mouth. Unbelievably, few by-owner sellers or realty agents play this technique for all that it's worth.

Make Your Sign Stand Out

> **Drivers must be able to read your sign without stopping their car.**

Use the largest for sale sign that the law (or HOA rules) allows. On your for sale sign, place as much appealing sales information as possible. Just like your flyer and classified ads, your for sale sign must grab *A*ttention, create *I*nterest, generate *D*esire, and motivate passersby to *A*ction (AIDA). You want someone driving by at 40 miles per hour to be able to learn about the great deal that you're offering.

---

1. Realtors have lobbied for laws that prohibit or restrict bird-dog fees. Check whether such restrictions apply in your area. If so, stay under the radar with your offer.

Sell with Honesty

Your sales message should sell the sizzle, but you still need to deliver the steak. You're entitled to tout the advantages of your property. No one's entitled to fabricate features that don't exist or cover up serious negatives that detract from the property. Go back to the agent flyer shown in Figure 9.2. By calling the property "beautiful," the agent-owner merely sets prospects up for disappointment. Had he advertised the property as a fixer (and priced it realistically), he would have sold it months before. By misrepresenting the property, owners lose credibility, waste their own time, and waste the time and efforts of homebuyers and investors.

> **Extol virtues, don't try to fake it.**

Entrepreneurial renovators strive to give their buyers the best deal for the money. They do not try to dupe them into paying too much for too little. Establish a strong reputation and potential buyers will come to you and ask, "When do you think that you'll have something else coming on stream? Please give us a call."

Sell the Property, Don't Just Show It

> **"Let me know if you have any questions" doesn't work as a sales presentation.**

Your promotional efforts have worked their magic. You're planning to show the property. Now what do you do? First, you put your mind into reverse. You rewind and erase forever that thought that you are going to *show* the property. No, you are going to *sell it,* not show it. Selling a property demands a much different perspective.

When people show properties, they assume a passive role. They let the buyer wander around and, if asked, they try to answer a question or two. When the prospect begins to leave, the passive show-man says, "Thanks for coming by. Let me know if you think you might be interested."

In contrast, the active seller knows that prospects arrive full of hopes, fears, and uncertainties. The active seller *prepares* to address all of these buyer concerns.

Prepare to Sell the Property

This morning I looked at a for sale by owner (FSBO) townhouse that was governed by a homeowners association. I asked the following questions:

Q. May I see a copy of the resale package? I would like to check the CCRs.

A.   What's a resale package? I don't know what you're referring to.

Q. Is there an attic?

A.   Yes.

Q. Where can I get to it? I would like to see it.

A.   The opening is in the laundry room ceiling.

Q. (After finding it) Do you have a stepladder I can use?

A.   No. We don't have one.

Q. Do you know if homeowner association rules or zoning would permit me to finish off the attic?

A.   No. Why would you want to do that? You would have to crawl up through that hole to get to it. (I then told her that you can buy a circular steel stairwell that's manufactured precisely for this purpose.)

Q. What's the status of that wooded area? (The townhouse property line abutted a large wooded tract of land.)

A. I don't know who owns that land or what they're going to do with it.

Q. Do you have an FHA or VA mortgage on the property?

A. FHA.

Q. How old is it and what's your rate?

A. 3 years. Around 8 and 1/4 percent, I think.

Q. 8 and 1/4 percent! Why haven't you refinanced? (FHA offers a streamlined refi that makes it easy and very cost effective to refi if rates drop by even 1 percent. At that time, 30-year fixed rates were at 6 percent.)

A. Our loan's only three years old. I think it would only save us about $50 a month.

Our conversation went on in the same vein. Neither she nor her husband (who was in a back bedroom getting ready for work) seemed to know anything about the property that a smart and informed buyer would want to learn. Indeed, although evidently unknown to the sellers, the financing issue was especially critical. Their FHA loan could have proved to be a powerful selling point. Owner-occupant buyers (but not investors) can assume the sellers' FHA mortgage at the same interest rate that the sellers are paying. Had these sellers refinanced at 6 percent, a buyer could have stepped into the property and the mortgage for just a few thousand dollars out of pocket. However, at 8 and 1/4 percent, the assumption wouldn't look attractive to most buyers (because most buyers wouldn't

> **Prepare to answer the questions that buyers *should* ask.**

know that they, too, could streamline the refi once their names went on the mortgage).

These sellers had elected the FSBO route because they had not accumulated enough equity in their property to pay the 6 or 7 percent Realtor sales commission. Unfortunately, although the means to their salvation lay at hand, they seemed oblivious to it.

Not an Isolated Case

I do not mean to indict these hapless souls for their lack of salesmanship. They represent the norm. Sellers and real estate agents alike routinely confuse showing a property with selling a property. As a result, they become adept at announcing rooms—"This is the kitchen. Here's the den. The master bedroom's at the end of the hall"—but they fail to make the sale.

They do not realize that (except in hot markets) sellers must give prospects reasons to buy. Sellers must anticipate and address the prospects' fears and hopes. Sellers must move to close the sale now rather than later.

Sales Success: Your 12-Step Program

To move past showing and on to selling, follow these 12 steps to a successful sale.

> **This 12-stop program will convert lookers to buyers.**

Back Up Your Sizzle with Facts Collect data on comps. Photocopy pertinent regulatory ordinances. Provide a home warranty. Show school rankings. Map out the convenience of the location to important linkages (employers, shopping, culture, nightlife, parks, schools). Whatever selling points you want to make, secure documentary proof or persuasive evidence. Otherwise, you're just puffing.

Establish Rapport   Find common ground for chitchat. Before you extol kitchens and closets, find out about their kids, cars, or hobbies. "I see you're wearing a Notre Dame sweatshirt. Is that where you went to college?" "Really, you did? My son's a junior there now. . . ."

Segue into Likes and Dislikes   Never begin talking features and benefits until you've learned the prospects' hot buttons and turnoffs. "What would you like to see first? What features prompted your call? Would you like . . . ?" Too often sellers and realty agents launch into a monologue about features that the prospects care little about. Or even worse, they tout a feature the prospects find unappealing, thus driving buyers into a socially distant position. Out goes your rapport.

Diplomatically Discover Their Feelings about Other Properties They've Shopped   You think that you're offering a great property at a competitive price. But what do your prospects think? Seek feedback about the market from the only people who really count—your potential buyers (renters).

Really Listen to the Criticism That Prospects Give You
You've worked hard to renovate the property to beat the competition. But, hey, none of us is perfect. Maybe you overlooked something. Ask your prospects for objections and weak points. Until you get a signed contract, keep searching for profit-enhancing improvements.

Translate Features into Concrete Benefits   Your prospects won't necessarily see the meaning of R-38 insulation, thermo pane windows, a southern exposure, or R-1B zoning. You must translate features into benefits. "This heavy grade insulation means that your heat and air costs will run less than $100 a month. Once this zoisha grass matures, your yard will look like a putting green and you'll never contend with crabgrass or weeds. Look at this photo. That's how the yard will look by the end of summer."

Inform the Prospects about Financing   First-time buyers, especially, may know little about down payments, monthly payments, and closing costs. They may not realize that they can buy your property with only a few thousand cash out of pocket (which may be borrowed from relatives). They may not realize that their after-tax monthly house payments can cost them less than rent.

Monitor the Prospects' Dialogue, Emotional Responses, and Body Language   Are they mentally moving their furniture into the home? Are they working through the financials in the context of their budget? Are they voicing seriously considered objections about price, terms, features, or neighborhood? Intensity of interest both positive and negative can signal that they want to buy—if you can alleviate their concerns and strengthen the facts and evidence that support your assurances.

> **Seek feedback. Don't give a monologue.**

Make It Easy to Close the Sale   Prepare your paperwork ahead of time. When you detect or elicit buy signals, move to the kitchen table (or sofa and coffee table) that you've brought into the house. If the prospects hesitate to commit, give more assurances along with the reasons why they really need to act now and not let this great property go to someone else. If necessary, agree to include short-term contingencies. However, retain the right to accept backup offers. If such an offer does come in, you agree to give the original buyers 24 hours (possibly longer) to clear their contingency or lose their chance to own the property.

> **Ask your prospects to buy.**

Set Up an Earnest Money Escrow   To seal the deal, you will want the buyers to put up an earnest money deposit. If they're smart, they won't want to make out this check directly to you. Prearrange an escrow account with a title company (or other escrow agent). The buyers can then write the check directly to the escrow account. This technique gives the buyers more assurance that you're playing straight with them.

Follow Up a Successful Close   When you successfully close your buyers, follow up to achieve two goals: (1) Make sure they proceed quickly to satisfy their contingencies (property inspection, mortgage approval, lawyer consultation); and (2) keep them motivated.

Some prospects suffer buyers' remorse. They begin to doubt their decision. You treat this disease with periodic positive updates. "A property down the street just sold for $10,000 more than you paid. The neighborhood elementary school has won an award for outstanding extracurricular programs. The city has pledged $500,000 to upgrade neighborhood streets and parks."

> You can't merely coast to closing. Remain alert for potential cracks in the pathway.

After buyers sign, they need assurance that they've made the right decision. Do what you can to bolster their high feelings of excitement and alleviate their low feelings of regret and worry.

Follow Up an Unsuccessful Close   When you first set up an appointment to sell the property, get the full names of the prospects and their telephone numbers. If you meet prospects through an open house that you're holding, ask visitors to register (name and phone number) for a door prize drawing. Or when convenient, you directly ask for their names and numbers and then write them down.

> Prospects who are "just looking" today may become your buyers tomorrow.

In some way, learn who your prospects are and how to contact them. Then follow up with a thank you note and additional persuasive information about the property. Too many FSBOs let uncommitted prospects walk out the door without any intent to follow up. Don't make that mistake. Try to spark their interest, desire, and action with periodic updates about the property, the availability of lower-rate financing, or other potentially motivating developments.

More Tips on Financing

As you'll recall, I chastised the townhouse FSBOs because they failed to tell me about their assumable FHA financing. Even worse, after I brought up the subject, these FSBOs never volunteered any information about the amount of outstanding balance on their mortgage or used its assumability as a selling point. To illustrate the importance of this failure, contrast the classified ad they ran with my rewrite using actual facts that I discovered through my sustained inquiries and investigations:

Original Owner Ad
3BR, 2BA, 1,600 sq.ft., huge master B.R. On golf course, stone fireplace, cul-de-sac, $83,500. 555 – 1234, apt.

My Rewrite
Easy qualify. 3BR, 2BA, 1,600 sq.ft. low maintenance, top condition patio home. Quiet cul-de-sac bordering wooded tract. Large attic storage (den/BR/study conversion possible). Priced at only $85,500. $4,800 cash-to-close, $489 per month. 2144 Park Lane. Open Sat. & Sun. 12 – 5. 555 – 1234.

First, you may wonder why I removed "on golf course" and "huge master" from their ad. Because neither was true![2] Also, the ad appeared in the "Houses for Sale" category, but it was not a single-family house. It was a common-wall patio home. Again, mis-

---

2. The golf course was actually behind the homes across the street from this property. At 15 feet by 15 feet, the master bedroom can hardly qualify as "huge."

leading. My rewrite not only accented the terrific financing (i.e., if the owners had refinanced at 6 percent)—it substituted true positives for deceptive wording.

Avoid Deception

Okay, I'm going to go off point a bit here. Primarily, I do want to emphasize the role that financing can play in your efforts to sell a property. Yet, this original seller ad pushes me to again warn you against using exaggerated and deceptive ads. Such ads only set up your prospects for letdown. Sure, "on golf course" will make the phone ring. But to what avail? As it was written, the ad targeted the wrong prospects and it failed to target the people who would most value the features and affordability of the actual property.

> **Misleading ads turn off potential buyers.**

Back to Financing

To successfully sell properties (especially to first-time buyers), plan ahead for financing. Ideally, to make buying easier, offer your buyers some type of owner financing or owner-assisted financing. Such financing includes, for example, seller seconds, contract-for-deed, lease option, and lease purchase. Or you could put an assumable mortgage on the property when you buy it and then pass that financing along to your buyers. (We discuss these possibilities in Chapter 10.)

As a minimum, develop a cooperative relationship with several mortgage lenders. Let them write up brochures or flyers that explain the down payment and monthly payment possibilities of the mortgage plans they offer. Then use these handouts to show buyers how little

> **Help your prospects "own" not just "buy."**

cash and income they will need to *own* your property. Although some of your prospects will have obtained a mortgage preapproval, many others will not. To make a sale, make financing easy.

(Note: Whenever you're talking with prospects, use the word "own" rather than "buy." As in "You can *own* this great house for just $15,000 cash to close and $1,600 a month. Given these figures, doesn't *owning* look a lot better than wasting money on rent?")

Should You Employ a Realty Agent?

Most owners who try to sell their own properties fail. They put out their front yard sign that they bought at Kmart, run a newspaper ad for a month or two, and then give up. Do these owner failures mean that you should forget your FSBO efforts and go ahead and list your property with a realty agent? No, not at all. It does mean, though, that to succeed where others fail, you must avoid their mistakes.

> **Most FSBOs fail to realize that sales agents provide a wide range of services for sellers.**

Most FSBOs simply do not realize that to sell properties, top sales agents go far beyond yard signs and newspaper ads. To get properties sold, top agents typically provide these services to sellers and buyers.

Services to Sellers

1. *24/7.* Agents work whenever they get called, and they remain on call morning, noon, and night every day of the week.

    Advice for FSBO sellers: You must make yourself available to show the property on a moment's notice at nearly any waking hour.

2. *Multiple media.* Agents use yard signs and newspaper ads, but they also rely heavily on referrals, networking,

web sites, cold calling, floor time, and personal and business relationships.

Advice for FSBO sellers: Get the word out about your property to everyone you know or come in contact with. Circulate those flyers.

3. *Pricing.* Agents inspect and show dozens of properties every week. They know properties, and they know the details of purchase contracts.

Advice for FSBO sellers: Look at properties in the neighborhood and nearby areas. Monitor sales prices, terms, and time on market. Price the property realistically in the context of other transactions.

4. *Home preparation.* Agents obtain feedback about properties from dozens of buyers each month. They learn the likes and dislikes of the market. They can use this knowledge to help sellers dress their house for success.

Advice for FSBO sellers: Monitor buyer feedback. Talk with realty agents, contractors, home remodelers, and sales consultants at home improvement centers. Give buyers what they really want.

5. *Selling presentations.* Top agents don't show properties, they sell them. They know how to encourage and recognize buy signals. They know how to overcome or deflect buyer objections. They diplomatically buffer hard-edged negotiations and persistently create trade-offs, options, and alternatives. They always maintain a supply of purchase agreements. They know how to get buyers to commit and sign.

Advice for FSBO sellers: Encourage your prospects and ask them to buy. Shy and passive won't make it. Remain flexible and open to offers. Give and take with tact and good nature. Persuasively lead your prospects into a buying decision. Don't wait for them to ask you.

6. *Troubleshoot problems.* Agents know that signed contracts don't close themselves. Someone must monitor the flow of paperwork and solve problems that can throw a sale off course.

Advice for FSBO sellers: Don't assume that you can walk the path from contract to closing without finding a few potholes to step over or around. Monitor the flow. Rely on a sharp escrow agent to diligently control the document shuffle.

Services to Buyers

1. *Market knowledge.* Agents know listings and can prescreen properties to save the buyers' time and effort.

Advice for FSBO sellers: Be able to compare and contrast your property with others on the market. Especially be able to highlight its competitive advantages.

2. *Agents help buyers with neighborhood selection.* People don't just buy houses, they buy locations. Agents know demographics, schools, trends, commuting distances, shopping, and culture. Buyers frequently depend on agents to compare and contrast the pros and cons of various neighborhoods.

> **Homebuyers rely on their agents for many services.**

Advice for FSBO sellers: Understand the neighborhood. Know how it compares to others. What are its advantages? Prepare a neighborhood flyer to complement the flyer you've prepared for the property itself. Homebuyers who are new to a city especially need this information.

3. *Pricing.* Buyers depend on agents to advise about pricing. In turn, agents provide buyers comp sales data. Agents also help buyers choose their offering price.

Advice for FSBO sellers: Provide prospects with comp sales data. Emphasize how your price, terms, and property features beat those offered by the competition. Do not push prospects to learn these facts on their own. Other owners (and their agents) will spin the facts to their own advantage—not yours.

4. *Financing.* Agents either qualify buyers or refer them to a loan rep who will provide this service. First-time buyers especially need someone to help them figure out how much home they can afford and the quality of their credit profile.

   Advice for FSBO sellers: Establish a relationship with several loan reps. Be able to discuss the parameters of various loan programs with prospects. Refer prospects to www.myfico.com where for $12.95 they can look at their credit report, learn their FICO (Fair Isaacs Company) credit score, and gain tips on how to improve their credit profile. Even better, help the buyers with owner-assisted financing or a mortgage assumption (Chapter 10).

5. *Negotiating assistance.* Many buyers, and especially first-time buyers, do not feel comfortable or competent in the negotiating process. In their role as facilitator and mediator, agents ease their buyers through the offer-counteroffer emotional roller coaster.

   Advice for FSBO sellers: Play softball, not hardball. Conciliate and contemplate. Help prospects feel comfortable in talking with you. Nurture trust. "Let's see if we can work out an agreement that will make us all happy." Not, "Look, take it or leave it. If you don't want the property, I'm sure someone else will."

6. *Follow through.* Agents help buyers follow through to submit their mortgage application and obtain a professional inspection of the property. They may also hand hold and troubleshoot for the buyers. The agent remains on call to provide assurances and intervene when an obstacle arises (low appraisal, mortgage turndown, encroachments, etc.).

Advice for FSBO sellers: Your sharp escrow agent can assist with some of these details. But you too must tell the buyers that they can call you at any time to assist with problems or answer questions about the property, the neighborhood, the mortgage loan process, or anything else that may concern them. You should also provide the buyers with the names of respected property inspectors, pest control companies (for termite clearance), and surveyors (if necessary).

Although, at several points I have repeated myself throughout this chapter, I have done so because I want you to succeed as a FSBO seller. If you follow the renovation and marketing process that we've gone through, you can outperform most agents. You will either earn a higher profit, give your buyers a better deal, or achieve some combination of both.

> **FSBOS "save the commission" only when they market their properties effectively.**

Nevertheless, understand that "saving the commission" usually requires thought and effort. If you prefer not to replicate the services that top realty agents provide, that's fine. Try the easy route that most FSBOs follow. Put up a sign, run an ad, and hope a preapproved buyer shows up with a checkbook in one hand and a written, full-asking-price offer in the other.

It does happen. And with a great property to sell, your chances of success do go up. But (except in red hot markets), experience teaches that you typically must go beyond the ordinary. Selling real estate seldom counts as the "lazy man's way to riches."

Co-op Sales

If going alone as a FSBO seller doesn't appeal to you, you could offer sales agents a 3 percent (more or less) commission to bring you a buyer. Essentially, you act as your own listing agent and pay the co-op percentage to the buyer's agent. Using this approach, you increase the chance of a sale, but if you find the buyer yourself, you owe the agents nothing.

Indeed, as soon as your FSBO sign goes up, realty agents will inundate you with telephone calls. Beware, though. Most of these agents don't care much about selling your property. They want to list it. To reach selling agents (i.e., those agents who work primarily with buyers rather than sellers), distribute your flyers to real estate offices.

> **Try a co-op deal.**

What about Lawyers?

Fortunately, the majority of my real estate transactions have occurred lawyer free. In those transactions of mine where lawyers have been involved, the lawyers created far more expense and trouble than they were worth. In fact, I do not know any small real estate investor who has much good to say about lawyers. As a rule, I will refuse to even deal with buyers who want to turn their negotiations over to their lawyer.

> **Lawyers can hinder as well as help.**

Nevertheless, it's becoming ever more difficult in our society to safely remain in a lawyer-free zone. And in some areas, such as New York City, lawyers routinely get involved in homebuying and other property transactions. (Lawyers in Maryland even went to the state legislature to lobby for a statute that would force all homebuyers to employ a lawyer—whether they wanted one or not.)

Understand that I am relating my personal preferences and experience. As a beginning investor, if you can find a competent, trustworthy lawyer who does not overbill and underperform, then by all means avail yourself of his or her services.

CHAPTER 10

Buying Your Property

Up until this point, you have explored many possibilities for creating value in real estate and then successfully marketing the product you've created. Now, in this chapter you're going to learn where to find your "fixer" properties and how to negotiate good deals.

Finding Good Properties

Where can you find good properties? Here are the leading sources:

◆ Real estate agents
◆ Newspapers
◆ Tour neighborhoods
◆ Networking
◆ Foreclosures and REOs
◆ The World Wide Web

Real Estate Agents

In most metro areas, real estate agents list about 60 percent of the properties that are available for sale. Another 20 percent consist of

> **You can often buy properties that aren't listed or advertised for sale.**

FSBOs (for sale by owners), and the remaining 20 percent include three other sources: property owners who are willing to sell but are not actively marketing their properties, foreclosures, and REOs (primarily foreclosed real estate that is now owned by banks, other types of mortgage lenders, and government agencies).

Advantages of Working with Agents

Relatively few investors go it alone in their search for properties. Even though investors don't need the hand-holding service that agents provide for first-time homebuyers, investors do value these four services:

1. *Screen properties.* Every day, new listings come onto the market, old listings expire, some listings cut their prices, and some properties get sold. Good agents will monitor these market activities. They will alert their preferred investors of all market developments that those investors could turn to their advantage.
2. *Save the investors time.* In screening properties and property transactions, agents not only alert investors to emerging opportunities but also save them enormous amounts of time and effort.
3. *Negotiating savvy.* Top agents can help investors craft their deals. They know how to present offers, create alternatives, and get transactions closed.
4. *Sources of money.* Top agents not only stay abreast of the institutional mortgage market—they also can uncover little-known sources of funding.

If you do choose to work with an agent, expect at least these four aforementioned services. To gain the most benefit, you will need to discuss what you're looking for, the types of financing that you might need, and how frequently you want the agent to contact you. Also, for maximum service, limit your buying activities to one

> **Your agent can screen properties that meet your criteria.**

favored agent—but only for so long as that agent fulfills the services and gathers the information that you request. Quid pro quo rules.

Disadvantages of Agents   Unfortunately, using a real estate agent can yield some negatives as well as positives:

1. *High fees.* Most sellers pay a sales commission of 6 or 7 percent of the selling price of a property. Absent these fees, you and the seller could "split the savings" and both come out ahead. The sales commission looms especially large when you're trying to negotiate a bargain price with a low-equity seller.
2. *Conflict of interest.* Agents only get paid when their sales close. As a result, some agents will try to talk you into a bad deal to earn the commission. Until you build a relationship of trust with an agent, accept all advice with a grain of salt. Weigh, consider, and verify.
3. *Too little knowledge.* After reading this book, you will possess more analytical knowledge about neighborhood and property analysis than a majority of sales agents. Consequently, you may need to weed through substantial incompetence before you match up with an agent who will fulfill your legitimate expectations.

> **Insist on an agent who knows how to work intelligently.**

Far too many sales agents think of their job as a numbers game. Talk to a lot of people, hand out 1,000 business cards a month, chauffeur prospects around, and *show* properties. Eventually someone buys something. Most sales agents (and FSBOs) do not realize that, first and foremost, selling requires service, knowledge, and integrity. When you find an agent who demonstrates those virtues, you've found someone who will earn those high fees.

Newspapers

When novice investors think about using the newspaper to help them search for properties, they needlessly restrict themselves to the Houses for Sale section of the classifieds and the Realtor display ads. But you can actually use the newspaper to discover properties in many different ways.

For Sale by Owner Ads   I have found more of my properties from by-owner ads than via any other source. Although most investors do prefer to work through agents, I prefer going direct. Usually, you can find your best low-down payment, owner will carry (OWC) sellers in the FSBO ads. In addition to calling current ads, I periodically call ads from 30 to 90 days back. If the sellers haven't sold

> **Read current and past FSBO ads.**

(and haven't listed with an agent), I often find them more open to offer. If a sale has occurred, I try to extract as much information as I can to bolster my knowledge of the market.

I telephone ads primarily on the basis of price and location. Many ads lack sufficient content, so I don't rule out properties based on omissions. Remember, you score your best bargains when you see possibilities and hidden values that the owner (or agent) misses.

Realtor Newspaper Ads   As mentioned before, ®Realtors place their ads primarily to generate phone calls. They want you to call so they can ask you what you're looking for and then try to set up an appointment to show you several other properties. That's okay if you're not currently working with an agent. If you are, then don't call the ad. Call your agent and ask him or her what they know about the property and whether it's likely to fit the property profile that you've specified.

> **Realtor ads often intentionally leave out important information.**

Lease Option　　I will discuss lease options in Chapter 12. But for now, I urge you to call about every lease option property that comes on the market in your targeted price range and neighborhood(s). Lease options give the ultimate low-cost method to control a property while you're completing your fix-up and renovations. Even better, write an assignability clause into your option agreement, and you can also achieve a low-cost exit strategy.

> **Lease options give you a low-cost way to control a property.**

House for Rent Ads　　Many property owners become accidental landlords or tired landlords. Even when owners are serious investors, they may be open to offers. If a rental house looks like it holds good promise, I'll ask the owners if they're interested in either a sale or a lease option. Given that these owners originally sought to rent the property, they're not counting on a huge inflow of cash. Their financial situation can easily permit them to offer flexible, low cash-up-front terms. Simply persuade them to do so.

> **Landlords are often would-be sellers. Ask them.**

Wanted to Buy　　Some investors use the Wanted to Buy section of the classified ads to locate distressed owners in hopes of snagging a bargain. Their ad might read something like this:

> I buy houses for cash. End your hassles with agents and tire kickers. Funds issued within 48 hours. All offers considered. Please call Tom anytime. (888) 888–1234.

Several ads such as this one run continuously in our local paper. The ads must work or someone is foolishly wasting money. Personally, though, I've never used the quick-cash gambit but I have succeeded many times with an ad such as the following:

> Experienced investor with cash, credit, and references seeks owner-financed houses and income properties. Please call Dr. Eldred, (888) 123 – 4567.

Or when I was just starting out, my Wanted to Buy ad similar to the following paid off with more replies than I could handle:

> Ambitious young investor would like to acquire rental properties. Owner financing preferred. Strong references. You enjoy the interest income, I'll do the work. Please call Gary, (888) 123 – 4567.

If you do run a Wanted to Buy ad, include a personal element with some indicator of credibility. In a world where the number of seniors is increasing and CD rates and stock returns are in the basement, I predict a large growth in owners who want to sell OWC to someone they perceive as low risk. In today's market, OWC mortgage interest provides an attractive yield.

Public Notices and Community News   Each day people marry, get divorced, or experience financial setbacks such as lawsuits, foreclosures, and job losses due to business failure, company downsizing, or plant closure. In addition, people die. Newspapers duly report all of these life-changing events. What do these events mean to you? They could signal that someone may need to sell a less-than-perfect house relatively quickly.

> You can find clues and leads throughout the newspaper.

That's why some hustling real estate agents rely on local news and public notices to provide them a fruitful source of potential sellers and buyers. You can do the same. If you can talk with some of these people before an agent gets their listing, you can often score a good deal.

Which Newspapers?   Up to this point, I've talked about "the" newspaper. But unless you live in a small town, your area probably supports anywhere from 3 to 10 newspapers. In addition to the standard local paper(s) that carry the city's name, you might consult real estate ads in the newspaper(s) published by the local college(s), want-ad–type papers such as the *Thrifty Nickel,* and newspapers that circulate in distinct communities where you might like to buy (e.g., in San Diego, the *La Jolla Light*, in Sarasota, the *Pelican* and the *Longboat Key Observer,* and in Oakland, the *Montclarian*). Given the high advertising cost of many major dailies, the smaller circulation papers often provide highly targeted, cost-effective leads.

I know a condominium developer in suburban Chicago who went broke buying display ads for his project in the *Chicago Tribune.* The investor who took over the development switched to advertising in the suburban paper that reached thousands of nearby apartment dwellers. This investor sold the condo project in four months. Target marketing works.

Drive, Bike, or Run Neighborhoods

Get out and regularly bike (or run as I do) your targeted neighborhoods. Okay, if you must, drive. But you discover much more when

> **Get out of your car.**

you're out of your car and you don't have to worry about slowing down traffic each time you hit the brakes to glimpse a better view of a potentially promising property.

For Sale Signs Of course, in touring neighborhoods, you're trying to spot for sale signs. But also take note of for rent signs and all property flyers. Your search process doesn't just alert you to properties you may want to buy. It's also intended to apprise you of what's selling and renting and at what prices and rent levels. If you notice available properties that aren't moving, you will want to investigate why.

When you see neighbors, tenants, or sellers of available properties, strike up an informal conversation. You want to gain insights that might not be as easy to come by in a formal purchase visit to the

> **Get firsthand information.**

property. I've found that neighbors and tenants can be especially forthcoming in a way that helps inform my negotiating strategy. "Why are they selling?" you might ask. "How long has the property been on the market? Do you know if the owners need or want a quick sale?" You're looking for all types of information that will help you size up the situation.

Verrry Interesting As you talk with neighborhood residents and tour the area, tune your hearing and sharpen your vision to pick up on such things as:

- ◆ Changes for good or bad that may affect future property values.
- ◆ People who plan to sell within the next 12 months.
- ◆ Properties that appear neglected, or even better, vacant or abandoned.
- ◆ Properties that display hidden value potential (conversion, oversized or double lot, rightsizing).

The more knowledge you possess, the quicker you can assess a property when potential opportunities present themselves. Likewise, with more knowledge, you can create your own possibilities.

Networking

> **Nearly everyone's a buyer or seller at some time. Ask them.**

Just as networking can help you sell a property, it can help you locate a good property to buy. Tell everyone you know that you're in the market and the kinds of deals that you would consider. As I have said before, networking offers far more possibilities than most beginning investors realize.

Most property owners prefer a quick, certain, and no-hassle sale at a lower price, rather than list with a realty firm and contend not only with paying a 6- or 7-percent commission but also putting their house and their lives on display for a period of months. Use these facts to persuade owners to sell to you at market value *less* the amount of the sales commission and some further discount (say $2,500 to $10,000) for fast, convenient, and low hassle.

Foreclosures and REOs

The foreclosure process offers you four shots at the same target:

- Preforeclosure workout
- Foreclosure auction
- Immediate postforeclosure purchase
- Lender REO

Preforeclosure Workout   At the beginning of the foreclosure process, the property owners have fallen behind on their mortgage payments and the lender is either threatening to sic its lawyers on them (iron fist approach) or the lender is pleading with the borrowers to come in, sit down, and try to schedule a payment catch-up or sell the property voluntarily (velvet glove approach). In the past, lenders relied far more on the iron fists of their lawyers to beat delinquent borrowers into submission. Today, lenders have wised up and are much more likely to cover those fists with a velvet glove that's holding an olive branch.

Your Role   Because lenders now generally favor workout to foreclosure, investors can sometimes step in to stop the growing losses of both the borrowers and the lender. Offer the defaulting owners some walkaway money. Offer the lender something less than the defaulting borrowers are legally obligated to pay, but something more than the lender would *net* from a foreclosure sale. Or, if the potential of the property warrants it, offer to take over the full obligations of the borrowers. In exchange, ask the lender for a reduced interest rate, an additional advance of renovation money, or other concessions in the terms or costs of financing.

In cases where the borrowers stand no chance of holding on to their house, lenders usually try to minimize their loses in lieu of chasing after dollars that they will never recover.

Show Empathy, Credibility, and Diplomacy   Once the foreclosure notice hits the newspaper, the foreclosure vultures will descend on the defaulting borrowers to scavenge what remains of their home equity and self-dignity. To succeed against these vultures, show empathy, credibility, and diplomacy.

> **Workouts require tact and perseverance.**

Empathy means that you sincerely try to fashion a solution that will permit the borrowers to salvage their credit record, home equity, and self-esteem. Credibility means that you prove to the borrowers that you're not just whistling Dixie. Prove to them that you can come up with the cash or credit to quickly close a deal. Diplomacy means that you listen more than you talk. That you're searching for a win-win-win outcome. That you're not just another "Take it or leave it" profit monger.

The Foreclosure Sale   When defaulting borrowers ignore their chance for workout (as they often do), the county sheriff (or other appointed officer of the law) sells the property to the highest bidder at a foreclosure sale. Unfortunately for borrowers and lenders, such sales seldom bring in enough to clear the balance on the mortgage, other liens, legal expenses, and unpaid property taxes. In fact, the foreclosure sale actually seems designed to fetch the lowest possible sales price.

Winning bidders do not receive a warranty deed to the property. They receive no disclosures about property defects. They receive no assurance of possession. (The buyer at a foreclosure auction may need to evict the existing tenants or owners of the property.) Winning bidders must pay cash for the property, and

> **Foreclosure sales typically go to risk-taking speculators or the foreclosing lender.**

their bid must not include any contingencies (such as a property inspection, termite clearance, environmental clearance, or lawyer approval).

Consequently, given these risks, the foreclosure sale only attracts two types of buyers: (1) foreclosure speculators, and (2) the lender who is foreclosing the mortgage. Contrary to the hype of those foreclosure gurus who deceptively peddle their books, tapes, and seminars, beginning investors can rarely play the foreclosure game without incurring large risks.

Immediate Postforeclosure   However, after the auction gavel comes down three times, beginning investors can spring back into action. For regardless of whether the winning bid comes from a foreclosure speculator or the mortgage lender, neither of these buyers typically plans to hold that property as a long-term investment. Both want out fast. The speculator wants to turn the property for a quick profit. The lender wants to clear its books of this nonperforming asset.

> **Buy from the winner of the foreclosure sale.**

Now, here's how you might work this situation to your advantage. Offer the winning bidder something more than the amount they've paid at the foreclosure auction, but something less than the "as-is" market value of the property. But also, condition your offer with a financing contingency, various inspections, and title insurance—all of which you should be able to satisfy within a week or two. If (when) everything checks out satisfactorily, the winning bidder gets a quick, easy, and profitable sale. You obtain a bargain price for the property without the risks of buying at foreclosure.

Shop the REOs   When lenders end up with a foreclosure, that property goes onto their books as an REO (real estate owned).

HUD/VA, Fannie, and Freddie   If the mortgage loan on that property was backed up by Freddie Mac, Fannie Mae, the Department of Veterans Affairs (VA), or the Federal Housing Administration (HUD/FHA), the lender will probably cash out its position in the property and require the backup company or government agency to step in and take the property. Then that company (or agency) puts the house up for sale and markets it according to that owning entity's specific rules and procedures.

Again, contrary to what most authors lead you to believe, Fannie, Freddie, HUD, and VA nearly always price their REO properties at (or very close to) market value. Typically, you can only score great deals in periods of severe market distress or when the owning entity wants to dump a severely distressed property (which probably involves high risks for the buyer). My book *Investing in Real Estate,* 4th ed. Wiley, 2003 devotes a full chapter to the REO policies of Fannie, Freddie, HUD, and VA. As a thorough investor, it will pay you to stay abreast of these types of REOs, but don't believe the hype. It's usually difficult to pick up these (or any other) REOs for dimes on the dollar.

Lender-Held REOs   When a lender can't get rid of its REO to a backup organization such as Fannie Mae or HUD, it will usually list the property with a local realty firm. That's why you should monitor the foreclosure auction and immediately contact the foreclosing lender before it lists the property. Nevertheless, in our quid pro quo world, many mortgage lenders who count on referrals for their mortgage business from realty agents won't deal directly with buyers. Still, even if you have to work through an agent, you might be able to negotiate a good deal on a lender-held REO.

> **Lenders usually list their REOs with realty firms.**

Every REO lender is open to offers. The longer they hold the property, the more money they lose in maintenance, upkeep, security costs to ward off vandals, and lost interest earnings. In addition, lenders who end up with too many nonperforming assets on their books look bad to shareholders and regulators. Sooner or later most lenders become motivated sellers. At that point, the lender may cut a deal on price, terms, interest rate, or some combination of the three. Also, when you concede on some issues, feel free to come back with a proposal that includes additional funds for renovations.

How do you know when the lender intends to move on a deal? You don't. To win with lender REOs, you must persist. Stay in touch. Keep your offers coming in. I know of more than a few instances where a lender has turned down, say, $100,000, and three months later accepted $75,000. Persistence can pay off.

The World Wide Web

Every method of finding properties that we've discussed now has its web site counterpart(s). The web devotes sites to realty firms, MLS listings, FSBOs, foreclosures, and REOs. You can network through investor groups and chat rooms. You can search and read the classified ads without ever buying a newspaper.

Through Mapquest.com you can pinpoint the location of a property with directions on how best to get there. To learn about comp sales in the neighborhood, school rankings, or crime rates, there are a dozen web sites that will give you this information. On some sites, you can even experience a virtual tour of the property.

> **You turn up your best information through personal contacts.**

Nevertheless, even though you might turn to the web for preliminary information, nothing beats touring neighborhoods, collecting facts from firsthand conversations, and talking with property owners, agents, sellers, and tenants. An old cliché still rings true: "Real estate's not about property, it's foremost about people." Use the web to begin or supplement your property search and fact checking. But your best information will be delivered to you personally.

Search for Agreement

Many inexperienced investors approach purchase negotiations with uncertainty and nervousness. They don't quite know what to expect. Some falsely believe, too, that a skillful negotiator dips into a bag of tricks and pulls out deceptive techniques like lowballing, weasel clauses (contingencies written primarily as easy escape hatches), running a bluff, shotgunning (multiple random offers), "dressing to impress" (pretending to be something you're not),

> **It takes two willing parties to structure an agreement.**

bad-mouthing (deflating the owners' high opinion of their home), asking for the moon and the stars, and eleventh-hour surprises (at the last minute before closing, insisting on contract changes in your favor). One book on real estate negotiating even advises, "Remember you are in a war and you must use every weapon available to win."

These hardball tactics might seem to make sense to those who use them, but experience shows that they often backfire. Successful investors don't primarily seek to win the negotiation. They negotiate to win an agreement that will actually close to the benefit of all parties. "The tendency of many sellers," says Realtor Bill Sloan, "is for them to stop listening if the purchase price offer is too low."

Sloan is pointing out a well-known fact. To most sellers, price stands out as the main event. Everything else is warm-up. That's why lowball offers knock negotiations off the track before they even get going.

> **Working "with" creates more deals than working "against."**

When you realize this fact, however, you can use it to your advantage. By not pushing the sellers too hard on price, you may get nearly anything else you want. Or if you really put bargain price at the top of your negotiating list, prepare to give the sellers enough other points to persuade them that your proposal makes sense from their perspective.

Deal Points

In addition to price, your purchase negotiations will include at least 8 or 10 other significant deal points such as the following:

> **Look for high-value–low-value deal points and trade-offs.**

1. *Terms.* Will the seller offer owner-assisted financing? If so, how much up-front cash? What interest rate? What amount of monthly payments? Exactly what type of financing assistance (lease option, lease purchase, land contract, first mortgage, second mortgage, etc.)?

2. *Closing costs.* In most areas, custom dictates who pays what settlement expenses. But negotiation can override custom. With settlement costs often amounting to upward of $5,000, smart investors put these amounts on the table for discussion.

3. *Earnest money deposit.* To show your commitment to a deal, you will bind your offer with an earnest money deposit. How much? That's subject to negotiation.

4. *Repair allowance.* In lieu of (or along with) a price reduction, you can negotiate a repair allowance for some of the fix-up work you plan for the property.

5. *Personal property.* Would you like the seller to include window air conditioners, appliances, or any other personal property in the sale? Write them into your offer.

6. *Financing contingencies.* If the seller does not provide all of your financing, you will probably include a financing contingency in your offer. This clause will give you a specified amount of time to raise the money you will need to close the deal. It will also set the terms (interest rate, loan-to-value, down payment, etc.) that you must be able to obtain. Otherwise, you're released from the agreement and entitled to a return of your earnest money.

7. *Inspection contingencies.* You will want to get the property professionally inspected for physical condition, ter-

mites, and environmental hazards. How long do you have to complete these inspections? Who pays how much for any unanticipated or previously unknown problems? Under what scenarios can you withdraw from the agreement without obligation? Negotiation can deal with all of these issues.

8. *Closing date.* To gain a bargain price, many investors offer a fast closing. Does your seller voice a strong preference?

9. *Possession date.* Generally, sellers relinquish possession on or around the date of closing. Sometimes, though, you may want a delayed closing with early possession (such as with a lease purchase or lease option). Or alternatively, the sellers may want to cash out fast, but remain in the property until, say, the school year ends or their new home is ready for them to move into.

10. *Warranties.* Is the seller providing you a home warranty or any specific warranties for components such as the roof, HVAC, or appliances? What exactly do the warranties cover, for what amounts, and for what period of time?

Every purchase-sale agreement addresses 10 or more significant deal points. Entrepreneurial negotiators never view any one of these issues as separate from the others. Instead, they try to find a combination that will work for everyone.

> **Work to find that right combination of deal points.**

Reduce Seller Anxiety

Often sellers will agree to accept a "probuyer" agreement—if you show them that you're a solid buyer and that the deal will actually close. Therefore, to persuade sellers and reduce their anxiety, draw from the following eight negotiating tactics:

1. Increase the amount of your earnest money deposit.
2. Produce a preapproval letter from a mortgage lender or other assurances that you have the money and credit to do the deal.
3. If you're paying cash or making a large down payment, emphasize that fact. Cash counts. If you've got it, use it to boost the credibility of your position.
4. Emphasize the strength of your character, stability in your job and community, how you plan to improve the property, and other positive factors.
5. Avoid weasel clauses in your offer. A weasel clause is any clause that lets you weasel out of, or easily escape from, a contract without obligation. One of the easiest and most obvious weasel clauses states, "This offer is subject to the approval of my attorney." If you need to consult an attorney, do it before you begin negotiations. (In some states, by custom, attorneys routinely get involved in negotiating property purchase agreements. Nevertheless, the same advice holds. The firmer your offer, the more likely the sellers will treat you as a serious buyer and make concessions toward an agreement.)
6. Avoid indefinite contingency clauses such as, "Offer subject to raising $10,000 from my business partners"; or sometimes homeowners write into their purchase offer, "Subject to the sale of our current home." Clauses like these raise the sellers' doubts, increase their anxiety, and generate reluctance to accept your offer.
7. When you write a contingency clause into the contract make it definite and short term. "Buyer will secure a property inspection report within five days." Or "Buyer agrees to submit mortgage loan application within 48 hours." Or "Sellers are released from obligation if buyers do not produce a letter of mortgage loan credit approval within three days." These clauses show that you're not going to drag your feet through the transaction.

8. Make your contingency clauses realistic. Don't condition your purchase on finding mortgage money at 6 percent if market rates are at 7.5 percent. Don't require a 27-year-old house to be free of all defects. The firmer your offer, the more willing the sellers may be to accept less than they originally had in mind.

Plan your offer with no more escape hatches than you need (but no fewer either). Many sellers will trade a lower price for the peace of mind of a near-certain sale. That's why buyers who pay cash nearly always gain more seller concessions than those who load their contracts with ifs, ands, or buts.

Win-Win Isn't for Wimps

Negotiators typically fit into one of three negotiating categories: (a) adversarial, (2) accommodating, and (3) win-win. Lawyers typically practice the adversarial style. Adversarial negotiators make outrageous demands. They push, pull, or threaten to move you as close as possible to their position. Adversarial negotiators don't care whether their opponents end up pleased. All they care about is winning for themselves.

In contrast to the adversarial approach, the accommodating negotiator tends to give in to every request or demand. Accommodators feel powerless to effect the outcome they want. They feel helpless due to lack of money, time, information, knowledge, or experience. Accommodators detest conflict. They would rather lose than stand their ground. When negotiating through a real estate agent or other third party, accommodators typically delegate too much responsibility. Accommodators often say things like, "Oh, just do what you think is best" or "Let's just sign and get the whole thing over."

When you negotiate win-win, you adopt some of the adversarial style and some of the accommodating style. But overall, you

> **Think multiple directions, not a win-lose continuum.**

adopt a cooperative perspective. Win-win negotiators recognize that every negotiation brings forth multiple issues, priorities, and possibilities. They also recognize and respect the other party's (not opponent's) concerns, feelings, and needs. They do not operate along a single line of contention (e.g., price). Win-win negotiators work to create a strong, mutually beneficial agreement that all parties want to see completed.

Yet in doing so, they never lie down in an accommodating position while the adversary hurls hardballs at them. When push comes to shove, win-win negotiators either shove back to reestablish a cooperative enterprise or they walk away with their dignity and finances intact.

Develop a Cooperative Attitude

Most importantly, win-win demands a cooperative approach. Bob Woolf, agent, attorney, and past negotiator for many well-known figures including Larry Bird, Larry King, and Joe Montana, says, "When I enter a negotiation, my attitude is, 'I'm going to make a deal.' I don't start with a negative thought or word. I try to foster a spirit of cooperation. I want the other party to feel that I'm forthright, cheerful, confident, and determined to reach their goals. If I'm sufficiently sensitive to the other party, I firmly believe they will be predisposed to make an agreement with me. To a degree, your attitude will become a self-fulfilling prophecy."

Bob Woolf's professional advice applies whether you are negotiating a big-time sports contract or a purchase agreement for a home. In fact, especially with a purchase agreement for a home, you're usually wise to display a cooperative "Let's reach an agreement" attitude. Act in good faith. Play by the rules of courtesy. You want to buy a property. The sellers want to sell a property. Your best chance for success comes when all parties cooperate to help each other.

> **To negotiate effectively, you must understand the sellers.**

Learn as Much as You Can about the Sellers

Some sales agents do everything they can to keep buyers and sellers away from each other, and for good reason. Agents have seen sales fall through because of personality clashes. Or they fear that sellers (since agents of yesteryear nearly always represented sellers) might give away a choice bit of information that will help the buyers.

"Why are you selling?" the buyers ask.

"Oh, Mack's been transferred," the sellers respond. "We have to be in Omaha by the end of next month."

Although the keep-the-buyers-and-sellers-apart sales strategy sometimes is best, as a rule I reject it. Before you make an offer, learn all you can about the sellers. What kind of people are they? Do they seem generous and open? Are they rigid and argumentative? Do they show pride in their home? Are they reluctantly moving? Are they eager to leave? Why are they selling? Have they bought another home? What are their important needs: emotional, personal, and financial? What are their worries and concerns?

What Do the Sellers Really Want?   The sellers aren't really trying to sell a house. They're reaching for more distant goals. Selling their home is a means to those ends. The sellers won't judge the price and terms of your offer by absolute standards. They will judge it according to how well it helps them move toward what they want to achieve. That's why you must get to know the sellers. Without understanding their needs, you miss a great opportunity to find high-value/low-value win-win trade-off deal points that can benefit both of you.

Say the sellers previously accepted two offers that fell through because the buyers couldn't arrange financing. With these experiences in their background, the sellers may be quite anxious. They don't want to be strung out again. If you can assure them that you have the resources to buy (bank statements, credit report, preapproval letter, job security), they likely will give you a lower price or other concessions.

Establish Rapport and Emotional Connection   Too frequently, investors and sellers aim their biggest negotiating guns toward price. The sellers want a higher price. The buyers want a lower price. Antagonism and stalemate result. Steer around this trap. Meet the sellers, talk with them, learn all you can about their perceptions, past home-selling experience, feelings, and needs. But keep in mind that agent concerns about personality clashes are valid. When meeting and talking with the sellers, follow these guidelines:

> **Play it cool. Avoid clashes with the sellers.**

◆ *Meet the sellers as soon as possible.* The sooner you get a fix on who they are and what they're like, the better you can begin to map your negotiation strategy. Sellers respond more openly with information when you first look at their property. At that point they're eager to please. They want to excite your interest. If you wait to meet them until after you've made an offer, they'll guard their admissions and concessions more tightly.

◆ *Get concessions before you begin negotiations.* "You're asking $225,000, is that right? Just so I can fairly compare your home to others I'm looking at, have you thought about how much less you would accept?" Or: "You're asking $225,000, right? What personal property—appliances, drapes, rugs, patio furniture, gazebo, and so on—are you planning to include?" Or maybe: "Have you considered how much financing you're willing to carry back?" By innocently suggesting concessions in this way, you're not negotiating with the sellers. You're not even asking for concessions. You're merely gathering information to rank the sellers' property against other houses that are up for sale. Sensing that you are exploring other options, many sellers will sweeten the deal before you write your offer.

◆ *Inquire, don't interrogate.* The way you ask your questions is far more important than the questions themselves. Phrase them as innocuously as you can. Don't intimidate, accuse, threaten, or debate. Remember Peter Falk as Columbo, the perpetually "disoriented" detective. Columbo didn't interrogate suspects. He gently probed. Use similar tactics. Encourage the easy flow of information. Don't try to extract it.

♦ *Establish rapport.* Find common ground. Talk about the last Cubs game, the weather, or perhaps a shared hobby. Negotiations are about people, not money. Treat the sellers as people, not merely owners of a property that you might want to buy.

♦ *Compliment, don't criticize.* As you walk through the sellers' home, sincerely note their beautiful grandfather clock. "Does it have an interesting history? How long have you owned it?" Comment on other belongings they seem to take pride in. What about the yard? Do the sellers have a green thumb? Can you genuinely admire their tomatoes or roses?

At this *first* meeting, put forth a cordial attitude. Establish a *relationship* bank account to draw on later when you will need it. To sharply criticize the sellers' home at this time won't loosen them up to accept a lower price. But it may very well turn them against you. Even though the property will need work and improvement, wait until later in the negotiations to start detailing all of the repairs and fix-up the house will need. On your first visit to the property, focus on learning— not lecturing.

> **Before you negotiate in earnest, establish a relationship bank.**

A Win-Win Example

In one of my earliest face-to-face negotiations, I learned the value of win-win. The sellers and I were sitting at their dining room table drafting a contract point by point. The first point was price. Although the sellers had their house priced fairly, I offered $5,000 less. The sellers rejected. I said, "Well, let's put that issue on hold and see if we can agree on some of the other points." In abbreviated form, I was able to get the sellers to agree to:

- A lease-purchase plan with closing 15 months after I took possession of the property.
- A cash deposit of just $2,500.
- A possession date within six weeks.
- Store all my household furniture in their den for the month prior to my taking possession of the property. (I had sold my previous home and was giving quick possession to my buyers, so I was going "homeless" for a month.)
- Include in the sale about $2,000 worth of furniture and appliances.

These people were among the easiest sellers I had ever dealt with. But when we eventually returned to price, they still didn't want to budge. After we talked some more, the husband said, "Look, here's what we paid for the property. At what you're offering us, we would take a $3,000 loss. We want to at least get what we paid."

Here's where negotiation experts differ. Some would say at this point you've got the sellers committed to everything but price. Hang tough and you can still get the price concession you want. The sellers are so close to a deal, they won't let you walk away. If they did, they would just have to start over again with someone else—if and when that someone else appears. If they're smart, the sellers won't take that risk.

For reasons explained earlier, I don't endorse this view. If the sellers have been willing to yield on every point that's important to you, why not let them score a point, too? Besides, once you've gotten nearly all you want, why push so hard you might upset the entire applecart? So, adopting a win-win approach, I increased my offer by $3,000 on the promise the sellers would cut down and remove a dead tree from the backyard. They quickly agreed. We had a deal that pleased us both. (Note: I really wanted this property because its floor plan and window alignments permitted me to create an accessory apartment and several value-enhancing views. The location was also superb and

> **Give and accept will help you sleep at night.**

the property was the lowest-priced property in the neighborhood. I knew that even at the sellers' price, I would make a good profit.)

How to Bargain for a Low Price

Let's return to the beginning of these negotiations. What would have happened early on if we had heavily debated price? Even if I had been able to pull the sellers down to my offer, that "success" probably would have destroyed my chances of getting all the other things I needed to make the deal work. A hollow victory indeed.

On other occasions, however, I have reversed this approach. When through early inquiries I've learned the sellers have needs stronger than price, I emphasize how I am willing to help them meet those needs (e.g., their preferred moving date, their need to know the transaction is actually going to close). Then, after the sellers understand that they are receiving nearly all of the terms and conditions they want, I can justify my request for their concession on price.

> **Most sellers take lowball offers as personal insults.**

The important thing to remember is that sellers don't demand their price for purely economic reasons. For many, price is laden with emotional content. A low offer doesn't just hurt their pocketbook. It affronts their psyche.

When you enter negotiations with the idea that you're negotiating price alone, more than likely one party will "lose" and the other party will "win." When you adopt the view that you are negotiating (searching for) an *agreement,* you and the sellers both emerge as winners.

Don't Compromise, Conciliate

In negotiation lore, the story is told of a mother who hears her two children bickering at the dinner table. Each child wants the only remaining slice of pie. Tiring of this debate, the mother takes the slice, cuts it in two, and gives half to Craig and half to Shawn. "There," she says, "as you get older you've got to realize that you can't have everything you want. You must learn to compromise. Remember this as an important lesson."

This well-intentioned mother thought she was teaching her kids a valuable lesson; in fact, she had imprinted them with one of the greatest obstacles to win-win negotiating. By splitting the difference before fully exploring her children's wants and a range of options, this mother mistakenly framed her kids' debate along a single continuum. Compromise simply meant deciding how to split the piece of pie.

Look for Ways to Make a Pie Bigger   Had the mother framed the problem multidimensionally, more than likely she could have figured out a better solution. What if Shawn really preferred the crust and Craig preferred the filling? What if the children shared a television set and each preferred different programs? What if the children shared after-dinner cleanup responsibilities? What if the children had money from an allowance? What if Shawn didn't really want the pie, but simply liked to torment Craig?

> **You can split a pie many more ways than one.**

Had the mother recognized a range of wants, trade-offs, and outcomes, she may have produced results more satisfying (or just) for both children. The true art of negotiating doesn't depend on one's readiness to strike a compromise. It depends on seeing beyond a single either/or issue.

Conciliation Sparks Creativity   Earlier, I told how sellers had agreed to let me use one of their rooms to store household furniture. Alternatively, I wanted an earlier date of possession and they wanted a later date. What would have happened had we focused our negotiations exclusively on possession date? I would have said, "I have to be out of my present home on February 1. I need possession on that date."

The sellers may have responded, "We can't get into our new home until March 1. A February 1 possession date is out of the question. We can't possibly give you possession before February 28."

"Okay," if I'm thinking compromise, I might say, "let's split the difference. I'll agree on February 15. I'm willing to meet you halfway."

Although meeting the sellers halfway has the ring of reason and fair play, in many situations it doesn't make sense, or it overlooks another more satisfying outcome. In this case, February 15 was actually undesirable for both of us. So that position never found its way onto the table. By looking at my real problem—what to do with my furniture for a month without incurring the high costs of multiple moves into and out of storage—we struck upon the solution of temporarily storing my household goods in a large room they used but didn't really need. We both were satisfied with this outcome.

> **Thoughtful conciliation beats lose-lose compromise.**

Nine times out of 10, thoughtful conciliation beats lose-lose compromise.

Compromise Provokes Extremes   People who negotiate to compromise typically open with offers at the extreme. If you believe the sellers will split the difference, it's to your advantage to offer $275,000 for a house that's worth $325,000. Should the sellers agree to meet you halfway, they will sell you the house for $300,000.

But few sellers are that obliging. The tactic of bid low and compromise is too familiar to work effectively. As negotiating expert Herb Cohen likes to emphasize, "A tactic perceived is no tactic at all." You're more likely to negotiate successfully if you bake a bigger pie. Expand your knowledge of wants, needs, trade-offs, and possibilities. To paraphrase Emerson, "Foolish compromises are the hobgoblins of little minds."

Learn the Sellers' Reasons and Reference Points

When the sellers say, "This house is worth at least $225,000," learn their reference points. Why do they think $225,00 represents bottom dollar? When the sellers say, "We need at least $225,000," find out why. When the sellers say, "We couldn't afford to carry back financing, we need every net dollar in cash," find out why. No matter what the objection to your proposal, never accept it as the final word. Find the real underlying reasons and the supposed factual foundation that the sellers are building on to support their decision (or their counterproposal).

> **Always find out where the sellers are coming from.**

Fast-talking sales agents deal with objections like a steamroller. They just charge forward and try to flatten the prospect's reluctance without bothering to slow down, let alone, stop, look, and listen. In contrast, I believe that you should never try to "overcome objections" by the methods taught in those high-pressure sales training classes. Rather, try to correct, alleviate, or eliminate the sellers' misperceptions through better understanding.

If it turns out that the sellers' facts or perceptions do make sense, try to solve their problem—not merely steamroll their objections. A confused mind will always say no. To get a yes, assuage the sellers' real concerns.

Use an Agent as an Intermediary, but Negotiate for Yourself

Writing in a national trade magazine for Realtors, sales agent Sal Greer tells of an offer he received on one of his listings. Sal says that after receiving the purchase offer from a *buyer's agent*, this agent told Sal, "This is their [first] offer, but I know my buyers will go up to $150,000."

"Of course," Sal adds, "I told my sellers that information, and we were pleased with the outcome of the transaction."

The lesson here is very plain. Never let your agent do your negotiating for you. Don't give your agent information you do not want the other side to learn. Don't let on to your agent that you're willing to pay a higher price than your first offer. Use your agent as a fact finder and intermediary. But guard your emotions, confidences, and intentions.

> **Never abandon control of negotiations to your agent (or your attorney).**

Many first-time investors mistakenly rely too heavily on their agents to actually come up with the terms of their offer and carry out their negotiations. These investors will ask their agents, "What price do you think I should offer? What's the most you think I should pay? Will the sellers concede points or agree to carryback financing?" The buyers then follow whatever the agent recommends.

Such buyers abdicate their negotiating responsibilities. If you follow their example and shift decision making to your agent, you run the following risks.

You May Be Working with a Subagent   Remember, you may be working with the sellers' subagent. As a subagent, a Realtor's legal duty is to the seller. In favoring the sellers' interests, the agent may persuade you to boost the price or terms of your offer. Or the agent may disclose your confidences to the sellers.

As a practical matter, many subagents don't strictly follow the letter of the law. Even though technically they're representing the sellers, in their heart and efforts they may feel more loyalty to you. I know many subagents who work hard for their investors—even to the detriment of their sellers.

Nevertheless, since you don't know for sure how your agent will use the information you share, carefully limit your disclosures. Likewise, when it comes to offering price and terms, rely on your agent for facts about the sellers, selling prices of comp houses, neighborhood statistics, and general market conditions. Listen to the agent's price recommendations and accept the benefits of his or her knowledge and experience. But don't delegate your decision making. You may be led into giving up more than you need to.

Be Cautious of Buyers' Agents   Increasingly, brokerage firms and sales agents have been promoting buyers' agents. Since sellers are represented by their own agents, buyers also need someone to look out for their interests. Marilyn Wilson, a Bellingham, Washington, real estate broker, says, "Buyers should think of their agents as attorneys. Would you want to have one attorney representing both parties in a divorce settlement?"

> **Buyers' agents, too, face conflicts of interest.**

Superficially, the idea sounds reasonable. Yet even if you choose to employ a buyers' agent, you still need to guard your disclosures and negotiating strategy. First of all, like the buyers' agent Sal Greer referred to earlier, even *your* agent may disclose confidences—either intentionally or unintentionally.

Second, we're all subject to subtle influences. A buyers' agent may talk you into offering a higher price or better terms because it will make his or her job easier. Under which scenario do you think your agent will work the hardest for you: When the agent knows you offered $185,000 but you've said you're willing to go up to $210,000, or when you offer $185,000 and say, "If they don't accept this offer, there's four or five other houses I'd like to look at"?

Watch What You Say   Regardless of whether you're working with a sellers' subagent, a buyers' agent, a dual agent, or a facilitator, watch what you say. Don't tell your agent everything and then turn the negotiations over to her with the simple instructions, "Do the best job you can," or "Why don't you try $235,000 and if that doesn't fly, we can go to $245,000."

In fact, it doesn't matter whether we're talking about lawyers, insurance agents, financial planners, real estate agents, or any other type of professional relationship, conflict of interest always lurks in the background. You must walk a fine line. Release enough in-

> **All types of agents sometimes compromise their principals (and principles).**

formation to achieve the results you want, but not so much that you invite your agent to sacrifice your interests to the interests of someone else (including herself).

The Deal's Not Over 'til It's Over

"I chose to work with a buyers' agent," recalls Barry Tausch. "I felt a buyers' agent would push harder to get me the best deal possible. As it turned out, I pushed too hard.

"I knew the sellers were getting a divorce. The wife had moved out of the house and in with her boss. Without income from the wife's paycheck, the husband was facing tough times. He couldn't handle the family expenses on his own. Although they had a lot of equity in the house, the husband was hurting for cash. He needed a fast sale. By using this information to my advantage, I got the sellers to come down at least $12,000 to $15,000 below market. Bad deal for them. Good deal for me.

"The only thing I had to agree to was a 30-day close. I didn't think this would be a problem because I already had been preapproved. But it was. There was one foul-up after another.

> **Beware of pushing too far, too hard.**

"In the meantime, the sellers got a backup offer for $7,500 more than my price. To make a long story short, the husband held such resentment against me for 'stealing' his house, he wouldn't cut me any slack. As soon as I missed the loan commitment date, he demanded payment. When I couldn't deliver, he pulled the contract and sold to the backup buyers."

Leave Something on the Table Negotiating expert Bob Woolf says, "There isn't any contract I have negotiated where I didn't feel I could have gone for more money or an additional benefit. Why leave money on the table? Because skilled negotiators know the deal's not over 'til it's over. If you push too hard, you create resentment and hostility in the other party." Even if they've signed a contract, they'll start thinking of all the ways they can get out of it. Even worse, if you stumble on the way to closing, they won't help you up. They'll just kick dirt in your face.

Especially in the purchase of real estate—where emotions run strong—you're better off leaving something on the table. The purchase agreement only forms stage one of your negotiations. Later, you might encounter problems with respect to property inspections, appraisal, financing, possession date, closing date, surveys, zoning, building permits, or any number of other things. Without goodwill, trust, and cooperation, unpleasant setbacks on the way to closing can throw your agreement into contentious dispute.

Let Your Profit Objectives Guide Your Negotiations   As a potential investor in fixers and renovations, you can become (1) a cutthroat shark (hardballer), (2) an accommodator, or (3) a win-win conciliator.

The Shark   As a shark you reach across the table and try to pull as many of the sellers' chips as possible into your pile. In most cases, that tactic will get you kicked out of the game. "That's okay," some investors retort, "I can always find another table at which to play. Sooner or later, I'll dupe the other side into losing a sucker bet."

It's true. On occasion, you can win big at the expense of someone else. How often? As the gurus who promote such tactics admit, "Maybe 1 out of 50 or 1 out of 100 times. You've got to persist. It's a numbers game." This approach works best for those people who can spend a huge number of hours looking at deals. For most investors, though, the big payoffs that do come in won't sufficiently compensate for the heavy commitment of time and effort.

The Accommodator   Accommodators never wish to offend. They never want to lose a deal. They fear rejection. They see the promise, but they fail to tally the risks. Accommodators buy a lot of properties, but they fail to make any serious money. Their enthusiasm for the deal causes them to give in too easily to the sellers' requests. As a result they make commitments they cannot honor. They agree to pay prices that can rarely yield high profits.

> **Never reject without first exploring a range of possibilities.**

The Win-Win Conciliator   Here's the style where real estate investors make the most money. As a conciliator, you won't quickly say yes, and you won't quickly say no. You will learn all that you can about the market, the sellers, and the property. Most importantly, you will know yourself.

What are your resources? What are your talents? What are the sources and amounts of your funding? What are your profit goals?

With knowledge of the market, the sellers, the property, and yourself in view, you then work cooperatively with the sellers to shape your deal points. Some in your pile, some in the sellers' pile. Ideally, to strike the best win-win deals, you will seriously negotiate only with those sellers whose most crucial wants and needs fit together with yours like the pieces of a jigsaw puzzle. The sellers need what you can give. You need what the sellers can give. The skilled conciliator brings all the pieces together to form a great profit picture.

CHAPTER 11

Easy Money for Owner-Occupants

If you think that lack of money or credit might prevent you from investing in real estate, you're in for a pleasant surprise. For no matter what your finances or credit look like, this chapter will show you how to raise the money to buy and renovate properties. First let's start with the easiest and best and then work from there.

Owner-Occupied Financing

> **Many new loan programs make buying easier.**

During the past five years, mortgage lenders have created dozens of little- or nothing-down payment mortgages for homebuyers. Although some of these loan programs restrict financing to buyers who have not owned a home for a period of at least three years, others are open to anyone with passable credit and a steady source of income.

Passable Credit

What is "passable credit"? Typically, a FICO score of 580 or above. This score level includes about 80 percent of the population. (To learn your FICO score, go to www.myfico.com.) Passable credit even includes people with previous foreclosures and bankruptcies—as long as these borrowers can reasonably explain their lapses and have reestablished sterling credit for a period of at least one and preferably two years.

Attention Current *Homeowners*

> **Owner-occupants receive the lowest interest and easiest terms.**

If you already own a home and are short of cash, I urge you to consider this strategy: Locate a property that offers strong renovation potential. Find a tenant for your current home. Then apply for a low-down payment, owner-occupied mortgage. Move into your fixer (obviously, I'm not talking about a house that's an unlivable junker) and work on getting the property renovated during your spare time. Naturally, this technique won't prove feasible for many investors. But if you can do it, this tactic may offer the following advantages—depending on the specific details of your renovation plan and the type of financing you use:

- ◆ Low or no down payment
- ◆ Easier qualifying for the mortgage loan
- ◆ No extra carrying costs during the renovation period
- ◆ Assumable financing for your buyer when you sell the property
- ◆ Lower cost of interest than you would pay with straight investor financing
- ◆ Possible tax-free capital gain on sale (if you stay in the property for two years, or if you move for "unforeseen circumstances" prior to a two-year residency)

If you want to build wealth fast, get into owner-occupied fixers. No legal technique that I know of offers as many advantages with so little risk. Whether you presently rent or own, definitely consider this profit-generating strategy.

FHA 203(k): The Homebuyer's Best Choice for Financing

> **Turn a fixer into fast profits with FHA 203(k).**

Like most other renters, Quentlin Henderson of Orlando, Florida, hoped to own his own home someday. Yet, with little savings, Quentlin thought he wouldn't realize his hopes for at least three to four years. He never dreamed that within six months he would actually own a completely renovated, three-bedroom, two-bath home of 2,288 square feet—more than two and a half times as large as his previous 900-square-foot apartment.

How did Quentlin manage this feat? He discovered the little-known but increasingly available FHA 203(k) mortgage loan program. FHA 203(k) allows any homebuyer to acquire and improve a rundown property with a low- or no-down payment loan. "The house needed a new roof, new paint, new carpeting; and a bad pet odor needed to be removed," says Quentlin. "There is no way I could have paid for the house plus the repairs at the same time. And there was no way I could have otherwise afforded a house this size."

Locate an FHA 203(k) Specialist   To use a 203(k) plan, your first step is to locate a Realtor or mortgage loan advisor who understands the current FHA 203(k) purchase and improvement process. In the past, FHA often stuck borrowers in red tape for months without end. But now with recent FHA streamlining and special computer software, Robert Arrowwood of California Financial Corporation reports that up-to-date, direct endorsement (DE) firms like his can close 203(k) loans in four to six weeks instead of four to six months.

Search for Good Value   Once you've located 203(k) advisors who know what they're doing, your next step is to search for a property that offers good value for the money. In Quentlin Henderson's case, his Realtor found him a bargain-priced, six-year-old house that was in a sorry state because its former owners had abandoned it as a result of foreclosure. "The good news for people who buy such houses," says Bob Osterman of HUD/FHA's Orlando, Florida, office, "is that prices are generally so low that after repairs are made, the home's new value often produces instant equity."

Not surprisingly, the term *instant equity* was also used by John Evianiak, a 203(k) buyer in Baltimore. "Not only can you buy a house and fix it the way you like," John says, "but you can buy a home for much below its market value, put some money into it, and create instant equity. There were a lot of other houses we checked out. But we were going by the profit margin."

Greg Gerin, a 203(k) loan specialist with Prosperity Mortgage, says his typical loan is with buyers who spend $50,000 to $100,000 for a property, add $20,000 to $25,000 in improvements, and end up with a home appraised at $100,000 to $150,000. Greg adds, for example, that one recent customer borrowed $148,000 to pay $98,000 for a home and $50,000 in renovations. Upon completion that home appraised at $190,000.

> **Only use a 203(k) loan specialist.**

Inspect, Design, and Appraise After you locate a property that you figure can be bought and renovated profitably, you next must come to terms with the owners on price and other conditions of sale. With agreement in hand, the home is then inspected, a formal plan of repair and renovation is designed, and the property is appraised according to its value after your improvements have been completed. The amount of your loan is based upon your purchase price plus your rehab expenses up to nearly 100 percent of the home's renovated value.

Eligible Properties and Improvements As long as you plan to pay more than $5,000 in rehab expenses, you can use a 203(k) mortgage to acquire and improve nearly any one- to four-

> **You finance almost any type of improvements.**

family property. In fact, using 203(k) money, you can convert a single-family home into a two-, three-, or four-unit property. Or you can convert a multifamily property into a duplex or single-family home. As long as you are creating value, you can rightsize the property in either direction. Under some conditions, you may even be able to borrow more than the property will be worth after you complete your improvements. In that case, you can give your buyer a zero-down purchase and loan assumption.

In terms of specific repairs and renovations, the 203(k) mortgage permits a near-infinite list of possibilities. As long as you stay away from luxuries (e.g., saunas and hot tubs—although you can spend to repair such items if they're already installed), you can do about anything you want. Here are some examples:

- Install skylights, fireplaces, energy-efficient items, or new appliances (stove, refrigerator, washer, dryer, trash compactor, dishwasher).
- Finish off an attic or basement.
- Eliminate pollution or safety hazards (e.g., lead paint, mold, asbestos, underground storage tanks).
- Add living units such as an accessory apartment or two.
- Add baths, bedrooms, a den, or a second story.
- Recondition or replace plumbing, roof, or HVAC systems.
- Improve aesthetic appeal (paint, carpet, tile, exterior siding).
- Install or replace a well or septic system.
- Landscape and fence the yard.

"One of the great features of this program is that it doesn't restrict the niceties," says Michael Noel of Pinnacle Financial. "If you want to install upgraded kitchen cabinets, you can do that. If you want to add crown moldings, you can do it. You can't borrow the money to install a swimming pool, but you can use the money—up to $1,500—to fix up an existing swimming pool."

FHA 203(k) Look-Alike Programs In addition to this
FHA loan program, Fannie Mae, Freddie Mac,
various portfolio lenders, and some city redevelopment agencies have offered mortgages that
roll property acquisition costs and renovation
expenses all into one loan. Also, some hard
money lenders (see discussion p. 255) will permit you to combine purchase and repairs in the
same loan. Absent this all-in-one feature, when
you otherwise acquire a fixer, you'll need to
supplement your purchase mortgage money with additional funding for renovations.

> **Fannie and
> Freddie offer
> 203(k) look-alike
> programs.**

Usually, that's not a problem. FHA and many other lenders
give property improvement loans. But applying for and taking out
two loans can stick you with more red tape and higher loan expenses. Nevertheless, because non-owner-occupant investors can't
use FHA 203(k), many, and possibly most, investor rehab projects
do involve multiple sources of funding.

Owner-Occupied Purchase Loans

Either an owner-occupant or investor with passable credit can easily obtain a mortgage with 20 to 30 percent down (and sometimes
as low as 10 percent down). With 20 percent down (or more), you
can borrow from just about any mortgage lender without any special type of loan program. However, if as an owner-occupant you
either can't (or don't want to) put more than 5 percent down, you
might choose from any of the following widely available types of
mortgage loans.

FHA Acquisition Mortgages   In addition to the FHA 203(k)
rehab loan, HUD/FHA authorizes easy-qualify, low-down payment
mortgages (3 percent to 5 percent) to buy condominiums, manufactured homes, single-family houses, and two- to four-unit apartment
properties (as long as you live in one of the units). FHA not only un-

derwrites 15- and 30-year fixed-rate loans, it also offers a complement of adjustable-rate (ARMs), graduated payment (GPMs), and property improvement loans.

> **Any borrower with passable credit can use FHA loans.**

Not Limited to Low Income   Contrary to what many authors write, FHA does not limit its loans to low-income families, first-time homebuyers, or low-priced properties. Anyone who legally resides in the United States can seek an FHA loan regardless of how many homes they've previously owned or the level of their income. As to mortgage amounts, FHA offers the following limits:

FHA Mortgage Limits

	Basic Limits	Higher Cost Areas
Single family	$154,896	$280,749
Duplex	198,288	359,397
Triplex	239,664	434,391
Quad	297,840	539,835

To learn the exact FHA mortgage limits that apply in your area, look under mortgages in the Yellow Pages of your telephone directory. Then find the display ad of a lender who specializes in FHA loans. These lenders are called direct endorsement underwriters. DE lenders can directly approve your FHA loan without submitting any paperwork to FHA. You can also learn about FHA (and HUD homes, too) at www.hud.gov.

> **FHA runs the largest loan program in the country.**

The Advantages of FHA   More than 1,000,000 homebuyers each year choose some type of FHA loan. FHA leads the low-down payment category by a wide margin because it offers the following six advantages:

1. You can roll many of your closing expenses and mortgage insurance premiums into your loan. This cuts the out-of-pocket cash you'll need at closing.
2. You may choose from either fixed-rate or adjustable-rate FHA plans. (As an aside, note that FHA ARMs give you lower annual and lifetime caps than most non-FHA ARM programs.)
3. FHA authorizes banks and other lenders to use higher qualifying ratios and easier underwriting guidelines. If your credit and income meet "passable" standards, FHA will do all it can to approve your loan. FHA wants to approve more loans for homebuyers.
4. If interest rates drop (and as long as you have a clean mortgage payment record for the past 12 months), you can "streamline" refinance your FHA loan at lower interest rates without a new appraisal and without having to requalify.
5. If you can persuade parents or other close relatives to "gift" you the down payment, you won't need to come up with any down payment cash from your own pocket.
6. Unlike most nongovernment loans, FHA mortgages are assumable. Someone who later agrees to buy your property won't necessarily have to apply for a new mortgage. When mortgage interest rates are high, an assumable mortgage will give your property a great selling advantage. As a fix and flip homebuyer/investor, you should find the assumability feature especially attractive.

FHA Drawbacks   Besides somewhat limited loan amounts (these may be raised soon, though), FHA mortgages display several other drawbacks. For one, you'll have to buy FHA mortgage insurance (MIP) to protect the lender should you fail to make your mortgage payments. This mortgage insurance initially will cost around 1.5 percent of the amount you borrow (e.g., $1,500 on a

$100,000 mortgage—remember though, if you don't have the cash, you can add this premium onto your mortgage loan balance). As another cost, your loan interest rate will be boosted by one-half percent to cover additional mortgage insurance premiums that you'll make along with your monthly mortgage payments.

> **FHA has helped more first-time buyers than any other loan programs.**

The Verdict on FHA   Unfortunately, much misinformation and general ignorance shrouds the FHA program in confusion. In reality, when you match the benefits of FHA loans to their costs, FHA comes out a real winner. Even better, President Bush and HUD Secretary Mel Martinez are working to make more improvements in these types of loans.

If you can start your fix-up career as an owner-occupant, closely compare FHA (especially 203(k)) to your other loan alternatives. Unless you find a liberal seller who offers OWC financing, FHA will often prove to be your best choice.

Fannie/Freddie Low-Down Loans   Fannie Mae and Freddie Mac do not directly loan mortgage money to homebuyers (owner-occupants) or investors (non-owner-occupants). However, these huge players in the mortgage market do set the underwriting standards for thousands of mortgage lenders throughout the country. And in recent years, both of these companies have substantially increased their 5 percent, 3 percent, and in some cases, even zero-down homebuyer loans. (Fannie and Freddie will approve loans for investors with 15 percent to 20 percent down.)

Typically, Fannie/Freddie loan products charge less for mortgage insurance than FHA. But they apply stricter credit standards. In addition, neither Fannie nor Freddie permit homebuyers to assume their fixed-rate loans (as do FHA and VA). However, Fannie/Freddie loans do carry higher loan limits than FHA (or VA):

Fannie/Freddie Mortgage Limits (2003)[1]

Single family	$322,000
Duplex	413,100
Triplex	499,300
Quad	620,500

Fannie Mae's 203(k) look-alike rehab program is called UFIXIT. Fannie/Freddie loans are called conventional, conforming mortgages. Nearly all major mortgage lenders in the country deal in loans underwritten by either Fannie or Freddie.

> **VA offers veterans a great mortgage program, yet most veterans don't use it.**

Department of Veterans Affairs   The VA mortgage is truly one of the best benefits offered to those who have worn our country's uniform. Last year alone, a record 600,000 veterans took advantage of this loan program. Here are several of the great benefits you'll get with a VA mortgage:

1. No down payment. With a VA loan you can finance up to $240,000 without putting any money down. If you want to buy a higher-priced home, you need only come up with 25 percent of the amount over $240,000. For instance, if the home you want to buy is priced at $280,000, you'll need a down payment of $10,000 (.25 X $40,000)—or just 3.57 percent of the purchase price.
2. Similar to FHA, VA loans offer liberal qualifying guidelines. Many (but not all) VA lenders will forgive properly explained credit blemishes. The VA loan also permits higher qualifying ratios. I've seen veterans with good compensating factors close loans with a .48 total debt ratio.

---

1. In Alaska, Hawaii, Guam, and the U.S. Virgin Islands, Fannie/Freddie limits exceed these loan maximums by 50 percent.

3. Often new homebuilders and cooperative sellers will pay all of the veteran's settlement expenses. In fact, new homebuilders sometimes advertise that veterans can buy homes in their developments for just one dollar total move-in costs.

4. Like FHA, a buyer may assume your VA mortgage when you sell your property. Also like FHA, if interest rates fall, you can streamline a no-appraisal, no-qualifying refinance.

5. But unlike FHA, when you use a VA loan, you won't have to buy mortgage insurance. You will, however, have to pay a one-time "funding fee" ranging between 1 and 2.25 percent of the amount you borrow. If you don't want to pay this fee in cash at closing, you can tell the lender to add it to your mortgage loan.

> **Always work with a VA lending specialist.**

As with many types of mortgages, VA loans require piles of paperwork and compliance with various guidelines that look into job history, property condition, home value (called a CRV), and seller prepaids. That's why you should work with a mortgage loan advisor who is skilled and experienced in the day-to-day job of getting VA loans approved. "The devil is in the details," says loan consultant Abe Padoka. Make sure you work with professionals who know the ins and outs of the VA (or FHA) loan approval process.

Community Loan Programs   When nationally syndicated ("Nation's Housing") columnist Kenneth Harney recently wrote, "Mortgage lenders devise more ways to say yes," he was primarily referring to various types of community loan products. "If you don't own a home because you assume that your income, cash savings, or job history rule you out, think again," Harney advises. "Banks, thrifts, and other mortgage lenders are actually rewriting their rulebooks to get you into home ownership."

> **Community loan programs may help get a neighborhood revitalized.**

When You Look, You'll Find Them   To locate community loan programs in your area, call banks, savings institutions, and various mortgage companies. Ask to speak to a loan officer or assistant vice-president who has knowledge of that lender's community lending or community reinvestment (CRA) loan programs. Some lenders also refer to these (or similar) easier-qualifying loans as "first-time buyer" programs. Because community lending has grown quite quickly, your efforts to locate the right program may take your fingers for a walk through the Yellow Pages. But your reward will make the trip worthwhile. "We are making money, we have no build-up of delinquencies or REOs, and we are in the risk management business," says Tobias Washington, a senior executive with a large mortgage lender. "We thought we needed to step out of the box a little more. People are basically honest and they need homes." So step out of the box they did. This lender introduced a 1 percent down payment program for first-time buyers for homes priced up to $200,000.

Nearly All Offer Low-Down, Easier Qualifying   Although it's unusual to find a 1 percent down payment community lending program, you're almost certain to turn up some type of relaxed qualifying, 3 to 5 percent down home-finance plan. Leave no stone unturned. Ask Realtors, loan officers, and friends who have recently bought homes. Closely read the mortgage loan ads in your local newspapers. Also, ask your Realtor to look through the monthly (or quarterly) magazine published by your state's association of Realtors. Often, these publications include articles and ads that describe new easier-qualifying home-finance plans.

Down Payment Assistance   From Oakland, California, to Atlanta, Georgia, from Boston to Miami, from Chicago to Houston, city and county governments and not-for-profit housing organizations

> **Local governments give buyers down payment money.**

have been providing down payment assistance to persons who have not owned a home during the past three years. Typically, these grants range from $1,500 to $5,000, but I've seen them go as high as $15,000. See, for example, the front-page *Wall Street Journal* article "Buyers Get Free Down Payments on Homes" (December 10, 2002).

To learn the types of down payment assistance that are offered in your area, telephone your city or county department of housing, finance, or community development. Often these programs fit right in with your efforts to buy and renovate fixers because they may be targeted toward neighborhoods to prime them for revitalization. The same government and not-for-profit agencies may also provide low-cost money to cover rehab and renovation expenses.

Owner-Occupied Assumptions

> **Real estate gurus popularized the non-quals.**

Up until the early 1980s, owners who sold their properties could generally transfer their mortgages to their buyers. In many cases, to take advantage of this mortgage assumption, the buyers weren't even required to go through any type of qualifying process. These loans (chiefly underwritten by FHA and VA) were called non-qual assumables.

> **Non-qual assumables have virtually disappeared.**

When the nothing-down gurus of the 1970s and 1980s told their readers, "No cash, no credit, no problem," these gurus were urging their readers to buy properties from sellers who offered non-qual assumable mortgages. "Find motivated sellers," the gurus advised. "Then talk them into a deal where you simply step in and pick up their mortgage payments. Equity? No problem. Give the sellers a second mortgage, or maybe trade them your RV."

The End of an Era   Alas, these simpler days are gone. By 1982, Congress, the courts, and mortgage contracts had terminated the *right* of assumption for conventional, conforming, fixed-rate mortgages. Then in the late 1980s, both FHA and VA removed their mortgage contract clauses that permitted non-qualifying assumptions from all of their future mortgage originations. Today, as a practical matter, you're quite unlikely to find any remaining non-quals that could work to your advantage.

> **Many types of *qualifying* assumptions are readily available.**

What Assumption Possibilities Can You Pursue?   Even though the non-quals have virtually disappeared, owner-occupants with *qualifying* passable credit may pursue several other types of mortgage assumptions:

1. *All outstanding FHA mortgages.* As an owner-occupant with passable credit, you can assume any fixed-rate or adjustable-rate mortgage.
2. *All outstanding VA mortgages.* With passable credit, you can assume any outstanding VA mortgage.
3. *Nearly all outstanding conventional, adjustable-rate mortgages.* With good credit (FICO of 620 to 680 or above), you can assume a Fannie/Freddie ARM and most ARMs written by portfolio lenders (those lenders who set their own underwriting standards apart from Fannie, Freddie, FHA, or VA).
4. *Nearly all outstanding conventional fixed-rate mortgages with lender approvals.* Unlike the assumption possibilities 1 through 3 above, conventional fixed-rate loans may *not* be assumed as a matter of right—regardless of the creditworthiness of the buyer. However, a

lender—at its sole discretion—may permit sellers to transfer their mortgage to the buyer of their home.

Implications for Owner-Occupant Renovators   Depending on the lender and the amount you borrow, a newly originated mortgage can typically cost you anywhere from $3,000 to $6,000 in settlement expenses. In favorable contrast, when you assume a mortgage, your settlement costs will probably run less than $1,000. Obviously, when you plan to fix and flip a property, mortgage origination costs can bite a large chunk out of your eventual profits, whereas if you buy a property and assume the current loan, you save those big settlement dollars for yourself.

When you talk with sellers, always learn the status of their present home (property) financing. What amount of balance remains outstanding on the original loan? How might a buyer assume the loan? At what interest rate? You especially want to pursue this line of inquiry when you're negotiating with owners who are behind in their mortgage payments. In such circumstances, even those lenders who need not allow an assumption may be persuaded to do so on quite favorable terms. (For a more extensive discussion of financing, see my book, *106 Mortgage Secrets All Homebuyers Must Learn—But Lenders Don't Tell* [Wiley, 2003].)

CHAPTER 12

Money for Everyone

We now leave the land of mortgages that are available primarily to owner-occupants and enter a world of property financing where everyone can play. First, we'll look at "subject to" purchases.

"Subject to" versus Mortgage Assumptions

Let's say that you would like to buy a property and take advantage of its current financing. Unfortunately, either the loan does not permit an assumption or for one reason or another (credit problems, uncertain or unprovable income, non-owner-occupant, etc.), the lender won't qualify you to take over the loan. Is there some other way to do the deal and keep the financing intact? Yes, it's called a "subject to" purchase.

> **"Subject to" can provide great short-term financing for fixers.**

Whereas under a qualified mortgage assumption, the lender releases the sellers from liability for their mortgage payments and permits you to step into their place, when you buy a property "subject to" the mortgage(s), you pay the sellers their equity (if any). The sellers then deed you their property. No one even tells the lender what's going on. You make the monthly payments for principal, interest, property taxes, and insurance. The lender still holds its mortgage against the property, but you're now the owner.

Is This Technique Legal?

Contrary to what some people believe, the "subject to" technique is neither illegal, immoral, nor fattening. However, it does trigger the so-called due-on-sale clause, which originally was paragraph no. 17 in the standard Fannie/Freddie fixed-rate mortgage contract. In part, the due-on-sale clause reads as follows:

> If all or any part of the [mortgaged] property or an interest therein is sold or transferred by the Borrower *without Lender's prior written consent...Lender may, at Lender's option, declare* all sums secured by this Mortgage to be immediately *due and payable.*

Notice that nothing in this paragraph prevents owners from selling their properties to their buyers without paying off their mortgage. This clause only gives lenders the right to call the mortgage due and payable if such a transfer occurs without "Lender's prior written consent." Thus, if and when the lender learns about this nonapproved transfer of the mortgaged property, it may write the sellers and demand payment of the outstanding mortgage balance within 30 days. If you or the sellers don't pay the full amount due, the lender could file a foreclosure action.

> **"Subject to" is perfectly legal.**

Should You Worry?

Note the key words above: *if, when,* and *may.* The lender can demand full payment only *if* and *when* it finds out about the title change to the property. Given the bureaucratic communication channels that exist within the organizational structure of most mortgage lenders, the sellers would not receive a demand letter for at least three to six months after you bought the property. Then the foreclosure process itself could easily drag on (or be purposely strung out) for another 3 to 12 months.

In other words, even in those situations where the lender gets wind of what you and the sellers have pulled off, you've almost certainly got at least six months to renovate and sell (or refinance) the property. For the great majority of fix-ups and renovations, a six-month window of opportunity will give you plenty of time to get in and out of the deal.

But this worst-case scenario presumes the lender will issue a demand letter. In practice, lenders generally do not push a performing mortgage into foreclosure. To do so would transform a paying asset into (more than likely) a losing asset. Because such a policy seldom makes economic sense, few lenders pursue it. Pay the mortgage, taxes, and insurance on time and as most lender operating procedures now stand, you need not lose any sleep worrying about a due-on-sale clause.

Short Term, Not Long Term

Note that in saying, "no worries," I'm referring to a short-term fix and flip or a short-term fix and refinance strategy. Over the long term, you could face a mortgage call risk if mortgage interest rates shoot up again. In that case, lenders might choose to aggressively enforce the due-on-sale clause.

> **Lenders may call long-term "subject to"s when interest rates go up.**

In fact, conventional lenders terminated the *right* of assumption clause because during the late 1970s and early 1980s high inflation and higher costs of deposits forced many savings and loans (S&Ls) into insolvency. S&Ls were paying depositors 8 to 12 percent interest on their savings and certificates of deposit, yet those old assumable mortgages that were still on the lenders' books were bringing in just 5 to 8 percent. Obviously, to profit and survive, lenders must bring in more from mortgage interest earnings than they pay in interest costs to their depositers. In times of rapidly rising interest rates, lenders want their outstanding low-interest loans paid off as soon as possible.

Risks to Sellers

As mentioned, under a lender-approved mortgage assumption, the lender qualifies the buyers of the property. Then, when the buyers pass muster, the lender issues a novation or "release of liability" to the sellers. The sellers now get off the hook. Whatever happens to that mortgage in the future does not concern them.

Not so with "subject to" unapproved property transfers. In those cases, the sellers' credit and finances remain at risk for as long as the mortgage remains outstanding. If the buyers pay the mortgage late, the lender forwards scurrilous remarks about the sellers to the credit bureau. If the property goes into foreclosure, the lender will chase down the sellers for any money (deficiency) judgments the court awards it. A "subject to" agreement places the sellers at risk.

Your Borrowing Strategy

When you apply for any type of property financing, you need to use solid evidence to persuade the lender that you will pay the money back as agreed. This same principle stands true for any type of seller-assisted financing. To make your case, you should rely on as many of the following criteria as possible:

1. *Credit.* If you've built a strong credit record, prove it with your FICO score, a credit report, or a letter from your landlord (if you're currently renting).

2. *Income.* Pull out your W-2s, 1099s, or your income tax returns. Show your financial capacity to make the payments.

3. *Property.* Emphasize your plans to create value for the property (but only to the extent that you don't weaken your negotiating position on price).

4. *Commitment.* Impress the sellers with your ambition and commitment to succeed as a homeowner or investor. Many older property owners like to help younger people get started. (This tactic certainly worked for me when I was starting out and relying on seller-assisted financing.)

5. *Character.* No one wants to do business with someone they do not trust. Throughout all of your rapport building and negotiation with the sellers, always present yourself

> **Many sellers need persuading.**

(both directly and indirectly) as a person of integrity. If you've experienced credit problems, explain them in terms of circumstances beyond your control—not financial irresponsibility.

At first, most property owners do respond coolly to "subject to" offers to purchase. But, when you put forth convincing assurances and protections, you often can slip flexible or motivated sellers into such an agreement.

Seller-Assisted Financing

Absent a workable mortgage assumption or "subject to" transaction, you might at least partially fund your purchase by drawing on some type of seller-assisted financing.

In fact, when the nationally syndicated real estate attorney and investor Robert Bruss, was asked, "Where's the best place to get a mortgage? At a bank, savings and loan, or credit union?" Bob Bruss answered, "None of these is the best. The best source of financing for your property is the seller." If you can persuade the sellers to help with your financing, you can often get easier quali-

> **Seller financing helps close sales that would otherwise fall through.**

fying and lower costs. Along this same line, here's what Realtor Robert Deimel says about seller financing: "In today's complex marketplace," Robert observes, "sellers and buyers don't always see the opportunity. That's why innovative sales people are often necessary to open their eyes. The key to making more transactions happen is to understand why and when sellers may want to offer the carrot of seller financing." What are the benefits of seller-assisted financing? Here are several:

1. *Easier qualifying.* Although many lending institutions have eased up on their qualifying criteria, they're still more rigid than most sellers.
2. *Flexibility.* Price, interest rate, monthly payments, and other terms are set by mutual agreement. You and the sellers can put together a financing package in any way that works for both of you.
3. *Lower closing costs.* Sellers seldom require points, origination fees, and loan application costs. Unlike lending institutions, sellers don't have to cover office overhead.
4. *Less paperwork.* Although sellers may ask you to provide a credit report, they won't require a stack of forms, documents, and verifications.
5. *Quicker sale.* Seller financing can help sellers get their property sold more quickly. Plus, for properties such as those that require extensive repairs or renovations, seller financing can make the difference between a sale and no sale.
6. *Higher returns.* Seller financing often gives sellers a higher interest rate on their money than they could earn in a savings account or certificate of deposit.

7. *Income tax savings.* Sellers can often achieve certain tax advantages by accepting installments for their property, rather than a lump sum at closing.

8. *Higher selling price.* Seller financing can help owners sell near the top of their home's price range. (Of course, from your perspective, you don't want to overpay. But within reason, many buyers do agree to trade off a slightly higher price for favorable seller's terms.)

The types of seller-assisted financing that you might use to help buy a fixer property are as varied as you or your Realtor's imagination. But be aware, many owners will accept seller-assisted financing even if they don't advertise their willingness. In fact, Robert Bruss says, "I've bought many houses with seller financing. But I can't recall a single one that was advertised 'seller financing.' Until they saw my offer, none of the sellers had informed their agent that they would help finance the sale."

So even when sellers haven't advertised OWC, don't hesitate to ask. Here are several types of seller-assisted financing from which you might be able to choose.

First Mortgage or Deed of Trust

In some OWC sales, the sellers will convey the title of their property to you and then record a mortgage (or in some states, a deed of trust) in the public records. This mortgage (trust deed) serves as a lien against the property. When you buy a property with a seller first mortgage (trust deed), your agreement with the seller establishes rights and responsibilities very similar to those of a bank-financed purchase.

> **Sellers can offer a mortgage just like a bank.**

Buy on the Installment Plan

In the highly popular silent film series *The Perils of Pauline,* Oil Can Harry repeatedly warned Pauline, "If you don't give me the deed to your ranch, I'm going to tie you to the railroad tracks." Oil Can Harry knew that if Pauline signed over the deed to her ranch, that deed would transfer the property's title to Harry. Although Oil Can Harry's no-money-down approach to property ownership was somewhat unorthodox (not to mention illegal), typically, when you buy real estate, you will receive a deed at the time of purchase. With the deed comes title and ownership.

In some sales, though, you won't receive a deed at the time of purchase. Instead, you pay for the property on the installment plan. In this type of purchase, you will give the sellers a small down payment and promise to continue making monthly installments. In return, the sellers turn over possession of the property and promise to deliver a deed to the buyers after they have completed their scheduled payments. This type of purchase agreement is known by various names such as *installment sale, contract-for-deed,* or *land contract.* For buyers and properties that do not meet the qualifying criteria of a lending institution, the land contract technique serves as an excellent way to buy property. I know from experience.

> **A contract-for-deed gives you rights to a property but delays transfer of the deed.**

> **Land contracts can get almost anyone started in real estate.**

Why Sellers Are Willing When I turned age 21, I wanted to acquire real estate as quickly as possible, and at the time, as I have said earlier, I was an undergraduate college student. I had little cash, no full-time job, and no significant credit record. My immediate chances for getting a bank to write a mortgage for me were zero. But this fact didn't deter me. I searched for properties that I could buy on an installment contract. By the time I completed my Ph.D., I had bought around 30 houses and small apartment buildings. The cash flow from these properties paid many of my college living expenses (and yes, for my Cessna and Jaguar XKE).

Land contract sellers can achieve all of the benefits listed on p. 245–246, but these four reasons especially apply:

1. *No bank financing available.* A property may not qualify for bank financing. The property might stand in poor condition, be located in a less-desirable neighborhood, or be functionally out-of-date (rooming house, apartment units with shared bathrooms, irregular floor plan). Also, many lending institutions won't write mortgages on condominiums or townhouses where more than 30 or 40 percent of the units in the complex are occupied by renters instead of owners. Of course, in many instances, land-contract properties offer excellent opportunities for value-creating entrepreneurs.

2. *High interest on savings.* Sellers who plan to deposit the cash they receive from a sale in certificates of deposit or money market accounts can get a higher return on their money by financing a buyer's purchase of their property. A 7- to 10-percent return from a real estate installment sale certainly beats a 2- to 4-percent return from a certificate of deposit.

3. *Tax savings.* When the seller is an investor, an installment sale of a property produces a smaller income tax bite than does a cash sale.

4. *Repossession.* If you default on making your monthly payments, the installment contract typically gives sellers a relatively quick and inexpensive right to repossess the property.

Follow These Guidelines   Because it's simple and low cost, the installment sale works well to help you pull off a highly lever-

> **Use a contract-for-deed as a short-term finance strategy.**

aged (low cash-to-close) purchase. For example, buy a property you can improve. Finance it with a low-down payment installment contract. Create value through fix up and renovations. Then sell or refinance the property based on its now higher value. To use this technique profitably, follow these guidelines:

1. *Buy the property, not the financing.* Don't let easy credit draw you into the purchase of an overpriced property. When circumstances warrant, you might in good judgment pay a price slightly higher than the as-is value. But you would not want to pay $5,000 for a 1995 Chevy from Easy Ed's "buy here, pay here" used car lot just because Easy Ed will sell it to you with nothing down and low monthly payments. This same principle applies to real estate. Beware of the guru's tactic to gain seller financing with the invitation, "You name the price; I'll name the terms." Verify value through your careful appraisal or other professional opinion.

2. *Beware of hidden defects.* A property that seems priced right might suffer hidden defects. Take care to obtain experienced and knowledgeable estimates for the repairs and renovations that you plan. Never "ballpark" or casually figure the costs necessary to bring a property up to the condition you want it. Get professional property inspections and cost estimates before you buy.

3. *Contract terms are governed by law.* A contract-for-deed places you and the seller in a relationship that is governed not only by the contract language but also by state laws and court decisions. Under an installment sale, your rights and responsibilities differ from those you acquire when you finance a property with a mortgage or trust deed.

Prior to negotiating an installment sale agreement, consult a real estate attorney who is experienced in reviewing these con-

> **Don't let the ease of a land contract deter your due diligence.**

tracts. Develop an understanding of contract law as it applies in your state so that you learn how to structure your deal in a way that you adequately protect your interests.

However, beware of lawyers who lack knowledge of this contract specialty. Some naysaying risk-averse lawyers warn against buying any property on the installment plan. (Using similar logic, such lawyers would advise against marriage because divorce can be so painful.) This type of lawyer looks at risks without considering benefits and opportunities. Get a lawyer who understands both. Then negotiate a contract-for-deed that can work for you and the sellers. Over the years, millions of Americans (especially cash-short and credit-challenged Americans) have successfully bought houses and small rental properties on the installment plan.

Lease Option a Property

> **Lease options also give you a low-cost, short-term way to control a fixer.**

The lease option combines a lease agreement for a house, townhouse, or apartment with an option (the right) to buy that property at a later date. In the early 1980s, Robert Bruss, the nationally syndicated real estate columnist and investor, called lease options "the most overlooked and underused" property finance possibility. At that time, most buyers, sellers, and real estate agents remained clueless about this technique.

Times have really changed. Awareness has mushroomed. When I travel throughout the United States, I always check through the local real estate classifieds. In most cities, I find real estate agents who regularly handle lease options and other low-down payment home-finance plans. I also have seen lease options promoted by home builders and developers of new condominiums and townhouses. In San Francisco, one ad from Bay Crest Condominiums boldly announced, "If You Can Afford to Rent, You Can Now Afford to Own: Exciting New Lease/Purchase Option."

With lease options moving into the mainstream, you can easily find lease option sellers. Indeed, when asked, even some "House for Rent" property owners will agree to lease option their rentals. Likewise, some sellers will agree to a lease option (or lease purchase) if you propose it. The lease option gives almost anyone the opportunity to become a homeowner or investor.

1. *Easier qualifying.* Qualifying for a lease option may be no more difficult than qualifying for a lease (sometimes easier). Generally, your credit and employment record need meet only minimum standards. Most property owners (sellers or lessors) will not place your financial life under a magnifying glass as would a mortgage lender.

2. *Low initial investment.* Your initial investment to get into a lease option agreement can be as little as one month's rent and a security deposit of a similar amount. At the outside, move-in cash rarely exceeds $5,000 to $10,000, although I did see a home lease optioned at a price of $1.5 million that asked for $50,000 up front.

3. *Forced savings.* The lease option contract typically forces you to save for the down payment required when you exercise your option to buy. Often, lease options charge above-market rental rates and then credit perhaps 50 percent of your rent toward the down payment. The exact amount is negotiable. And once you have committed yourself to buying, you should find it easier to cut other spending and place more money toward your "house account."

4. *Reestablish credit.* A lease option also can help renters buy when they need time to build or reestablish a solid credit record. Judy and Paul Davis wanted to buy a home

before prices in their area once again rose above their reach. But the Davises needed time to clear up credit problems created by too much borrowing and Judy's lay-off. The lease option could be the possibility that helps the Davises achieve their goal of home ownership.

5. *100-percent financing possible.* Lease option a property that can be profitably improved through repairs, renovation, or cosmetics. By increasing the property's value, you may be able to borrow nearly all the money you need to exercise your option to buy. Suppose your lease option purchase price is $175,000, and by the end of one year, your option deposit and rent credits equal $7,500. You now owe the sellers $167,500. Through repairs, fix-up work, and redecorating, you have increased the home's value by $25,000. This property is now worth around $200,000. If you have paid your bills on time during the previous year, you can finance your purchase with the full $167,500 you need to pay off the sellers. Or, as another possibility, you could sell the property, pay the sellers $167,500, and use the remaining cash from the sale to buy another property.

> **Make sure your lease option gives you enough time to complete your improvements.**

Obviously, the lease option technique achieves the same objectives as does a land contract installment sale. However, the land contract actually finances the purchase of a property, whereas the lease option puts you on your own to come up with the money to close the deal—before your option to buy expires.

Lease Purchase Agreements versus Lease Purchase Options

Although some people use the terms *lease option* and *lease purchase* interchangeably, technically there's a big distinction. With a lease purchase agreement, you're actually agreeing to buy a property. Your lease period merely gives you time to renovate the property, build up cash (or rent credits) for a down payment, or perhaps shape up your financial fitness. With a lease purchase *option* (or more frequently called a lease option), you can walk away from the property at the end of your lease period. You would forfeit any option money or rent credits you have paid. But the sellers couldn't require you to go ahead and buy the property if you chose not to.

> **Some sellers prefer a lease purchase (over a lease option) because it seems more solid.**

To buy a property through a lease purchase or lease option agreement, here are several key issues to talk over with your Realtor, an attorney, and the sellers:

1. *Purchase price.* Verify that the price you're offering is in line with other comparable properties that have recently sold in the neighborhood. If you apply for a mortgage at some future date, your property must appraise high enough so your loan-to-value (LTV) ratio will be approved. Some "lease-to-own" sellers grossly overprice their properties.

2. *Move-in cash.* Whether you lease purchase or lease option a property, you'll have to negotiate the amount of your "move-in" money. The sellers will credit this cash toward your purchase price when you eventually buy. Typically, if you choose not to buy, the sellers will keep all (or part) of this money.

3. *Lease period.* How much time will you need before you're able to buy? Sellers often want to close relatively quickly—sometimes within 6 to 12 months. However, make sure you give yourself enough breathing room. If you can't renovate the property, sell it, or come up with permanent mortgage financing at the end of your lease period, you may lose your move-in cash. On the other

hand, if you can close sooner than the date specified in your agreement, most sellers would gladly accommodate you. (But make sure your agreement gives you that right.)

4. *Rent credits.* As noted, many lease purchase/lease option sellers now apply rent credits toward your purchase price. These monthly credits also can count as part (or all) of your down payment. But remember, lenders won't count the full amount without question. They count only lease amounts paid in excess of market rent levels. You pay $1,000 a month, market's at $800, the lender will allow $200 per month. If you're planning to use rent credits as part of your cash to close on permanent financing, make sure your lease agreement fits within the lender's guidelines.

5. *Right to assign.* Include a "right to assign" clause in your agreement. Then if you don't complete your purchase, you can sell (assign for a payment) to someone else your right to buy the property at your option (or purchase) contract price. That way you won't forfeit all of your rent credits and move-in cash. After you've improved the property, you can assign your right of purchase to your buyers and profit nicely.

6. *Inspections and title check.* When you buy a property, get the property inspected by a specialist who knows houses. Unless you're buying at a steep discount, don't run the risk of unexpected major repairs. Likewise, you'll want a title insurance company to check the seller's rights of ownership. Too many lease option/lease purchase buyers omit these precautions and put themselves at risk. Discuss this issue with an attorney. Be especially careful about waiting for the title check if you're giving the seller a fairly large amount of move-in cash.

Lease purchase and lease option agreements are two more good techniques you can use to acquire a property. Remember, though, both of these techniques raise questions and risks that differ from a mortgage transaction where the sellers deed the property to you without a waiting period.

Easy Money—Hard Terms

> **Be careful. These "easy-money" lenders don't play in the same league with FHA/VA or Fannie/Freddie.**

When other types of property financing fail, you've got one more possibility that I hesitate to recommend, but will do so only in the cause of thoroughness. In some limited situations, you may want to turn to an easy-money lender. Within the real estate industry, such lenders actually work under the label of "private money" or "hard money." I call them "easy-money" lenders because they will loan money to buy, improve, or refinance about any type of property as long as the borrower can fog a mirror.

Predatory Lending

In fact, some easy-money lenders loan funds to people who stand very little chance of paying it back. Why? Because these lenders *want to foreclose* the property. Such lenders profit from this tactic for three reasons:

1. *Low Loan-to-Value (L-T-V) ratio.* Easy-money lenders only make loans where the property value greatly exceeds the amount borrowed.
2. *Immediate collection.* Unlike reputable mortgage lenders, these easy-money folks don't know the concept of forbearance. Miss a payment and they will sic the lawyers on you as soon as legally possible.
3. *High late fees and penalties.* Not only do these predatory lenders go after the amount owed on the mortgage,

they make sure that the delinquent borrowers pay dearly for their failure to make their payments as scheduled.

Both the state and federal governments have initiated an enforcement campaign against illegal predatory lending practices. Two such lenders (Citigroup and Household Lending) recently paid a total of $700 million to settle charges of bilking tens of thousands of their mortgage customers. Although easy-money lenders do make borrowing easier for the credit impaired, such lenders also expect to receive a huge (and perhaps illegal or unconscionable) return.

Why Would You Want to Deal with This Type of "Easy-Money" Lender?

Generally, lenders who specialize in easy money with hard terms appeal to three types of borrowers: (1) the poorly educated who don't really understand the terms and costs of the loan, (2) those who need money so desperately that they'll sign away their future for immediate relief from some financial difficulty, and (3) optimistic investors who care nothing about the hard terms of the easy money because they imagine high profits from their venture. Assuming that you're not a type 1 or 2 borrower, I will focus on a type 3 situation.

The Optimistic Entrepreneur

Say you find a desperate (aka motivated) property owner who is willing to sell you his $100,000 as-is property for $75,000 if you can come up with the cash within 10 days. You know that after putting in $15,000 and some sweat equity into the property, you could sell the house for at least $135,000. You want to grab this deal before someone else beats you to it. But how can you raise $75,000 on such short notice?

The answer: An easy-money–hard-terms lender. What will this loan cost you? Can't say for sure because the private mortgage in-

<table>
<tr><td>

Hard-terms lenders specialize in fast-cash deals.

</td><td>

dustry includes thousands of small players as well as some of the major mortgage lenders like Citigroup (who runs its hard-money operations through no-name subsidiaries). Each player sets its own costs, terms, and loan-to-value ratios. The structure of the deals also varies over time. Sometimes too much money is chasing too few borrowers. At other times, too many borrowers

</td></tr>
</table>

are chasing after too little money.

With all of these caveats in view, here's how your deal to borrow $75,000 in this situation might look:

	Cash You Pay
Interest @ 15% p.a. (6 months)	$ 5,625
Settlement costs	6,000
Mortgage broker fee @ 5%	3,750
Mortgage payback	75,000
Total cost	90,375
Net cost of funds for 6 months	15,375

	Your Expected Profit
Sales price of renovated property	$135,000
Marketing costs @ 6%	8,100
Cost of funds	15,375
Acquisition cost of property	75,000
Costs of improvements	15,000
Profit (before tax)	21,525

Are these numbers realistic? Yes. Do they reflect a norm? No. As I said, easy-money lenders are highly idiosyncratic. Each deal is negotiated according to the particulars of the loan, the property, the lender, and the borrower. No Freddie Mac or Fannie Mae rules over this domain. Plus, this deal showed a great buy on the property, which is possible but not typical.

> **Before you sign up for hard money, take off your rose-colored glasses.**

Nevertheless, this example does indicate that, on occasion, you can earn a good profit—even after paying the high costs of a hard terms lender. Before you enter into such a loan agreement, though, take off your rose-colored glasses. Sharpen your pencil. Critically work through the numbers. Remember to include a liberal amount for the oops factor. If the profit still outweighs costs and risks, go for it.

Where to Find This Easy Money

The classified ad section of many newspapers includes a cate-gory entitled "Loans," "Financing," or perhaps "Money to Lend." Quite often, these advertisers represent easy-money–hard-terms lenders. Also look in your telephone book's Yellow Pages under mortgages and mortgage brokers. You're looking for listings that use language such as "credit problems okay," "nonconforming," "secured," "fast closing," "investor loans," "rehab acquisitions," "we buy mortgages and land contracts," or "no income verification." Box 12.1 shows a sampling of easy-money ads from *The New York Times* and a local newspaper.

Cash to Close

Up to this point you've seen that you can fund your property purchase in many different ways. Surely, one or more of these techniques will work for you. However, you're not yet in the game because nearly all of these funding techniques will require some cash to close the deal. Where can you get this cash? Here are the most widely used sources:

- ◆ Personal savings and investments
- ◆ Unnecessary assets
- ◆ Home equity loan

Box 12.1   Newspaper Ads for Hard Money Lenders.

♦ Partnership ventures
♦ Second mortgages
♦ Cash advances

Personal Savings

How much cash can you raise from your personal savings and investments? If your answer comes in at anything under five figures (not counting decimals!), you need to work through some fiscal fitness exercises. (For a philosophy that leads to sensible spending and wealth building see *The Millionaire Next Door* by Thomas Stanley and William Danko.) Virtually every financial expert agrees that before you can invest profitably, you must learn to spend *well below* your means.

But even if your bank balance isn't even high enough to get you a free checking account, recall that you might use money from your IRA, 401(k), Keogh, and several other types of tax-deferred accounts (TDAs). The Wall Street mutual funds want to keep that secret from getting out. To tap these funds for your real estate investing, you set up a self-directed account with a third-party administrator. The process follows some complicated rules, but your plan administrator can keep you legal. For more details, go to www.midoh.com. That's the web site for Mid-Ohio Securities, one of the leading companies that shows individuals how to invest their TDA money in real estate of their choosing.

Sell Unnecessary Assets

> **Nearly everyone owns assets that they could sell to raise investment cash.**

Can you sell, trade, or downsize any assets such as cars, boats, jet skis, or furniture? What about that no-longer-pursued stamp or coin collection? I recently talked with one of my readers who wanted to invest in properties but said she lacked cash. "What would you recommend?" she asked. When I queried her about assets that she could draw on, she admitted that she and her husband owned a vacation property at Lake Tahoe with $150,000 of equity.

"Why don't you sell that property and put the money to more productive use?" I said.

"Well, we've been considering that idea. But we really love our weekend getaways," she responded.

"How often do you use the property?" I asked.

"Oh, we don't get over as much as we would like. Maybe four or five times a year."

Do you see the problem here? All of us love our possessions. We don't want to give them up. But ask yourself whether all of

Learn to live with less so you can eventually enjoy far more.

those assets are truly worth the price you pay to retain them. I recently owned a Porsche 911. Obviously, that's a car that I loved to drive. But when I calculated my out-of-pocket costs of ownership plus the money I could earn by investing the cash that I had tied up in the car, the decision to sell became a no-brainer.

Your decision to sell unnecessary assets becomes even more important when you're shelling out money for monthly payments. Those assets not only capture your cash equity, they also can drag down your credit score and borrowing power. Get rid of those unnecessary assets now. The returns you earn over time will permit you to later replace them many times over. (Also, you may find as I have that simplifying one's material possessions can actually lead to a higher quality of life.)

Obtain a Home Equity Loan (or Downsize the House) and Free Up Investment Capital

A low-cost home equity loan makes an excellent source of cash to expand your real estate wealth.

If you've owned a home for a number of years, you've no doubt built up tens (perhaps hundreds) of thousands of dollars in equity. Through either a home equity loan or a cash-out refinance, you can raise money at quite favorable rates. In fact, I know of some homeowners who are refinancing their homes with larger mortgages and then using the net proceeds for cash bids on fix-up properties at discount prices.

If your home has proven to be a good investment, now's the time to leverage up. Put some of that equity into buying and renovating properties. Don't let that cash sit idle when you could use it to accelerate your wealth building.

Bring in Partners

> **Right now, millions of people with money would like to invest in real estate.**

> **Partners can provide the money. You provide the talent and time.**

Whom do you know that would like to earn the profits that real estate can provide but lacks the time or interest to take an active role? Such investing partners can provide cash to the deal and they also may enhance your credibility and borrowing power.

Although space here doesn't permit a full discussion of the legal, tax, and practical issues that partnerships can entail, I will urge you to look into this approach to raising cash for investment. I have brought in a partner on a number of my property purchases. All have worked out well for both me and the partner(s).

Attract Money with a Business Plan
Once you gain experience and credibility, you will be able to raise money based on your reputation and achievements. When you're just getting started, though, I recommend that you write out a business plan for two reasons:

1. *Think it through.* Writing out a plan forces you to think your project through from start to finish. As you write, you clarify. You see glitches (and perhaps opportunities) that more casual analysis frequently misses.
2. *Credibility.* Which of these approaches would most persuade you to invest in a project? Someone simply asks you, "Hey, how would you like to invest $20,000 in a rehab deal I'm putting together?" Or she says, "Here's a copy of my business plan for a rehab project that I'm doing. As you can see from this market and financial analysis, a $20,000 investment will pay you back $30,000 within six months."

To write this plan, you would highlight the market and property data that we discussed in earlier chapters as well as the expenditure, revenue, and profit calculations as shown in Figure 3.1. To further enhance your credibility and forthrightness, you should also pinpoint risk factors and how you're prepared to deal with them. For example,

> **Don't overpromise. Anticipate risks.**

◆ What if interest rates go up?
◆ What if renovation costs exceed the estimate?
◆ What if the renovations take longer than planned?
◆ What if sales (or rental) prices begin to soften?

All smart entrepreneurs realize that no one can perfectly predict the future. You can, though, anticipate problems. Then take steps beforehand to alleviate, reduce, or eliminate them. "What if" scenarios should stimulate you to build safeguards into your plans and prepare contingent exit strategies.

Favored Partners   Since even the most promising partnerships (aka marriages) can break down into contentiousness, choose your real estate partners carefully. You want someone who's reasonable, easy to get along with, and lives by a personal code of integrity and fairness. If plans go awry, as they sometimes do, you want a partner who will sit down and look at reasonable and fair ways to resolve the cause of the detour and cooperatively steer the project back on track.

> **Choose a person with character first, money second.**

You do not want a partner who insists that you sign a 10-page, fine-print partnership agreement that has been drafted by his or her lawyer. The more you let the lawyers intercede into your agreement, the more likely you and your partner will come to discord. Of course, here I'm talking about small deals—not multimillion-dollar agreements, when like it or not, the lawyers will probably actively participate in the partnership negotiations.

Most lawyers would like you to believe that a good partnership requires an "airtight" partnership agreement that nails down precisely each partner's rights and responsibilities. Wrong! A good partnership requires good people as partners. If, for small deals, you (or your partner) think you need a 10-page, fine-print document of legal jargon to set the terms of your agreement, that partnership is headed for trouble.

In your eagerness to do a deal, never jump for the money until you're perfectly confident that your investor will make a great partner. No contract can ever substitute for the character of the people involved.

Second Mortgages

Assume that you've found a great property, a motivated seller, and a low-interest rate assumable (or "subject to") mortgage. You face only one problem. The existing mortgage has a balance of $190,000, the owner wants a price of $225,000, and you can only come up with $20,000 in cash. How can you cover the $15,000 gap? Use a second mortgage.

> **Seller seconds reduce the amount of cash you need to close.**

First, ask the seller to carry back a $15,000 security interest in the property. If the seller won't or can't oblige you, turn to an institutional or private mortgage lender to provide the money. In the world of investment real estate (and increasingly, too, in the world of homebuyers), cash-short buyers use second mortgages to help close the gap between the amount of the primary financing and the purchase price of the property.

Cash Advances

In today's world of easy credit, you probably receive dozens of credit card offers every month. In taking advantage of these multiple offers, some investors build up cash advance credit lines of $25,000, $50,000, or more. Then, when they need ready money for a down payment, fix-up costs, or even total funding for a property acquisition, they draw on their multiple cards for quick cash.

Should you pursue this method of financing? Yes, as long as you stick to these strict guidelines for borrowing and payback:

1. *Bid limits.* Never use easy money to boost your bid limit for a property. Ready credit (either OWC or cash advances) can lure investors into overpaying. Work the profit potential of the deal (see Figure 3.1). Then hold fast to your numbers. Excess credit does cause too many beginning investors to abandon their good sense.

2. *Productive versus unproductive borrowing.* Even worse than overpaying for a property, some would-be investors squander their credit lines on unproductive consumer spending (vacations, clothes, jewelry, home decorating, entertainment). If you can't resist temptation, avoid multiple credit cards.

3. *Rapid payback.* When you do use your cash advance credit lines for acquisition or renovation, pay the money back as soon as you can generate your profits through a property sale or refinance. Not only is credit card borrowing expensive, it will reduce your ability to borrow mortgage money in the future.

4. *FICO credit score.* Even without borrowing, holding 6 to 10 credit cards with tens of thousands of dollars in available credit may pull down your credit scores. If such a tactic brings you down to a FICO of 740 from 780, that's no reason for concern. However, if multiple cards moves you from a score of 628 to 575, you should probably not try to build your credit lines through credit cards. (For more on credit scoring, see myfico.com and creditaccuracy.com.)

Overall, credit card cash advances can really boost your ability to quickly snatch up good deals when they come your way. But, as you undoubtedly already know, unwise (profligate) use of credit card debt has ruined the fiscal fitness of many hopeful wealth builders. Don't take the risk unless you're confident that you can discipline both your borrowing and your payback.

Summing Up

Since the 1970s, various real estate gurus have promoted various "no cash, no credit, no problem" techniques of investor financing. Undoubtedly, many of these gurus exaggerate the possibilities and understate the risks of their proposed deal making. Nevertheless, you can do it. In real estate, knowledge of properties, knowledge of the market, and an entrepreneurial vision count far more than ready cash or 780 FICO scores. Experience proves that if you will put the knowledge gained from this book into practice, you will build wealth in real estate.

I wish you the best. Should you have any questions or comments about investing in real estate, please telephone me (800-942-9304, ext. 20691) or send me an e-mail (garye@stoprenting now. com). I enjoy hearing from my readers.

INDEX

A

Accessory apartment, 135
Acquisition costs, 38
Aesthetics, 116–117, 134
Affordability, 16
Agency relationship, 219–222
AIDA, 167, 177
Appraisal process, 30–31
Appraisal strengths, 25–26
Appraisal weaknesses,
    26–28
Appreciation potential, 29

B

Bargain price, 29
"Bargain price" approach, 3–4
Bids, 48–51
Bird-dog fee, 177
Bootleg contractors, 52–53
Bruss, Robert, 101–102, 151–152,
    244, 250
Building codes, 86–87
Buyer's eyes, 92

C

Cash advances, 264–265
Change orders, 47
Cherry picking, 50
Classified adspeak, 172
Cleanliness, 119–121
Community action, 149–150
Community loans,
    234–236
Community Reinvestment Act,
    158
Comparable sales, 23–24
Concessions, 213
Condition, 121–122
Contract for deed, 247
Conversions, 133
Co-op sales, 191–192
Cost estimating, 125–127
Cost-plus pricing, 39
Credit, 225–226
Credit scoring, 265
Credit standards,
    243–244
Curb appeal, 99–100

D

Deal points, 207–208
Dealer, 41
Deceptive ads, 185–186
Deed of trust, 246
Deed restrictions, 153
District concept, 64–67
Down payment assistance,
    236–237
Due diligence, 250

E

Easements, 62–63
Echo boomers, 160
Emotional appeal, 117–118
Energy efficiency, 128–129
Entrepreneurial approach, 6
Entrepreneurial difference, 2
Entrepreneurial fixer, 16–17
Entrepreneurial vision,
    30–31
Environmental laws, 87–88
Exterior, 100–106
    appearance, 101–103
    condition, 103
    maintenance, 104–105
    roof, 101

F

Fannie Mae, 233–234
Fencing and driveways, 99
FHA advantages, 231–232
FHA drawbacks, 232–233

FHA loan limits, 231
FHA loans, 230–234
FHA 203(k), 227–230
FICO, 225–226, 265
Financing costs, 38–39
Fix and flip, 13–15
Fixer (defined), 5
Floor plan, 111
For sale signs, 177
Foreclosure vultures, 202
Foreclosures, 201–203
Franklin, Ben, 92
Freddie Mac, 233–234
Freddie/Fannie limits, 234
Free-agent nation, 74

G

Gentrification, 147
"Greenlining," 158
Gross bid, 38, 49–50

H

Hard money, 255–258
HOA rules, 153
Holding costs, 39
Home equity loans, 261–262
Homeowner associations, 59–61
Homes for Dallas, 158–159
Housewise, 5, 13

I

Improvement costs, 38
In Search of Excellence, 20

Income taxes, 41
Instant equity, 228
Insurance restrictions, 62

L

Land contract, 247
Lease option, 197, 250 – 252
Lease purchase, 252 – 255
Legal compliance, 124 – 125
Lien release, 51
Livability, 111 – 112
Loss leader repairs, 101 – 102
Lowball offers, 216

M

Market strategy, 10
Market value, 22 – 23
Myers, Kevin, 2
Minimum improved value (MIV),
    36 – 37
Mortgage assumptions, 237 – 239,
    240
Mortgage helper, 139
Mortgage restrictions, 61 – 62

N

Negotiating, 207 – 215
Neighborhood nuisances, 152 – 153
Neighborhood revitalization,
    144 – 161
Networking, 200 – 201
Newspaper ads, 165 – 166
Newspapers, 196 – 199

Noise, 118 – 119
Noise ordinance, 76 – 77
Nonconforming use, 78 – 80
Non-qual assumables,
    237 – 238

O

Oops factor, 40 – 41
Opportunity costs, 40
Owner-occupant financing,
    225 – 227

P

Paragraph no. 17, 241
Partners, 262 – 264
"Payback," 44 – 45
Piecemeal renovation, 45
Predatory lending, 255 – 256
Preferred value proposition
    (PVP), 33
Profit formula, 35
Project plan, 46 – 48
Property brochures,
    168 – 177
Property insurance, 129 – 130
Property taxes, 129

R

Realty agents, 187 – 192,
    193 – 195
"Redlining," 158
REOs, 203 – 204
Resale package, 60 – 61

Rightsizing, 113 – 114
Rose-colored glasses, 91 – 92

S

Safety and security, 130 – 131, 156
Schools, 155 – 156
Second mortgages, 264
Section 1031, 15, 42 – 43
"Sell the sizzle," 164
Seller anxiety, 208 – 209
Seller financing (OWC),
    244 – 246
Selling costs, 39
Sequencing, 47
Site analysis, 93 – 100
    buildable lot, 95
    configuration, 93 – 94
    easements, 94
    encroachments, 94
    "hidden value," 95 – 96
    size, 93 – 94
Site placement, 105 – 106
Site quality, 96 – 98
    landscaping, 97 – 98
    soil conditions, 97
    topography, 97
Small claims court, 153 – 155
Square footage, 107, 110
    comp houses, 110
    measurement errors, 108
    quality, 108 – 109
Storage, 115 – 116
Strategic improvements, 22

"Subject to" mortgages,
    240 – 243

T

Target market, 112 – 113
Thorton Park, 147
Transformation, 9

U

UFIXIT, 234
Unconditional release, 51
Utility bills, 127 – 129

V

VA funding fee, 235
VA loans, 234 – 235

W

Watts, 146
"What if" calculations, 36
Win-win, 210 – 216

Z

Zoning ordinances, 64 – 67
Zoning restrictions, 67 – 78
    floor area ratio, 70 – 71
    height, 68 – 70
    historical properties, 76
    home businesses, 73

lot coverage ratio, 70 – 71
occupancy, 71 – 72
parking, 72 – 73
rezoning, 84 – 85
setbacks, 68 – 70

sideyards, 68 – 70
special uses, 74 – 75
sunlight, 77 – 78
variance, 83
views, 77 – 83